Food and Identity in the Caribbean

Food and Identity in the Caribbean

Edited by Hanna Garth

B L O O M S B U R Y

LONDON • NEW DELHI • NEW YORK • SYDNEY

Bloomsbury Academic
An imprint of Bloomsbury Publishing Plc

50 Bedford Square
London
WC1B 3DP
UK

175 Fifth Avenue
New York
NY 10010
USA

www.bloomsbury.com

First published 2013

British Library Cataloguing-in-Publication Data
A catalogue record for this book is available from the British Library.

ISBN: HB: 978-0-85785-357-8
PB: 978-0-85785-358-5
ePub: 978-0-85785-359-2

Library of Congress Cataloging-in-Publication Data

Food and identity in the Caribbean / edited by Hanna Garth.
p. cm.
Includes bibliographical references.
ISBN 978-0-85785-357-8 — ISBN 978-0-85785-358-5 — ISBN 978-0-85785-359-2
1. Food habits—Caribbean Area.   2. Food—Caribbean Area—
Psychological aspects.   3. Identity (Psychology)—Caribbean Area.
I. Garth, Hanna.
GT2853.C27F66 2012
394.1'209729—dc23   2012022576

Typeset by Apex CoVantage, LLC, Madison, WI, USA.
Printed and bound in Great Britain

Contents

Notes on Contributors

Barrett P. Brenton is an Associate Professor in the Department of Sociology and Anthropology and Associate Director of the Center for Global Development at St. John's University.

Hanna Garth is a Ph.D. candidate in the Department of Anthropology at UCLA.

Lidia Marte obtained her Ph.D. in cultural anthropology from the University of Texas at Austin, and is currently faculty at Brooklyn College, CUNY.

John Mazzeo is an Assistant Professor in the Department of Anthropology at DePaul University.

Gillian Richards-Greaves is a dual Ph.D. candidate in Ethnomusicology and Social-Cultural Anthropology at Indiana University, Bloomington.

Heather J. Sawyer is a Ph.D. candidate in the Department of Anthropology at the University of Kentucky.

Ryan N. Schacht is a Ph.D. candidate at the University of California, Davis, in the Department of Evolutionary Anthropology.

Richard R. Wilk is Provost's Professor of Anthropology at Indiana University.

Marisa Wilson is an Assistant Professor in Human Geography at the University of the West Indies.

Lauren Wynne is a Ph.D. candidate in the Department of Anthropology at the University of Chicago.

Preface

The topics that scholars *do not study* can be much more revealing than the limited range of subjects they do choose to work on. Topics and issues are constantly moving in and out of a zone of visibility. While some are firmly emplaced as legitimate, others seem to hover in the fringes, either stuck in the permanently marginal position, or in motion, coming into focus as they move towards the mainstream, or edging out into invisibility. Funding and publication opportunities tend to move towards topics that are central, which are often matters of public debate and political controversy.

Food studies have been a peripheral part of anthropology and other social sciences for a very long time. While ecological anthropologists have long been interested in food production, what happened after the harvest was often relegated to a section called "daily life" in classic ethnographic monographs that described entire cultures and peoples. Since the early generations of European and North American anthropologists were overwhelming male, it should not surprise us that they paid little attention to what their own cultures defined as women's work. Real men studied kinship systems, religion, politics, and law. Feasts appeared important at funerals and other life-course events, but the hard work and skill involved in cooking all those pigs and sweet potatoes usually went unnoticed. Classic ethnographies often describe staple diets as simple, unchanging, and monotonous, lumps of starch with sauce, as if everyone had the same tastes and preferences.

Even when food did appear on center stage, in the hands of structuralists it was just another means of getting to something deeper, cultural grammars, maps of social hierarchies or structures, or evidence of the way the "savage mind" categorized the world. Anthropologists also followed other disciplines in mincing the study of food into bits that could be handed out to specialists in nutrition, agriculture, kinship, gender, ritual taboos, and the environment, despite the overarching ambition of "holism."

What would anthropology have looked like if it had taken food and eating as a central object in its first fifty years, instead of topics like kinship and social organization? It is hard to say, but I suspect we would not have started out by dividing up the world into discrete territories inhabited by separate "tribes" each with their own language and customs. Food is far too mobile and fluid to allow us to spend decades trying to reconstruct the genealogies and histories of individual "cultures." We certainly would not be studying food as a behavioral key to another more important topic like kinship. Instead we might be studying politics or religion as a way to better understand food, rather than the other way around. Or at least we would be thinking about how daily routines of eating are actually ways in which we construct and enact kinship, religion, and politics.

This book appears, therefore, at a pivotal moment when food is emerging as a legitimate topic *in itself*, at the same time that food has also entered public and political discourse in many parts of the world, connected with ideas about cultural preservation, sustainability, sovereignty, security, the dangers of monopoly, rights, and risks. But we bring food to center stage against a good deal of academic resistance, founded in the structure and history of social sciences in general and anthropology in particular. What are the sources of this resistance?

We can begin with the ethnocentric identification of cooking with female gender and nurturant mothering. It is also clear that food is caught up in ideas about modernity that are built upon a separation between the public and private spheres. Food production is generally done in public, and is managed by complex laws and ideas about cleanliness and health. The public is a legitimate location for politics and debate, research, and policy. The domestic, on the other extreme, is private and protected from scrutiny. We are all free to observe people in public and engage with them as individuals. But the domestic sphere is still protected and non-commodified, and we can enter only with elaborate forms of permission. The domestic lives of the poor and destitute are labeled as deviant and dysfunctional, so they lose the protection of privacy and are diagnosed and treated, like diseases and other "dangers to public health."

Resistance is also prompted by the very complexity of food, its mutability and the way it uncomfortably mixes pleasure and necessity. Like sexuality, it is can be deceptively simplified as a biologically based drive, since we eat to satisfy the body's hunger. It may be a cultural construction, but eating also has biological limits. At the same time, like language, food is a topic only partially accessible to the user; people can talk endlessly about food, but they do not know the deep historical and structural rules they follow in their everyday eating. Like music, food often has an improvisational element like jazz that is unscripted, while other kinds of cooking are rigidly programmed and rehearsed like symphonic performances.

While food is extremely complex and difficult, it can also be crushingly boring and mundane. People often eat in a "mindless" and automatic way, and habit guides most of what people eat. In cultures where people depend on their own subsistence farming, they may eat the same main dish at every meal, all year long. While there are many cultures where people talk endlessly about their food, in other places people show little overt interest in the topic. Food is often taken for granted until it is suddenly changed, becomes scarce, or rises in price.

In countries where most people are shoppers rather than farmers or hunter-gatherers, food draws anthropologists away from their traditionally comfortable locations for fieldwork. While some meals are taken at the traditional kitchen table, a setting where ethnographers are often most comfortable, in cities and suburbs food draws us into supermarkets and restaurants, busses and shopping malls, street markets and offices. We may have to visit factories and even landfills and sewage treatment plants. None are traditional haunts for ethnographers.

Fortunately, the studies in this book do not look away from the domestic. Instead of working from the public to the private, most begin with a prosaic daily dish like mangú, tamales, or cookup rice, and take this as a departure to work outwards into larger public issues like nationality, ethnicity, land ownership, and new forms of livelihood. They show a refreshing irreverence for national and conceptual boundaries in tracing connections among migrants and homelands, local and global, domestic and public. Collectively the chapters define a new kind of food studies in anthropology that (1) is grounded in history and political economy; (2) emphasizes the mutual interaction between global and local instead of seeing them as opposites; (3) treats authenticity as a complex and constant process, rather than a steady-state or a quality of goods or products; (4) views the nation state as an only partially successful entity, one that is often resisted, undercut, and even destroyed; and finally (5) this volume does not start analysis by reifying boundaries or bounded groups, but looks instead at the ways that flows and movements of culture may create or challenge boundaries.

In saying that food studies are developing into a new kind of anthropology, I do not mean to say that the scope or methods of this work are being invented anew. We have many venerable ancestors who have laid the groundwork, from Audrey Richards to Sidney Mintz. Anthropology is more like a palimpsest than an open book. Each generation re-inscribes itself on top of an only partially-faded text, in a way that allows some of the earlier work to remain legible, while other parts are obscured.

One of the great pleasures of reading the chapters of this book comes from seeing how cuisines are also palimpsests. They are constantly being remade and revised, and even when the cook tries to recapture or replicate a dish or a food from the past, it never comes out the same way, for it is always being produced and consumed in a new social context. No meal can be an exact repeat of the ones before it, because of the irreversibility of time; the diners will have aged, the tablecloth accumulates stains, the vegetables you buy this year are subtly different from the ones you cooked last year. You simply cannot eat the same food twice. To borrow a metaphor from Mark Twain, food and cuisine in the present can rhyme with those of the past, but they can never be perfect reproductions.

This paradox frames many of the ways the authors in this book engage with the ideas of tradition and innovation, continuity and rupture with the past. While once anthropologists were in the business of authentification, certifying that something was indeed being done in a traditional fashion, with authentic ingredients, implements, and procedures, we no longer rush to issue such pronouncements, at least in print. Authenticity, we assert, is a social construction, with a political, economic, and social context, and we seem happiest when we can show how something that people feel is timeless and a profound basis for their identity is actually something out of a box, an import, based on new ingredients.

But denying the reality of tradition or the authenticity of foods and practices is just as much a political act as standing behind the Parmesan cheese and saying, "this is exactly the same cheese that was made here 500 years ago." We may know that *moros y cristianos*, or *gallo pinto*, or red beans and rice, are relatively recent inventions, but we must also recognize that authenticity and tradition are things that many people fervently believe in. We may no longer be a part of the authentification industry, but cookbook authors, food processors, advertisers, and popular artists still celebrate both the traditional and the modern in a constant mass-mediated din that cannot be avoided or muted. Each of the chapters in this book engages, in some way, with this question of time and temporality, of how people forge relationships between old and new. They show us how a cuisine can absorb and domesticate foreign elements while rejecting others, how people can change identity by learning new food practices, or refuse absorption by insisting on the uniqueness of their own tradition. But each chapter does this while keeping food in the center of the table, no longer a marginal side dish or spicy sauce, but the main dish, satisfying in itself.

In putting these papers together as a group, Garth is bringing us closer to understanding classical anthropological issues like continuity and change, migration, and nationalism. She also invites us to think more deeply about the continuing significance of culture-areas, and demonstrates once again how comparison is such a deeply important part of our social science. The result is refreshing, readable, and useful at a number of levels. Hopefully it will also prompt some readers to fry some mashed plantain, try out a pepperpot recipe, or enjoy the ironic pleasure of imagining that KFC is an authentic Trini experience!

Richard R. Wilk
Indiana University

Figure 0.1   Map of the Caribbean.

Introduction: Understanding Caribbean Identity through Food

Hanna Garth

This volume is an extended conversation about the ways in which people in the Caribbean maintain and adjust their ways of eating as local food systems change. Through the focus on food, these works help to illuminate how issues such as globalization, neoliberalism, and migration are experienced in everyday life. Food often carries some significant social meaning, and by consuming foods with those meanings we symbolically incorporate them into our identities. Food consumption connects to a wide range of social processes related to identity, from class distinction (Bourdieu [1979]1984, 1993) and religious practice (Walker Bynum 1997), to cultural preferences (Barthes 1997; Counihan and van Esterik 1997; Sahlins 1990; Weismantel 1988) and nationalism (Appadurai 1988). Foods and cultural groups' culinary preferences also help to define one's place in society. Food reflects who we are, but as we create and recreate cuisine we may change the way that food expresses identity.

Collective identities have long been strengthened and forged under situations of distress caused by changes in local food systems (Escobar and Alvarez 1992): this phenomenon continues today as "the vagaries of modern life undo and remake people's lives in new and ominous ways" (Biehl, Good, and Kleinman 2007: 1). Identity is always a relationship, not a property. According to Richard Wilk's (1999) analysis of consumption practices in Belize, as food systems change individuals are able to construct "imaginative scenarios" of the kinds of people they wish to be as they consume and identify with a range of new commodities and media images (Miller 1995: 149). For instance, Roseberry (1996) has demonstrated a link between class identity and the growth of a specialized coffee market in the United States; at the time of that study Americans tended to associate drinking so-called fancy coffee with an upper or upper-middle class identity. Pilcher (1998) examines the role of food and everyday life in Mexican national identity, showing the ways in which corn-based foods, once considered to be lowly peasant foods, became a symbol of national heritage that today are proudly associated with Mexican identity.

Caribbean scholars and food scholars alike have connected the cultural, social, and economic practices relating to Caribbean food production and consumption with efforts to define and mobilize national identity (Derby 1998; Wilk 2006a). In addition to national and class identity, foods are tied to many different facets of peoples' identities, from gender and ethnicity to counterculture and resistance movements. Historically, anthropologists have studied the link between identity and consumption by outlining changes in traditional behavior as modern and neo-liberal economies have emerged across the globe. Anthropologists have tended to link increased individualism with capitalist "neoliberal consumption." The rise of large transnational corporations and growth of individual and household purchasing has been associated with the erosion of tradition. Several of the contributions in this volume reveal some of the ways in which changes in food systems, access to new foods, and related knowledge can challenge local hierarchies and ideologies and bring about positive change. While some contributors show how new foods can be empowering and help people to challenge established hierarchies, others show that the maintenance of long-standing culinary traditions can also be an empowering form of resistance. As Ryan Schacht's chapter shows, for the Makushi the consumption of cassava is connected to their struggles to stay alive and maintain their cultural identity despite hundreds of years of colonialism and postcolonial global capitalist influence that push them to change their cuisine and in turn their way of life.

When cuisine has long been linked to place, how does the relationship between food and identity change as regional characteristics dissolve or people migrate away from their ancestral locations? The contributors to this volume consider how these relationships between food and identity shift as identity constructs destabilize through changes in economic and political systems, new migration patterns, and movements of foods to and from the Caribbean through the global food system. Lidia Marte explores how *mangú*, a staple dish in the Dominican Republic, is now a prominent site of self-representation for Dominicans in New York City, and is used to perform in Dominican "identity politics" on and off of the island.

Another theme cross-cutting this volume are the ways in which race and gender are affected by the destabilization of longstanding links between food and identity. As I outline further on, several chapters reveal the ways in which identity is truly intersectional, hybrid, and multiple. For instance, Lauren Wynne's chapter illustrates that consuming new foods and identifying with broader Mexican culture allows women in Juubche to become more versatile and respected members of the community, thus shifting longstanding local gender dynamics. Through the ability to manage new foods and successfully integrate them into local life, they become resident culinary experts. These new foods and consumption practices may lead them to reshape their understandings of the body and the universe.

Theories of Identity in the Caribbean

> This is a region where Pentecostalism is as "indigenous" as Rastafarianism, where some "Bush Negroes" were Christians long before Texas became "American," where some "East Indians" find peace in "African" rituals of Shango.
>
> —Michel-Rolph Trouillot, "The Caribbean Region," 1992: 24

Defining "the Caribbean" is a very difficult task. Social and cultural life varies almost as much as cuisine from place to place. One common factor is that the region,[1] roughly comprised of the territories that touch the Caribbean Sea, was the first of many European colonial experiments in the New World.[2] Early on, colonialism brought large numbers of people and new foods from Europe. In the 1500s, Spain was the dominant colonial force in the Caribbean. Spanish colonial rule quickly exhausted natural resources (including native foods) and decimated native populations. The region is characterized by hundreds of years of European colonization and plantation economies based on the chattel slavery of Africans and others. As European colonizers expanded into the region, the slave labor plantation system began to thrive (Mintz and Price 1985: 4). Over the seventeenth, eighteenth, and nineteenth centuries, millions of Africans were forced into chattel slavery in the Caribbean, and hundreds of thousands of Chinese and other Asian indentured servants were brought to the region to support the plantation economy.[3] Just as people came to the Caribbean from all over the world, so did many of the foods and culinary traditions.

Many who migrated to the Caribbean came on their own without large family networks; they had to learn to "deal socially with others" (Mintz 1993: 201). The social and physical interactions between Africans, Europeans, Natives, and other migrants manifested in the "creolization" of the people and cuisine within region—that is, the social, cultural, and biological mixture that ultimately led to new identities. Movement to and within the Caribbean has been a normal part of life there since before colonization, and self-awareness in comparison to Others has long been a part of the way that people in the Caribbean come to understand their identities. Caribbean cuisines also became mixtures of ingredients and cuisines from all of these different groups of people.

These circumstances gave rise to what Sidney Mintz (1993) has called "the first modernized peoples in world history" (191). For Mintz (1993), modernity in this context refers to a new awareness of cultural differences and variety that is open to the Other and to rethinking one's own ways of living and thinking. This understanding of modernity also tends to illuminate to the subject their relative smallness in the world and a lack of control over rapid and ongoing change (Mintz 1993). Furthermore, these forms of social contact and the resulting economic situation, which creates "new tensions between needs and desires," has been characterized as the departure point for theories of the modern subject (Epele 2002: 164). Modern food consumption, like migration, is a global process embedded in particular historical, political, and social contexts. At the same time social scientists began to focus increasingly on the Caribbean in the 1980s, consumption research also became increasingly important within the social sciences. Consumption practices, food consumption in particular, are among the many ways in which people come to understand their world and develop their sense of identity (Douglas and Isherwood 1979). Identities are not fixed essences; they are socially and culturally constructed through interpersonal performances, relations, and behaviors.

Because of the ways in which people and goods come together in the Caribbean, scholars who focus on that region have long been interested in theories of identity. In Trouillot's review of Caribbean anthropology, he reminds us that "in the Caribbean, there is no 'native' viewpoint, there is no privileged shoulder upon which to lean" (1992: 24). Although this is not true for some parts of the greater Caribbean—such as Columbia, Venezuela, and Guyana, where there are still large indigenous populations today (see Schacht, this volume)—the larger Caribbean islands' native populations were reduced to such small numbers that their viewpoints and practices are largely absent from the regions island nations today. Due to the lack of an observable native perspective, the Caribbean was not a central focus of early social scientists and those who did study there struggled with how to characterize the people of the area (Mintz 1993; Scott 2004). During a time when anthropological research focused on native populations in their indigenous environments, the relatively marginal role of Amerindians and the ongoing influence of colonial and international political economic forces contributed to the lack of anthropological attention on the Caribbean. Instead, focus on the African diaspora has been central to a growing number of ethnographic studies of the Caribbean. Studying the Caribbean under circumstances of colonization, migration, and political change, early scholars tended to focus on understanding factors associated with cultural change in Caribbean slave societies. Yet the very factors that kept anthropologists from studying the Caribbean in the past have been precisely what have made Caribbean anthropology so rich today. From issues of ethnicity and representation to local connections to world systems, Caribbean anthropology has been engaged in issues that have become increasingly important to the discipline (cf. Bhabha 1994; Hannerz 1990). The notions of creolization, transculturation, and hybridity (on which I elaborate further on in this chapter) emerged as theoretical constructs used to understand identity in Caribbean societies.

Through their studies of the African diaspora in the Americas, European American anthropologist Melville J. Herskovits (1941) and African American sociologist E. Franklin Frazier (1957) established two distinct social theories. Herskovits attempted to alleviate the forms of racism that he felt were present within the academy by showing what he saw as retained "Africanisms"—cultural or linguistic features that are thought to be characteristically African—in New World black culture that reached back, and endured through, the years of slavery. This theory of identity is known as *syncretism*, that is, the notion that cultural, religious, linguistic, and other kinds of traditions that originated in Africa continue to be carried out in the New World African diaspora.[4] By contrast, Frazier contended that the sociocultural shaping of people of African descent under slavery and colonialism in the New World stripped them of their cultures and led to their development as "disadvantaged Americans" (Yelvington 2001: 230). Frazier argued that the horrific process of forced migration and chattel slavery had eliminated any African cultural traits in this population. Frazier's approach is one version of "acculturation." For many years these two approaches were in opposition within the social sciences, along with the theory of creolization, another framework developed as a critique of Herskovits's work, which I outline further below (cf. Apter 2004).

In their 1976 work, Mintz and Price reject the idea of retention of Africanisms in the New World, arguing that "an African cultural heritage, widely shared by the people imported into any new colony, will have to be defined in less concrete terms, by focusing more on values, and less on sociocultural forms" (Mintz and Price [1976]1992: 9). Emphasizing the ethnic diversity of the African diaspora, they argue further that sociocultural characterizations of the diaspora must take into account the conditions of slavery in the Americas. They illustrate the ways in which sociocultural changes that began to take place as soon as Africans were forced onto the slave ships to America significantly influenced New World culture. This process, known as creolization, continued in the New World as the process of cultural interchange between the African diaspora and various other ethnic groups who were residing in the Caribbean. The interplay of these groups caused shifts in language, art, food, dress, and social customs, which created a new and unique social system. For many early scholars, creolization was very similar to acculturation; it was a slow process whereby less civilized people ascended the social hierarchies to become more similar to the dominant classes. However, Mintz and Price, among other scholars of creolization, began to recognize it as a process of mutual exchange through which groups of people from all ends of the social hierarchy were transformed.

As I outline in chapter six, Fernando Ortiz developed the notion of "transculturation" as an alternative to the idea of "acculturation" that was more open to mutual exchange (Ortiz [1940]1963). In order to develop a theory of Caribbean identity, Ortiz conducted an analysis of the cultural attributes of different groups of people in Cuba. He focused his analysis on cultural expressions through music, religious ceremonies, and oral traditions. Ortiz then attempted to link these cultural traits to different places of origin in Africa (Barcia 2008). Ortiz worked to explain and bring value to black and mulatto cultural practices, which were generally shunned, marginalized, and denied by the light-skinned elites during his era.[5] In his book the *Cuban Counterpoint* ([1947]1995), Ortiz traces the development of sugar and tobacco as Cuba's central agricultural products; he examines their role in transculturation, drawing a parallel between the crops and the people who cultivate them.[6] Using a food metaphor about a Cuban stew called *ajiaco*, Ortiz developed the notion of transculturation as an improvement on the term acculturation:

> I am of the opinion that the word transculturation better expresses the different phases of the process of transition from one culture to another because it does not merely consist in acquiring another culture, which could be defined as deculturation. In addition it carries the idea of the consequent creation of a new cultural phenomena, which could be called neoculturation. (Ortiz 1995: 102–3, as cited in Ryer 2006: 34)

Transculturation also allows for continuous change and the ongoing addition of new elements to identity. It is more aligned with Stuart Hall's notion that theories of identity must allow for hybridity. For Hall, the experience of Caribbean identity is defined "not by essence or purity, but by the recognition of a necessary heterogeneity and diversity; by a conception of 'identity' that lives with and through, not despite, difference; by hybridity. Diaspora identities are constantly producing and reproducing themselves anew through transformation and difference" (Hall and du Gay 1996: 235).

The concept of transculturation has been criticized for being too idealist and not accounting for differences across demographic lines, such as race, age, gender, or class, to name a few (cf. Larsen 1990). Kimberlé Crenshaw (1991) uses the concept of "intersectionality" to get beyond the reductiveness of many identity theories. She specifically does not think of the concept of intersectionality as just another "totalizing theory of identity," but rather as a way to "denote the various ways in which race and gender interact to shape the multiple dimensions" of experience (Crenshaw 1991: 1244). That is to say, identity overlaps in complex ways; one can not simply add black identity and female identity to get black female identity, which in reality is a specific identity to the particular combination or intersection of being black and being a woman. She discussed this concept in relation to black women in the United States, looking closely at the intersection of race and gender, but apart from race intersectionality it has been extended to include sexual orientation (Boellstorff 2007), class (Mullings 2002), and citizenship (Rottmann and Marx Ferree 2008). Like many other theories of identity, intersectionality has been critiqued because it is extremely difficult to study due to the fact that social life is so irreducibly complex. The complexity of social life makes it nearly impossible to create fixed categories upon which to base a study and to find the right methods with which to analyze intersectional identities (McCall 2009).

Individuals, groups, and cuisine also have multiple and hybrid identities (Hall and du Gay 1996; Hernandez-Reguant 2006).[7] Theories of identity tend to emphasize the common traits of a group, contrasting these with others in order to better understand collective identities and how individual members envision their belonging. Zygmunt Bauman, following Siegfried Kracauer (1995: 144), conceives of these groups as

communities of "life and fate" whose members "live together in an indissoluble at-
tachment," "welded together solely by ideas or various principles" (Bauman 2001: 11).
Unfortunately, these theories of identity often deemphasize heterogeneity within
groups and individual identity. Not only is there heterogeneity within groups, but
also individual identity is not fixed and can change over time and space. Individual
identity may be fragmented, multisided, and present in different ways in different
settings. The possibility of multiplicity and hybridity adds another layer of complexity to intersectional identity; continuing with the example from above, black female
identity is not the same for all black females, and it may even vary over time and
space for one black female individual.

Food, Political Economy, and Family Structure

Although there is a great deal of variation and complexity in Caribbean identity, there
are many common factors that influence identity across the Caribbean. Focusing on
the Caribbean as a unified entity, Cabezas (2009: 8) notes that "since colonization the
Caribbean has been seen by Europe and America as a place for extraction" (see also
Robotham 1998). Colonists took advantage of Caribbean climates and land to grow
export crops such as sugar, coffee, and fruit. Since then the Caribbean has been and
continues to be a place from which companies, governments, individuals, and other
entities from all over the world purchase or appropriate goods, labor, and resources.
International trade agreements allow for the purchase of Caribbean produced goods,
including food products, at extremely low prices. The hospitality industry has long
capitalized on the beauty of Caribbean beaches; unfortunately the profits from Caribbean tourism often go to local or transnational elites. For the most part, tourism has
done little to develop or improve the everyday lives and food consumption practices
of those who must live and work in the Caribbean.

Caribbean scholars and food scholars alike have connected local foodways—the
cultural, social, and economic practices relating to food production and consumption—
with efforts to define and mobilize national identity (Derby 1998; Wilk 2006a). Because the Caribbean was shaped economically, culturally, and politically by the colonial plantation system (Cabezas 2009; Smith 1962; Smith 1956; Trouillot 1998),
understanding the Caribbean today requires a focus on political economy, national
identity, and resistance to hegemony. For the most part, the economy of the Common-
wealth Caribbean (former colonies of the United Kingdom) is based on a Keynesian
welfare state, where markets are thought of as a means to allocate resources in
exchange for a steady rise in living standards (Dominguez 2003: 11).[8] Even after
colonialism and plantation economies, the Caribbean continues to have many structural linkages to the global economy. For instance, in the 1970s, Jamaica and Guyana were the first Caribbean nations to obtain International Monetary Fund (IMF)

assistance in order to pay off international debts. These loans coupled with the structural adjustment policies that were implemented to establish so-called free-market economies where agriculture shifted to export crops and food was imported for domestic consumption, and in many cases this structure plunged Caribbean countries into poverty, bankruptcy, or heightened unemployment. In many instances, these policies led to decreased purchasing power and decreased quality of life for people living in these countries. Furthermore, many Caribbean nations have become export-processing zones with tax-free incentives to multinational corporations and exemptions from labor laws. Several eastern Caribbean states created an official Caribbean Community (CARICOM) with the Caribbean Single Market and Economy (CSME), which allows for easier movement of people, goods, and services.[9] These political economic systems significantly affect food systems and in turn the food consumption practices of Caribbean families.

Although political economic systems do not determine identity, the common experience of living under similar political and economic conditions does relate to and influence identity in various ways. For instance, Amy Bentley (2001) has also written about the relationship between identity and food riots. She argues that food riots are motivated by more than hunger. Because foods are so deeply tied to identity, these riots are often triggered by efforts to maintain group and individual identity when confronted by political economic systems. In the Dominican Republic, the poor quality of life in the early 1980s erupted into a food riot in 1984 that led to a wave of violence throughout the country (Cabezas 2009; Walton and Seddon 1994).

Issues relating to gender and kinship also have similarities across the Caribbean. Studies of sexual reproduction, family, and kinship have always been central to understanding Caribbean societies. Some of the seminal works of Caribbean anthropology, including the works of R. T. Smith (1956) and M. G. Smith (1962), have focused on kinship and family structure. Slavery created ruptures in traditional kinship patterns; people within slave societies developed nuanced ways to create and conceptualize kinship. Sexual reproduction and the family are the center of the social mixing that is so central to creolization; family and household are also often the setting in which the connections between food and identity can really be explored ethnographically. Family and kinship establish and reinforce certain cultural forms, and at the same time, sociocultural norms and broader macrolevel processes shape the gendered dynamics of family life. As economies have shifted away from predominantly rural agrarian societies, and toward urban cosmopolitan societies, labor structures and living dynamics have shifted as well. These shifts in the sociopolitical organization of society lead to changes in living arrangements, household dynamics, and the social dynamics of food consumption. They also contribute to changing kinship patterns. With these changes in social organization, people often shift the way that they eat, and in turn, as new ways of eating are integrated into society, individuals often change their lifestyles. For instance, the low cost of fast food and pre-prepared meals may lead to decreases in how much cooking and eating is done in the household. As it becomes increasingly common for families to be split between the city and the countryside and across transnational borders, the social dynamics of daily life are shifting and these changes may affect identity. Ethnographic studies of family life are still extremely important given the ever-present migratory flows within and from the Caribbean.

Food Consumption and Everyday Life

The chapters in this volume use food as the object of study to illuminate social issues directly and indirectly related to consumption. Early work in the anthropology of food tied food consumption habits to "traditions" and local cultures of more simple societies. This early work (Lévi-Strauss 1968; Mennell 1996; Mintz 1985b, [1974]1989) showed that food consumption, like many other aspects of traditional societies, has not been static and has long been influenced by contact through trade and migration. But this sort of slow change and integration of new items into already established cuisines appears somewhat different from many of the types of eating habits that are being studied today. The sociocultural dimensions of food as an object of study within the social sciences has taken off in recent years, and more research focuses on complex social and economic systems (Magdoff and Tokar 2009; Nestle 2002; Pollan 2006, 2008). Revealing some of the ways in which food is just as central to local economies as it is to everyday household life and so many aspects of human life, the anthropological study of food illuminates rich and detailed information about how people experience the complexities of daily life.

While early studies of food focused on traditional food consumption habits, recent studies more often focus on food production and distribution (Bestor 2004; Pollan 2006, 2008; Schlosser 2002). Anthropological studies of global systems of food production have detailed the ways in which production systems and global trade affect local consumption patterns (Inglis and Gimlin 2009; Mintz 1985a; Wolf 1982). Jack Goody (1997) outlined a history of food preservation practices that gave rise to the global movement of (once) perishable foods. Mintz's (1985a) work on sugar reveals how the Caribbean plantation system and the flooding of European markets with cheap sugar radically shifted household consumption patterns that led to long-lasting changes in labor practices and other aspects of global production. Many anthropological works on food production align with the work of development sociologists McMichael and Myhre (1991), which shows that much of the world's contemporary food production is controlled by just a few very large transnational corporations, and as these corporations take over there is a decrease in national regulation and control over food production. To understand the food systems and consumption patterns of a household within any single country, it is necessary to understand how the local food system embeds within the global food system.[10]

Changes in global food production have changed food distribution not only with respect to the items for sale in markets but also regarding the rise of new forms of distribution such as fast food restaurants. Much of the work in this area has focused on "single commodities and substances" (Mintz and Du Bois 2002: 102), weaving together stories of historical production and consumption practices and then tracing the commodities through to the contemporary dinner table. Recently there has been increasing attention on "globalized cuisine" and the rise of new and innovative forms of food processing that lead to different consumption practices. For instance, Watson's (1997) volume illuminates local responses to McDonald's in five different countries where invariably fast food eventually becomes a local institution. The chapters in Watson's volume reveal the ways in which McDonald's consumers relate their fast food experience to their identity, whether it is a connection to modernity, class identity, or American food culture.

Despite the rise of globalized cuisine, there are still places where people don't eat this way. Even when production is no longer local but becomes transnational, corporate, or global, consumption can remain grounded in local identities. Continuing with studies of McDonald's, Melissa Caldwell's (2004) research illustrates how local groups can take something often seen as generically global and make it into their own. Caldwell shows how Russians incorporate McDonald's into the personal aspects of daily life, by pulling the transnational corporation into local ideas of what is meaningful, and thus making it local.

With this volume we seek to open a dialogue, an investigation on the subject of food and identity in the Caribbean region, to show how the relationships between food and identity can shape the experience of everyday life in the Caribbean today. Through ethnographic research, each of the chapters brings a unique approach to the study of food and identity in the Caribbean. The chapters address connections to food and precolonial histories, as well as the ways in which more recent political economic changes and development in the region have manifested on the contemporary dinner table. Whether analyzing identity and nationalism, migrations and diaspora, or tourism and authenticity, all of the chapters in this volume shed light on how people in the Caribbean struggle with their culinary identities.

Outline of the Chapters

Ryan N. Schacht's chapter opens the volume by describing nearly five centuries of cassava cultivation, preparation, and consumption among the Makushi of southwestern Guyana. Despite centuries of suffering through diseases and slave raids, the Makushi maintain cassava consumption traditions. Postcolonial conflict between the Makushi and other Guyanese gave way to increased isolation of the Makushi who remain living in remote communities, and who must grow most of their own food— this is yet another reason for the maintenance of the cassava consumption tradition.

In fact, it could be the nutritional benefits of this staple crop that allowed them to live through the difficulties of colonialism. In stark contrast to the non-Amerindian diet, which is rice-based, the Makushi people talk about cassava as "we food," clearly aligning it with their cultural identity. Schacht shows how despite hundreds of years of sociopolitical struggle and a changing national food system, cassava remains inextricably tied to Makushi identity and an outward expression of what defines them as a group.

Heather J. Sawyer's chapter uses an analysis of tourism and tourists' desires to show how particular representations of local cultures may or may not be so-called authentic forms of identity for local people. Sawyer's chapter explores the impacts of economic development efforts via conservation-based tourism development on shifting seafood accessibility in Roatán, an island located approximately fifty kilometers (thirty miles) off the Caribbean coast of Honduras. The residents of Roatán (who are primarily English speakers of Caribbean descent) view themselves as distinct historically, culturally, linguistically, politically, and economically from those living on the Honduran mainland. The subsequent emergence of an islander identity separate from the Honduran mainland has been fostered by the strong linguistic and trade connections islanders have with other English-speaking enclaves in the Caribbean and U.S. Regional trade relations, local ecological availability, and the island's history have shaped islander food identity. Sawyer discusses the relationships between Roatán's declining fishing industry and the rise in tourism. Sawyer analyzes the ways in which this problem is ignored in an effort to please tourists and serve them the "local cuisine" as they imagine that authentic Caribbean island cuisine should be. Tourists come away with a satisfying experience that reinforces false stereotypes about island life and covers up the devastation of local ecology and traditional cuisine.

The chapter by Lauren Wynne also reveals the ways in which tourism affects local food consumption patterns and notions of authentic local cuisine. Wynne's piece focuses on shifts in culinary expertise and ideas of the body in one rural town in Yucatán, Mexico. The town's residents are of mostly indigenous descent and their everyday cuisine is the product of Mesoamerican roots and centuries of Spanish influence. Their cuisine is more similar to that of neighboring Caribbean islands than to that of central Mexico. A history of relative isolation from the rest of Mexico, as both colony and nation-state, left many of Yucatán's established culinary features intact, such as tamales cooked in banana leaves, the use of habañero peppers, and a reliance on sour oranges. While some food traditions remain intact, Wynne shows the ways in which families integrate subtle innovations that fit within the existing material conditions of life there. For her informants, the production, preparation, and consumption of foodstuffs has been the primary way in which they continue to identify with their local cosmology, one that roots the most basic of human needs within the universe's cycles of life and death. As in other parts of the Caribbean where tourism has radically altered the ways in which residents make their livings, the rural cuisine of Yucatán today reflects the global influences and influxes of cash that accompanied the rapid development of a massive regional tourist industry. Wynne examines how the development of tourism, along with shifts in farming and mass media, have led to the accumulation of new wealth and expertise with implications for how residents engage with these recent additions to the local culinary landscape. In doing so, they embrace what they envision to be Mexican, middle-class, and cosmopolitan while retaining the cultural richness that reflects Yucatán's unique place in both Mexican and Caribbean history.

Gillian Richards-Greaves draws on nearly five years of data collection in Guyana and among the Guyanese diaspora in New York City to illustrate the role food has in Guyanese constructions of race and identity. In the chapter, Richards-Greaves explores the ways in which the influences and intersections of race and gender are embedded within communal processes of cooking and eating what research participants view as distinctively Guyanese cuisine. She specifically examines religious influences on ritual performances and identity negotiations amongst African Guyanese in the two communities. She also shows how food is a powerful weapon in Guyanese national politics, given that cuisines may be racially tagged and that each racial group has their own dishes that they tie to group identity. Although some dishes are clearly associated with a particular race, Richards-Greaves also illustrates that often dishes are not such rigid representations of a singular racial group, and that there has been a lot of mixing, borrowing, and blending between the dishes over time and across groups.

Lidia Marte's chapter analyzes the intersections of gender and nationality through the Dominican dish *mangú*, a dish of boiled and mashed plantains. Since the early 1500s, mangú has remained a major staple for the majority of Dominicans in the Dominican Republic (DR) and in the Dominican diaspora. Mangú is not claimed openly in the Dominican Republic as "national" but is now a prominent site of self-representation for Dominicans in the diaspora, specifically in New York City. Marte examines three mangú preparations and the associated narratives in order to help shed light on the axes of intersecting identities—gender, sexuality, class, and race—as sites of contested national belonging and of the transnational search for a sense of "home." She shows how this low-prestige staple allows for examination of the many strategic self-making roles that food is made to perform in Dominican identity politics.

My own chapter analyzes the ways in which Cuba's nationalized food rationing system has affected local food consumption patterns, and local ideas of how food and Cuban identity are related. I elaborate on Fernando Ortiz's idea of transculturation and his use of food metaphors to illuminate that idea. Two of the dishes featured in this chapter, *spaghetti con picadillo* and *arroz con pollo*, are overwhelmingly common in everyday Cuban households, but they are not infused with the same sense of cultural identity as other dishes consumed in Cuba, such as rice and beans (or *congris*), *hallaca* (a local version of tamales), and other foods that participants characterize as specifically Cuban. I demonstrate how Cubans struggle just to get food on the table, and once that is accomplished they try to take the ingredients and resources that they have, which may not be the same as the so-called traditional foods, and make them into something that is still uniquely Cuban. The examples show that despite changes in the Cuban food system, which shift access to particular types of traditional foods, Cubans are still able to consume a type of cuisine that remains distinctly Cuban in their eyes, though not traditional foods that they see as their own.

Marisa Wilson's chapter outlines general Caribbean and more specific Trinidadian histories of modernization and imported food consumption. Wilson connects this history with Trini consumerism today, showing how tastes for expensive imports and a general dislike of local products are connected with hundreds of years of socialization and connections between modern consumption, identity, and social hierarchies. She uses examples of shopping in local markets versus commercial grocery stores; local efforts to increase domestic food production; rampant consumerism during Christmas; and the Trini love of Kentucky Fried Chicken (KFC) to illustrate the ways in which particular foods are associated with Trini identity. She shows that within that association further distinctions along class and social lines are determined by where people purchase the products and where the products are produced. Wilson shows how the foreign can become associated with the local, and that mass-produced globalized brands can come to stand for authentic local identity. While she finds this to be true among many of her Trinidadian subjects, she also shows that the "localize it" movement, appealing to the economic and environmental effects of uneven development, is trying to change these attitudes.

John Mazzeo and Barrett P. Brenton approach the concept of food identity through an examination of how the development of hybrid seed threatens peasant production. This chapter examines the implications that the introduction of hybrid seed as part of a response to the 2010 earthquake in Haiti raises for food security, food sovereignty, and cultural identity. They argue that the peasantry derives its identity through its ability to be autonomous and independent producers, offering an ethnographic look at how modified food technology can impact local identity by transforming production. This chapter examines the peasantry and the peasant movement around the area of Papay, Haiti. The Haitian peasant class highly values autonomy and their ability to control the means of production, which is threatened with the introduction of hybrid and genetically modified (GM) seed. They define themselves in contrast to wage laborers or plantation workers and place great value in the independence and freedom their livelihood provides them. After the January 2010 earthquake, access to sufficient quantities of nutritious food remains an issue for millions of Haitians. Haiti, like many Caribbean countries, relies heavily on imported food—at least 50 percent of national requirements are imported. This chapter reviews the role and motives of large multinational seed companies and partnering international aid organizations in providing new hybrid seed varieties, including seeds suspected of being genetically modified, as a form of humanitarian aid. Accounting for important links between food and identity, the chapter highlights the role of anthropologists in identifying local perceptions of food justice and the realities of food security as critical for developing and supporting sustainable food systems and healthy communities.

Recently many anthropological and sociological studies have emphasized the disruption and despair that accompany globalization, famine, migration, and other shifts in everyday life. It is our hope that this book will offer a different perspective. We use ethnography and historical analysis to study practices and experiences in the Caribbean and its diaspora to illuminate how contemporary politics, economics, and culture shape the relationship between food and identity. The chapters illuminate contemporary issues of food and identity as grounded in practice. This collection brings together chapters that look at the relationship between food and identity in the Caribbean and in Caribbean diasporas. The chapters use histories of food, slavery, colonization, migration, and community to illuminate issues relating to and concepts of identity today.

Cassava and the Makushi: A Shared History of Resiliency and Transformation

Ryan N. Schacht

For every society, there is no more important set of cultural traits than the one related to subsistence. Food, and its necessary growth, gathering, and preparation, is fundamental to the existence of human life. If one would like to know what lies at the very heart of a people, then surely food must be seen as its visible manifestation. Societies throughout time and the world have developed complex ceremonies, rituals, rites, taboos, and beliefs surrounding the growth, harvest, preparation, and consumption of food. The Makushi of southwestern Guyana and their staple foods are no exception. Cassava (*Manihot esculenta* Crantz, Euphorbiaceae) and its products are inextricably tied to Makushi identity and are the outward expressions of what defines them as a group.

Amerindian (the term used to describe Central and South America's indigenous people) societies and cultures have undergone profound transformations through colonization, disease, and missionization. Charles Schomburgk, a German explorer, painted a grim picture of the future of Amerindians after his travels through Guyana in the 1830s.

> Driven from their lands, now in possession of the Europeans and their descendants, they have wandered from their ancient homes, strangers in their own country, and diseases and vices introduced by the settlers and feuds among themselves, have all but annihilated the rightful owners of the soil. It is a melancholy fact, but too well founded that wherever Europeans have settled, the extermination of the native tribes has succeeded their arrival. (Schomburgk 1840: 48)

The Makushi represent a striking example of Schomburgk's depiction because they were nearly wiped out themselves by diseases introduced in the years following European contact with South America (DeFillips, Maina, and Crepin 2004). This was not alarming to the colonial regime at the time because, as one British official stated, Amerindians held "little or no social value and their early extinction must be looked upon as inevitable" (Rowland 1892: 56). However, far from disappearing as victims of "progress," the Makushi have rebounded to become the second largest Amerindian group in Guyana and the fourth largest in Brazil (Forte 1996b; Conselho Indigena de Roraima 1993). This return from the brink has been nothing short of amazing, and much of their resilience resides in their dietary staple: cassava.

Makushi men and women regularly refer to cassava and its associated products as "we food." This simple statement encapsulates a complicated history of conflict, colonization, and upheaval that has at times destabilized a people. This chapter will explain the history of the Makushi and their subsistence patterns, and reveal the importance of cassava in their daily lives. In the face of major social and political upheaval, the fact that this food staple has remained integral to what it means to be Makushi is a testament to the importance of cassava to both group livelihood and identity.

The Makushi

The Makushi are a Carib-speaking people living in the Rio Branco-Rupununi Savannahs in northern Brazil and southwestern Guyana. Historical evidence dating back to the early eighteenth century marks the earliest Makushi presence in the region (Hemming 1994). Settlement of the area was a result of their southern neighbors, the Wapishana, an Arawakan group, driving them north (Evans and Meggers 1960). The Wapishana were themselves responding to external forces, pushed north and eastward as Brazilian settlers began populating the area (Riviere 1963). In southwestern Guyana today, the forested Kanuku Mountains, which run east–west, provide a natural dividing line of the Rupununi savannahs with the Makushi generally found in the north and the Wapishana in the south.

Linguistic, cultural, and ethnohistoric evidence places the Makushi in the tropical forest culture complex (Myers 1993), with their origin centered in the Xingu basin of western Amazonia (Evans and Meggers 1960). The groups from this area all share a complex of subsistence traits that include hunting, fishing, and gathering, as well as the cultivation of cassava through shifting (slash-and-burn), cultivation, and a semi-nomadic lifestyle. Makushi settlements historically were dispersed and politically decentralized (Whitehead 1994). Individuals and households were highly mobile, leading to temporary and distant settlements. A household was a self-sufficient entity in terms of production of food and craft staples and could contain three to four generations under one roof.

Although the Makushi are still alive and well today, much of their way of life has changed since the Europeans first made contact in the Americas. Cassava and its products are still central to the idea of what it means to be a Makushi; however, due to contact a greater reliance has been placed on wage earnings and this has influenced the once strict gender division of labor. Thus, in order to understand how this change came about, as well as to understand the importance of cassava to the contemporary Makushi, it is essential to understand Guyana's colonial history.

Guyana's Colonial History

The first Europeans came to the Guianas in search of new trade routes, spices, and gold. Early voyagers initially saw little of consequence in the interior and often felt themselves in an impenetrable and meaningless green blanket as they attempted to explore the rainforest. In stark contrast, Amerindians in the Guianas lived in relative ecological synchrony with the forested surroundings and had a thorough knowledge of plants and animals (DeFillips, Maina, and Crepin 2004). The Europeans mostly stayed out, but they entered deeper into the forests of the interior as stories spread of the golden city of Manoa and King El Dorado. They began working their way into what was, at least for the European, uncharted territory, using rivers as highways into the interior. Although they never did find El Dorado, and Sir Walter Raleigh lost his head for nearly bankrupting King James I in his series of misguided voyages in the late sixteenth and early seventeenth centuries, they did find areas ripe for colonial exploitation through the development of plantations (Gillian 1963).

The Dutch were the first Europeans to develop permanent settlements in Guyana beginning in 1616, putting their knowledge of building levees, canals, and locks to "recover" the earth from mangrove and tidally flooded swamps (Daly 1974). Initial contacts with Amerindian populations were friendly and the Dutch expressed a keen interest and surprise in the amount of food and crafts they could exchange for cheap European goods. However, this relationship quickly changed, as the colonists needed additional laborers to work in the ever-expanding sugarcane fields. The coastal tribes were first enlisted, with force when necessary, but these overtures were eventually met with resistance and abandonment of plantation life. Because of this, the Dutch in 1686 named four tribes they had contact with immune from slavery and employed them as slave-catchers (Forte 1996c). The Arawak, Carib, Warrau, and Akawaio were not to be used as slaves, but they were to bring other men and women from interior tribes to work in their place.

These slave-raiding exploits carried out by the four immune tribes led to what is known to the locals as the "tribal wars." Stories abound of Makushis being forced to retreat to higher, more remote areas of the Pakaraima Mountains and deeper into the rainforest to avoid the slave-raiding coastal tribes. The Makushi were at a disadvantage as they were not equipped with European goods such as guns and cutlasses (a local term for machetes). Their southern neighbors, the Wapishana, were under the same pressure from the slave-raiders and there were reports that they were living in the savannahs by day, but at night retiring to cliffs and caves that were defended by palisades (Butt Colson and Morton 1982).

Accounts from Sir Walter Raleigh's failed expedition in search of El Dorado may have mentioned the Makushi living in the Rupununi savannah as early as the seventeenth century, but the names of tribes and their descriptions are unclear (Gillian 1963). Before the European presence in South America, the Rupununi savannah likely was unpopulated and the movement of people into the area was either as a consequence of colonizers pushing out tribes from their traditional areas or those seeking refuge from slave-raiding, or both (Williams 1991). In 1793, however, the Dutch government outlawed Amerindian slavery in Guyana and the Makushi subsequently drove the Caribs out of the Rupununi (Forte 1996c). Then, shortly thereafter, the Dutch were themselves driven out by the British at the turn of the nineteenth century. The focus now was wholly on African slaves providing the colonial workforce. This was not to last though as slavery was abolished in 1834 and, without African slaves providing the workforce, the British sought out other plantation workers. Initially the Portuguese were enlisted as indentured servants, but once their period of servitude was completed they quickly began filling the merchant class and expected the same rights as the British. The British had set up a system of social stratification by race in Guyana (as they had in other colonies) and the Portuguese would not stay on as plantation workers after their service period ended. Because the British were not looking to bring in those who would expect equal standing in society, but instead were looking for lifetime laborers, the next experiment was with the Chinese. However, the colony was unable to bring them over in any sizeable numbers and it was at this time that the first boats of indentured East Indians began arriving. In total, over 240,000 East Indians were brought to Guyana (Daly 1974). At this time the colony of India also included Pakistan and as such both Hindus and Muslims were carried over. The Africans had mostly been converted to Christianity (Anglican), followed by the Amerindians during the twentieth century, and thus a multiethnic colony composed of multiple religions was produced.

As some colonists moved from the coast and into the interior they saw much that needed changing in terms of the Amerindian population. This sentiment was felt most profoundly by the missionaries. The intimate lives of the indigenous people—childcare, the home, sexuality, marriage, gender relations, and even bodily adornments—came under the scrutiny and condemnation of the colonizers (see Jacobs 2009). This contributed to social and cultural upheaval as missionaries worked to replace many of the local philosophies that formed Makushi social organization with European Christianity. Polygyny (men taking multiple wives) was banned, nuclear settlements were directed, and men were expected to be the head of the family (Myers 1993). This upheaval was further compounded by the new diseases people brought into the area (even throughout the first half of the twentieth century, epidemics were still killing large numbers of Makushi people) (Jones 1952).

Along with the colonists also came new opportunities for subsistence. Because of the expansive savannahs, the Rupununi was looked to as an ideal area for cattle ranching. Initially brought over from Brazil in the late 1800s, grazing cattle in the open grasslands and savannahs became a common sight in the area (Myers 1993). The balata bleeding industry also took off during this time period (Baldwin 1946). Balata is a rubber substitute extracted from the bullet wood tree (*Manilkaria bidentata*), which is generally found deep in primary rainforest. For these two industries, workers were needed and recruited from local villages. Traditionally, men and women stayed close to their families and homes, but with the advent of wage labor many young adults moved to areas providing jobs. These industries and others had major demographic consequences, affecting cassava demand and production throughout the Rupununi. Balata bleeders, ranchers, and *vaqueiros* (Portuguese word for cowboys) often spent weeks or months alone or in small groups far from settlements (Myers 1993). As such, they needed a portable food source and this led to a demand for the increased production of cassava. These industries also concentrated the demand for cassava products in new population centers, resulting in many farmers expanding their farms and producing more cassava than needed for their own subsistence for the first time.

Contemporary Guyana and the Makushi

As a result of its colonial history, Guyana today is both a multiethnic and multi-religious state. Of the nation's roughly 750,000 people, 90 percent live along the urbanized coastlands, which is only about 5 percent of the country's landmass. The remaining 95 percent of the country is either sparsely or completely un-populated. Inland from the coast, Amerindians compose the majority of the popu-lation. There are currently approximately 24,000 Makushi, with 9,000 living in Region Nine (Upper Takutu-Upper Essequibo, one of ten administrative regions) of southwestern Guyana (Ricardo 1996; Forte 1996b). Throughout the region, there are twenty-seven principle Makushi villages as well as a number of smaller satellite communities (Forte 1996c).

Geographically, Guyana is part of the South American continent but culturally the major population centers on the coast are Caribbean. Much of the interior, including the Rupununi, is more closely connected with the markets and industries of Brazil. Partly this is the result of the inland regions of Guyana being isolated from coastal populations. To this day there is only one road that connects the coast to the interior and it is unpaved and frequently impassable during the rainy season. Because of the interior's remoteness from the coastland and the close ties to Brazil, much of what happens in the interior is disconnected from the capital.

The racial politics on the coast, created by colonial policies, were (and are) fo-cused solely on the competition between the Afro- and Indo-Guyanese groups for power. After independence in 1966, the paternalism of the colonial government was replaced by a strident nationalism colored by racial overtones (Colchester, Rose, and James 2002). This led to those in the interior, who were neither Afro- or Indo-Guyanese, feeling left out of the political sphere because their needs were not being addressed by the coastally-focused government. A rebellion led by ranchers followed in 1969 and was provoked by many reasons, including "insecure pastoral leases, am-bitious government proposals for reallocating land in favor of settlers from the coast, racial suspicions, lack of control of cattle rustling from Brazil, and ill-documented ru-mors of meddling from neighboring countries" (Colchester, Rose, and James 2002: 125).

This uprising was quickly put down by the Guyana Defense Force, and the cattle heyday of the Rupununi was ended overnight as the livestock that had not been rustled by Brazilians was taken by the government. A military base was installed in the capital of Region Nine, Lethem, and settlements of Coastlanders (primarily Afro-Guyanese) were made in traditional Amerindian lands with the purpose of bringing the coast to the interior (Forte 1996b).

This rebellion fueled suspicions that the Makushi were not loyal Guyanese and it poisoned relations between inhabitants of the interior and the coast in a manner that endures to this day. Many government services were suspended including veterinary, rangeland, abattoir and refrigeration, and air transport. Because these connections with the coast were allowed to deteriorate, the ranching economy went into decline (Colchester, Rose, and James 2002). As a consequence, most of the Makushi of Guyana live in remote communities, removed from the national political and economic power and have much more in common with the Makushi in Brazil than with coastal Guyanese (Vereecke 1994; Forte 1996b). The result has been that the economy of the Rupununi is more focused toward the Brazilian state capital of Boa Vista than to Georgetown. Many Makushi in the region now move to Brazil for work because of the decline in the cattle industry (as well as that of the balata industry around 1970). The Brazilian government has also encouraged this movement of people by recently completing a bridge over the Takatu River connecting the two countries near Lethem, making the trip to Brazil even easier. It is quite the transformation to cross into Brazil over this bridge, leaving behind the dusty (or muddy, depending on the season), red, pitted, two-wheeled vehicle tracks of the Rupununi for the paved, illuminated roads of Guyana's more industrialized neighbor.

The geographical remoteness of the Makushi, as well as most of Guyana's Amerindian population, exacerbates their marginal status as a group—socially, culturally, and economically—within a country dominated by other ethnic groups (Henfry 2002). Throughout the Caribbean, indigenous contributions to national identity and cultural diversity are rarely recognized, and Guyana is no exception (Palacio 1995). The attention of the coastal Guyanese generally is focused north in the direction of the Caribbean and North America. Very few ever even visit the interior and as a consequence ignorance and misconceptions of the area abound among the general public (Henfry 2002). From the point of view of the coast, much of what happens in the interior is unimportant and there is a sharp social and conceptual divide between the coastal dwellers and those who live in the "hinterland" as it is known. Those in the interior are generally viewed as poorer, less educated, and uncultured, and as such are viewed as having a lower social status than the average Coastlander. As a Guyanese anthropologist noted, "Amerindians comprise the poorest and most neglected stratum of Guyanese society, both when measured in terms of gross annual earnings and in the popular perception of where they fit in the local hierarchical ranking—in both instances, on the very last rung" (Forte 1996a: 5).

Thus the contemporary Makushi people of Guyana are stuck in a land in-between. They are Guyanese but are viewed as less so than those from the coast. Consequently, most have removed themselves even further from the politics of "Town," as the capital city is called. There is little chance that a remedy exists even within the current public education system. This system follows a pan-Caribbean curriculum and as such does not hold much relevance to the requirements of interior life. Thus, successful students in this system are more likely to be alienated from their home areas rather than be equipped to help solve problems there (Forte 1996b; Lea 1968). Traditional social organization of the Makushi has been characterized by individualistic tendencies, loose social structures, and lack of formal social groupings and this all lies in contrast to the hierarchical and centralized systems of governmental decision making (Gillian 1963). Thus, because of their lack of conforming to the national model, they are viewed as impediments to development (Forte 1996b).

This coastal view of the Makushi being "impediments to development" can be best described by the word the Coastlanders often use when referring to them (as well as other Amerindians). It is not uncommon to hear the Makushi being referred to as "bucks" or "buck-people." When asked what this refers to the speaker will quickly point out that he or she is comparing the Makushi with the term for male deer, which are common in the hinterland. The use of this word is not always meant to be an insult; however, it does have the effect of further exacerbating the commonly held belief on the coast of the Amerindian as an uncultured, uneducated being.

Although the Makushi do feel left out of the politics of "Town," and are aware of the stereotypical view an average coastlander has of them, this has, generally, led to a strong sense of a shared identity both amongst themselves as well as other Guyanese Amerindians. Rather than simply becoming victims to this term, many Makushi now embrace the word "buck" and refer to themselves as "we buck people." Many will also make statements about the importance of "we food" (as mentioned earlier) and the pride they feel in knowing that their diet is much different from the rice-based foods of the coastal populations (as well as the fact that Coastlanders generally cannot stomach their food). In order to understand the source of this pride that the Makushi feel of their subsistence staple, one must understand the shared spiritual origins of the Makushi and cassava.

Cassava and Creation

Cassava is an extremely resilient plant that has many uses. Originally from South America, today cassava is grown worldwide and is the third largest source of carbohydrates in the world. A perennial woody shrub that produces long tapered tubers resembling sweet potatoes, cassava can be classified as sweet or bitter depending of the amount of toxic cyanogenic-glucosides in the tubers (Elias, Rival, and McKey 2000). The bitter variety is quite poisonous and the toxins must be extracted through a laborious process before the tubers can be safely consumed. Although potentially toxic, bitter cassava is the staple crop throughout much of the Amazon and has been so for over 3,000 years (Renvoize 1972).

Because of colonization, and especially missionization, much of the Makushi's original oral histories and folklore have been lost, subsequently transforming Makushi cosmology and notions of spirituality. Indeed, such "traditional" knowledge has been replaced with cosmologies of Western religion and their concomitant cultural norms, despite the fact that these imposed beliefs conflicted with traditional ideas related to gender relations, parenting, the family, and marriage (de Oliveira 1994). However, stories of the spiritual origins of cassava can be pieced together from past accounts detailed by early explorers and ethnographers as well from conversations with those still knowledgeable of these origin myths. This knowledge is needed to appreciate the importance this food crop holds in the psyche of the contemporary Makushi.

Makushi folklore and their conception of creation indicate they were an animistic people who did not believe in or worship a single omnipotent god. They instead saw their world inhabited by spirits and, of these, there was one Great Spirit known as Makunaima (Roth 1915). Makunaima had a twin brother Pia and these spirits were the result of the sun coupling with a woman who had been carved from a tree by Alligator. Because both Makunaima and Pia inhabited the same world the Makushi lived in, the spirits' influence on people's lives was both expected and unavoidable. The folklore that surrounds Makunaima and Pia can be viewed in a similar light to the stories from Greek Mythology regarding the gods and their exploits. They were mischievous, fickle, and cunning. The stories of their adventures abound in Makushi folklore; such stories, for example, include: the killing of Tiger in retaliation for him killing their mother, the burning of Tiger's mother Frog, and the unfortunate hunting accident in which Makunaima lost a leg while hunting Tapir—you can still see the stump of his leg to this day if you look into the night sky at what we know as Orion's belt (Roth 1915).

However, for the Makushi the most important tale involving Makunaima is their creation story. As the legend goes, one day Makunaima climbed a large tree with his stone ax and began to cut pieces of wood. He then cast these pieces into a nearby river and they, once wet, became animate beings. These newly created people were the Makushi and they began to populate the area. Yet Makunaima did not make their existence an easy one and they and all the other animals were starving because they had nothing to eat. One animal, though, the tapir, always appeared sleek and fat. The other animals noticed this and sent the opossum to follow him. The opossum did what he was told, following the tapir deep into the forest. When he saw the tapir pause, the opossum found himself under an enormous tree bearing all of the food types any creature, man or animal, could want. The opossum went back and reported this and then led the humans to the tree. They picked up all they could, but once this food was consumed the only food remaining was very high up in the branches of the tree. The tree trunk was too smooth to climb and, after a brief discussion, they decided to cut it down. Yet this was a very large tree and took the people many days of chopping with stone axes. The tree finally fell and, alongside the other animals, the people gathered all that they wanted.

However, the people were novices and had no idea how to propagate and prepare some of the foods they had collected. Many were not poisonous, such as corn, and others were edible raw, such as pineapple, but one in particular, bitter cassava, required special knowledge to become suitable for eating. A most helpful bird explained to the Makushi how to grow each food type they collected and most importantly how to prepare the bitter cassava and extract its toxic juice (Roth 1915).

Since this time, it is said that bitter cassava has been the staple of the Makushi. Although bitter cassava may seem like an odd choice for a dietary staple because it is so labor intensive to process in comparison to sweet cassava, the Makushi and bitter cassava are well adapted to one another. The bitter variety is preferred by the Makushi for a number of reasons but primarily because the processing results in products that are resistant to spoilage in a tropical environment. This is an important benefit because, in general, any food not consumed immediately will spoil and go to waste. And, as will be described in more detail further on, bitter cassava is an ideal crop for the demanding and variable physical environment in which the Makushi live.

Farming

Makushi farming practices are in response to their environment, which is punctuated by two seasons: the rainy and dry. During the rainy season (April through September), rains fall heavily and the savannahs become flooded. During this time the Guiana Shield and the Amazon Basin meet, and along their confluence there is a proliferation of plant and animal life. This is the one time of year that the watershed of the largest river in South America, the Amazon, and the third largest river, the Essequibo, connect, and lead to some of the highest levels and concentrations of biodiversity in South America (Lowe-McConnel 2000). However, during the dry season (October through March), rainfall is low and the temperatures rise, causing the creeks to stop flowing, savannahs to dry, and grasses to brown.

The Makushi generally make their homes in the savannah areas, but because of the poor nature of the grassland soil and its exposure to weather extremes, including flooding in the rainy season and severe parching in the dry, the savannahs are inadequate for growing crops. As such, farming is primarily done at the foot of the jungle-covered Kanuku Mountains as well as in forest galleries along rivers where the soil stays moist year round (Elias, Rival, and McKey 2000). This landscape has remained largely unchanged since colonization and was described eloquently by Charles Waterton:

The finest park that England boasts falls far short of this delightful scene. There are about two thousand acres of grass, with here and there a clump of trees and a few bushes and single trees scattered up and down by the hand of nature. The ground is neither hilly nor level, but diversified with moderate rises and falls, so gently running into one another that the eye cannot distinguish where they begin nor where they end . . . The beautiful park of Nature is quite surrounded by lofty hills, all arrayed in superbest garb of trees: some in the form of pyramids, other like sugar-loaves, towering one above the other, some rounded off, and others as though they had lost their apex . . . and ridges of others resemble the waves of an agitated sea. Beyond these appear others, and others past them, others still farther on, till they can scarcely be distinguished from the clouds. (1825: 30–31)

Farming practices do vary among the Makushi, but each household has at least one bitter cassava field. Each field varies in size but they are generally no smaller than one-half acre and rarely larger than two acres (Elias, Rival, and McKey 2000). The Makushi have historically harvested only what they needed for survival. Today, however, although most are still subsistence farmers, crop surpluses are often carried to the market to be sold. One main benefit of cassava, compared to a crop like corn, is that there is no conflict between what is edible and what is needed for replanting because cassava can be propagated vegetatively (without seeds) and the non-edible stalks are the sources of new plants. In order to replant cassava, the stalks of the cassava plant are cut into roughly twelve-inch segments and are planted at about a forty-five-degree angle one to three inches in the ground. Many farmers have a second field where they grow plantains, bananas, and other fruiting trees such as papaya. This field also commonly includes additional root vegetables, pepper plants, watermelon, pineapple, sugarcane, and pumpkin.

Most cassava fields are only used for two or three years before being abandoned. The reasons for this vary but the most common are that the soil fertility declines and produces smaller and poorer quality cassava; as the forest begins to reclaim the field and pests begin to cause more damage than what the plot produces, weeding becomes an unmanageable chore. One of the dreaded pests of every farmer is known locally as the *acoushi* ant (leaf-cutter ant, *Atta* spp.). The ants are seen as the number-one threat to any farm and there are a number of natural remedies that range from introducing other ants and wasps that defend against the *acoushi* ant to the pouring of fish poison made from local plants down their burrows (Forte 1996b, 1996c).

Depending on the size of the household and their occupant ages and associated needs, as well as abiotic and biotic environmental factors, at least one new field is cut every year. This provides each household with several fields of varying maturity at one time. These areas are generally selected in the rainy season and then cut during the dry season. In preparation for the arrival of the rains, farmers begin burning these cut areas. The fire consumes the vegetation cover, reducing the labor time needed to weed the field and resulting in a layer of ash that provides nutrients for the first crop. Some farms also include larger trees that were felled and failed to burn through. These are left where they lay and act as ground protection from erosion as well continuing to contribute nutrients to the farm as they decay. Some crops, such as watermelon and pumpkin, are preferentially planted near tree stumps and fallen logs to take advantage of this (Forte 1996a).

As mentioned previously, these farming practices ensure that each household has two to three fields at varying stages of maturity. Bitter cassava also comes in a staggering number of varieties and each has varying times of maturity, which further influences crop availability. A recent study found that the Makushi in one community cultivate over seventy-six different varieties and that each farm, on average, grew sixteen different varieties. This may seem like needless variation, but having so many varieties serves quite a few purposes. Environments vary and what at one time may do poorly may do quite well in another set of circumstances (Elias, Rival, and McKey 2000). For example, some varieties are more drought tolerant while others are more flood tolerant. Although there are two distinct seasons in the Rupununi, a year or two of drought may be quickly followed by extensive flooding. In this sense, having only one type of bitter cassava growing at a farm is quite risky in terms of supplying a growing and, often times, multigenerational family with food. Diversity is also good for protection against disease and pests (Elias, Rival, and McKey 2000). Because all varieties vary in their ability to grow and develop in spite of climatic or biotic factors, this variation is important to maintain because at any point in time the environmental factors could change, exposing the farm to new pressures.

Farmers are always on the lookout for new varieties and will willingly trade stalks from their farm for a new variety. Cassava stalks may also be given as gifts to those just beginning their first farm, those new to the area, or those who may have lost their farm to drought, flooding, or pests. Thus, exchange networks are created, often beyond kinship ties, and are reinforced through the reciprocal trade of cassava types. This trade leads to further bitter cassava diversity maintained by farmers throughout their fields. Because of the varying rates of tuber development of the different cassava varieties, as well as varying ages of farms, a family generally has harvestable cassava available to them all year. Tubers of some varieties are ready in as little as three to four months, whereas other varieties require at least a year to develop and will still produce edible tubers for up to two years. As such, the risk of crop failure is low because the risk is spread out over various fields planted at different times of the year with numerous varieties, each with its own speed of development. This adaptability and resiliency of the cassava tuber are a source of pride for the Makushi. Although any one variety is not integral to an individual or shared identity, the intrinsic flexibility of cassava is. An individual Makushi will speak of how much has changed culturally over his or her lifespan but point out that cassava is still "we food." The pride comes from the fact that as much as everything has changed, they and their food staple have been able to adapt and survive.

Cassava Processing and Gender Specialization

For the Makushi, the process of turning bitter cassava into an edible food product has resulted in a fairly rigid gender-based division of labor. These gender-based differences are a fundamental feature of the social, economic, political, and ritual organization shared among all societies in the Amazon. For most Amazonian groups, relationships between the sexes are generally asymmetrical with the women in a subordinate position (Wilson 1999). Although the Makushi have a well-defined division of labor between the sexes, with men as the primary hunters and fishers and women as the producers of the products of cassava (Myers 1993), this general pattern of gender subordination does not seem to apply. Iris Myers, who conducted the most extensive ethnography of the Makushi in the 1930s and 1940s, described women as having a high level of independence and high standing relative to their contemporaries in other Amerindian societies (Myers 1993). This female independence within the household arguably still holds true to this day. In order to better understand this division of labor as well as the relationship between the sexes, it is important to understand the most fundamental aspect of each household: the processing of cassava.

The most labor-intensive aspect of cassava-related work is the cutting of the field, which is done by the males. Traditionally, this would have been conducted through a collective action of sorts called *mayu*, or self-help (Elias, Rival, and McKey 2000). In order to get other men to help cut a new farm, the male head of household would have his wife make *parakari*, a beer-like beverage made from the cassava tuber, and invite local men to participate. The men would gather, consume some of the drink and then begin the work of clearing the farm. At various intervals throughout the day, breaks would be taken and more parakari drunk. Although alcoholic, it is a filling beverage and is quite often used as fuel to keep a farmer going even when not participating in a mayu. Once the farm has been cut, and ideally not before, the men will then put down their tools and celebrate together until the parakari is completely consumed. However, the importance of this collective work has diminished—although it does still occur—because the Makushi have become more market-integrated and many expect to be paid for work provided. Therefore, a man today usually goes with his sons or brothers to cut a new field. Once the area is dried, the men then burn the farm in anticipation of the rains. Either before or after the rains begin, the entire family will clean the farm. The men then hoe the soil into mounds in which the women plant freshly cut cassava stalks generally taken from a recently harvested field. The subsequent weeding and care of the farm is up to the women, but the children help as well. When harvesting the cassava tubers, the men and women work together and, if it is the first or second crop, plant stalks in the same area in freshly hoed banks (field notes 2011). The more fertile the soil, the more consecutive cassava crops can be planted in the same area before moving to another field.

Gender specialization in cassava processing becomes apparent once the cassava is brought home. Women are the processors of the cassava tuber—a labor-intensive procedure of extracting the poison and transforming it into edible form. The finished cassava products range in preparation, consistency, and use. However, for all end goods, the initial steps of processing are the same. The tuber is first scraped and washed. The cleaned tuber is then grated using a grater that consists of a board about three feet tall, embedded with small rock chips across one side. More modern graters substitute thin metal strips for rock chips; or, if possible, a household will buy a grater from Brazil that can be powered by a bicycle. This latter method is preferred as it saves hours of back-breaking up-and-down grating motions. In order to detoxify the cassava, the grated pulp is placed into a three- to five-foot-tall woven *matapi*, or what looks like a giant finger trap. The top is hung from a branch or rafter and the bottom has a loop through which a pole is passed. A woman will then sit on this pole and a container will be placed below the matapi to collect the juice that escapes as the matapi is constricted. From this point forward, further processing techniques are based on the desired product.

Yellow tubers will be made into toasted granules called *farine* (from the Portuguese *farinha*, similar in size and texture to Grapenuts cereal). Once squeezed, the pulp from the matapi will be passed through a woven sifter (approximately two by two feet) to remove any larger pieces. The sifted mass will then be placed in a large pan over a hot fire and roasted until all of the moisture has been parched from it. Farine will not spoil unless wet, and acts as the staple for the Makushi. A favorite snack is a quick scoop of farine, a dash of water, and spoonful of sugar.

White cassava tubers provide the base for another essential product: cassava bread. The processing of cassava to make bread differs in that the pulp from the matapi is pushed through a sifter with smaller holes than for farine. This finer flour is placed on a hot pan and is shaped into a circle about two feet across and when cooked resembles a crispy flatbread. This bread, once dried, normally on the thatched roof of the household, has a long shelf-life as well, which is important in the tropics. It is often eaten with a Makushi dish known as *tuma* pot (described further on).

Parakari, the alcoholic drink mentioned above for the mayu, is made using cassava bread that has been baked until one-half inch thick and slightly blackened. These "loaves" are then torn into pieces and placed on banana or other waterproof leaves, sometimes in the main area of the household. Old cassava leaves that have been dried in the rafters of the house are then crushed and sprinkled on each layer in order to introduce the yeast (*Rhizopus* spp.) that begins breaking down the starch and producing alcohol. Once a thick layer of cotton white yeast has formed over the bread (approximately forty-eight hours) and the mash is sweet to the taste, the parakari has "woken up" as they say and can be added to water, strained, and drunk. If strong parakari (higher alcohol content) is called for, then this mass will be placed in a container to continue fermenting and will be consumed some days later.

The water collected from the squeezing of the matapi, known as the cassava water, will not be thrown out, but will be further processed. The color is reminiscent of vehicle antifreeze, and if left unprocessed, can be even more deadly. The first step for processing this water is to let it sit and then separate the liquid from the starch that has settled at the bottom of the container. This starch can be made into tapioca by roasting it in a similar manner to farine. The remaining liquid is not thrown out either and is a favorite addition to two Makushi dishes. The first is known as tuma pot and is regularly served with cassava bread, as mentioned earlier. This dish generally consists of the cassava water, fish, sweet cassava or other root vegetable, and hot peppers. The boiling makes the dish safe to eat and the cassava water helps to flavor the food. The other option is to continually boil down the cassava water until it becomes thick syrup, like molasses, called *cassareep.* This syrup is a necessary addition for a dish known as pepperpot (see Richards-Greaves, this volume), which would include meat, hot peppers, and any root vegetables available. Some houses have a constantly boiling pot to which they simply add more food and cassareep from time to time.

At the beginning of the twentieth century, for the first time, more and more women were now making cassava products not just for their families' consumption but to sell to others. Although this change may seem minor, it had fundamental cultural consequences. In light of the equitable gender roles of the Makushi, this shift may have been what gave the women more independence, value, and control within the household. Women were the ones who supplied the goods that provided money for the family. Although men still generally acted as the go-betweens for trade, the women made it all possible. More men were also gone throughout the year working, and as a result it was up to women to provide for their families in their partners' absence. In addition, the men now spent considerably more time processing cassava because of the increased demands for farine. The older generations laugh when asked if men parch farine or make cassava bread, but younger men routinely identify themselves as capable of processing cassava. This work is now seen less as "women's work" but rather an important source of income for the family.

Summary

The Makushi of today live quite differently than those who came before them. Because of the effects of contact with Europeans, they, as a people and culture, have fundamentally changed. Initially, their population was decimated by disease, even before physical contact with the colonizers. They were then pushed out of their traditional areas because of pressures placed on them by both European settlers as well as from other tribes that were themselves being displaced. For nearly 300 years slave-raiding was also a constant concern, and as a result was culturally damaging as it further scattered a reduced number of Makushi people into ever more remote recesses of the mountains and forests to escape the superiorly equipped coastal tribes. After slave-raiding ended, the Makushi were able to return to a more traditional way of life—living in the savannahs and farming in the wet, fertile soil of the forests along streams and at the foot of the mountains. However, this return to their customary practices was short-lived, as colonizers began entering the area. New diseases were introduced and epidemics occurred, even up until the 1950s (Jones 1952). Part of this susceptibility to disease was due to the effects of missionization. The Makushi were nearly wiped out as they began clustering around densely populated mission settlements (Forte 1996b). These settlements provided the perfect vectors for diseases to spread quickly through people accustomed to living in dispersed, small, kin-based groups. Because of this decimation due to disease, as well as the conversion process, Makushi culture itself was also nearly destroyed. As missionaries began conversion, they condemned many of their traditional beliefs and practices. The influence of church and mission schools, with their ethnocentric disapproval of "savage" and "pagan" customs, led to the disappearance of much of the Makushi material and cultural life (Forte 1996c). Family composition, childcare, marriage, sex, and many other aspects fundamental to the Makushi identity were also changed under the scrutiny of the missionaries.

Although much has changed since initial European contact, one constant for the Makushi has been the reliance on cassava and its associated elaborate processing techniques. Cassava, the staple of the Makushi, and its resilience helped them weather the various storms that battered them. Although traditional beliefs were replaced with (often conflicting) Christian teachings, and Western family models were imposed, the Makushi never lost the arguably fundamental aspect of any culture—their food. Processing techniques of the bitter cassava are necessary for its consumption and have been reliably passed down, generation to generation. As a result, so have some fundamental stories related to creation, spirituality, and subsistence. The efficient aspects of gender specialization have also remained largely intact. The production of food out of bitter cassava has stayed, for the most part, the work of the women, although men more commonly help now than they once did. As a consequence of the increased importance of the work of women through their increased economic productivity, female status within the household is higher than other Amazonian groups.

Makushi people speak with pride and talk about cassava as "we food," which lies in stark contrast to the non-Amerindian diet that is rice-based. Most Makushi are proud that their diet differs from those from the coast, as they have done little to endear themselves to those of the interior. Governmental policies have focused on the acculturation of the Makushi, while at the same time belittling them for their faults—faults that were imposed by the very same government and that stem from a lack of infrastructure, land rights, and economic opportunities. Although so much has been lost because of enculturation, missionization, disease, and migration, the ability to process bitter cassava into edible food and drink products has remained—including the associated tools, crafts, and stories. In the face of overwhelming cultural change, the fact that this complex has remained fully intact, while so many other traditional practices and beliefs are fading, is a testament to the importance of cassava to the Makushi in terms of group livelihood and identity.

-2-

Transformations in Body and Cuisine in Rural Yucatán, Mexico

Lauren Wynne

Many twentieth-century ethnographic accounts of the rural Yucatec Maya analyze the accruement of culinary knowledge as a crucial part of the process of socialization by which children become adults (e.g., Gaskins 2003; Greene 2002). Indeed, in the rural town of Juubche, fairly predictable culinary milestones continue to mark the lives of girls and women. Some young women, however, are using their access to new foods and related knowledge to challenge both local hierarchies of expertise and ideologies of racial difference. For many young women in Juubche, there is a link between consuming new foods and identifying oneself with larger Yucatecan and Mexican cultures. Yet, rather than disavowing their rural Yucatec Maya community, these women are establishing themselves as versatile and respected members of that community. Part of this process entails identifying oneself as someone who can manage new foods and successfully integrate them into the everyday rhythms of local life. In doing so, these women render themselves local culinary experts and expand the possibilities of alimentary pleasure for themselves and for their community. They are also reshaping a cosmology already in flux as they and these new foods complicate understandings of the body and the universe.

The conditions under which these young women live are the product of a century of governmental efforts to economically and culturally integrate the peninsula into the Mexican nation-state, yet these conditions also reflect centuries of ties with neighboring islands and an ecosystem more similar to that of those islands than to that of central Mexico. Though Yucatán's staple crops for centuries—corn, beans, and squash—are roughly the same as those in central Mexico and other parts of Mesoamerica, the local cuisine holds other daily foodstuffs in common with its Caribbean neighbors: habañero chilies, sour oranges, and sugarcane, among others. During the colonial period and even after Independence in 1821, the peninsula's remote location and powerful local elite shaped a strong regional culture that reflected its cultural and economic ties—and a shared history of slavery—with Caribbean islands and the southeastern United States (Joseph 1986; Torres-Saillant 2006: 20).

Today, the region shares an economic reliance on tourism with many of its Caribbean neighbors. Juubche's proximity to the large urban and tourist centers of Cancun and Playa del Carmen has changed the patterns of everyday life since the development of regional tourism in the 1970s. Though wage labor is not a new phenomenon, only during the last few decades has it begun to fully replace farming for many families.[1] The rise of tourism on the Peninsula largely coincided with a number of other factors that have shaped the ongoing decline of work in the *kool* (cornfield).[2] Prior to this, and despite a long history of outside intervention and engagement, agricultural practice and its attendant religious beliefs reproduced shared logics and values for the region's Maya population since the Conquest. The preparation and consumption of staple crops such as corn were central to the cycle through which Maya communities sustained themselves and their spiritual worlds. A gendered division of labor ordered the domestic landscape and produced largely self-sufficient households in which men produced and women processed food. Though never static, everyday and ritual consumption patterns generated community cohesion and maintained human and spiritual hierarchies. Beliefs, such as those embedded in the hot-cold syndrome, root individual bodies and their imperative for balance within a larger social order that seeks to also maintain balance within the multiple cycles—seasons, life spans—that characterize the existences of living beings, including supernatural forces (Villa Rojas 1981, 1983).

Located in the eastern part of the state of Yucatán, the town of Juubche has a population of around 2,600, almost all of whom are native speakers of Yucatec Maya. Most men now commute weekly to the Caribbean coast for work in construction or service industries. Some continue to farm full-time and others part-time, either seasonally when the crops demand labor, or when jobs in the cities wane, as during the global financial crisis that began in 2008. A small number of men live full-time in town but commute to work at a nearby archeological site or in service-industry jobs in Valladolid. Other men, though still a minority, supplement or opt out of agricultural labor to tend cattle in neighboring ranches.

Women's labor is based largely in the home; very few migrate for work, and when they do it tends to be only until they marry. The bulk of women's time is spent preparing food, cleaning the home and clothing, and caring for young children. Several women sell prepared foods and snacks to students at the local schools, and a small number—all unmarried and relatively young—commute daily or weekly to factory jobs in or near Valladolid. Many women also embroider *iipils* (a type of women's dress popular in the region), weave hammocks, and sew clothing to sell locally or in regional tourist markets. Depending upon the volume they produce and whether or not they sell directly to consumers, the degree to which this sort of labor contributes to household income varies tremendously. Additionally, most women have gardens in which they grow produce such as habañero chilies and cilantro for their own use and for sale, and men and women sometimes sell excess fruit from trees surrounding their homes. The sale of these foodstuffs tends to make up a small portion of household income. Women usually manage any money they earn, and in many families, women also manage the earnings of their male partners.

Contemporary Cuisine and Culinary Education

Due to the fact that farming is no longer a universal among men and that it often fails to meet the food needs of many families, most residents now buy staple foods such as corn, beans, and squash from neighbors with a surplus or from a store in town or in the nearby city of Valladolid.[3] Residents supplement these staples with store-bought goods such as sugar, instant coffee, and crackers, and most also buy rolls and sweet breads from itinerant bakers. Chicken, beef, and pork are consumed at most a few times a week and are almost always freshly slaughtered, either within the household or by fellow residents. When wage labor jobs are few and far between, many more men hunt for local game such as deer, agouti, peccary, and gophers. Eggs, often from residents' own hens or neighbors' hens, are a more common part of the everyday diet and often make their way to the table every other day. Soft drinks have been a regular part of most residents' diets since the construction of major roads in the 1980s. The roads also allowed for the transport of mass-produced alcohol, particularly beer, into Juubche, and these beverages now fuel the weekend binges in which some local men indulge.[4]

Despite changes in the origins of many staple foods, the gendered division of food labor has not radically changed in recent decades. Although men continue to prepare certain ceremonial foods, women are still responsible for daily cooking. The processes by which girls and young women learn to do this work are similar to the culinary initiations of earlier generations. As school-age children, girls are often sent out to have corn ground at one of the local corn mills. All of my informants, who ranged in age from eighteen to eighty-six, learned to *pak'ach* (prepare tortillas) between the ages of eight and fourteen. Some women learned on their own out of necessity after a mother fell ill or passed way. One woman remembered: "My mother's head was hurting . . . Who made my father's serving? Me! With a spoon! With a knife! . . . I learned on my own like that."

More frequently, girls learned through observation and then by joining older girls and women at the table, subjecting their tortilla-making techniques and final products to critique. This learning process is often a slow one. Not all women—especially younger ones—are experts in tortilla making. In fact, girls are rarely those manning the fire; they tend to play a supporting role, patting out tortillas while an older female relative judges "cooked-ness" on the *xamach* (griddle). In some cases, girls who marry particularly young—at fifteen or sixteen—may have not yet perfected their tortilla-making skills. Still, even in those families for whom hand-patted tortillas are not the norm, tortilla making is required female knowledge, understood as crucial to the complementary gender roles that have organized household production for centuries (Landa [1566]1941; Redfield and Villa Rojas 1934).

Learning to prepare savory dishes, which are known as *ki' waaj*, is an even lengthier process. Many girls are too busy patting tortillas, running errands, or attending to younger siblings to study the more in-depth food preparation usually undertaken by their mothers. They may observe and even participate in chopping vegetables and herbs, juicing oranges and limes, and beating eggs. Those activities that require more skill and are thus more highly valued—for example, cutting meat, judging cooked-ness, and seasoning dishes—are generally left to the older women in the household. Preparing more basic everyday dishes like boiled black beans, scrambled eggs, and sautéed squash are learned through trial and error or casual observation, rather than direct instruction. One woman recounted to me how she learned to make ki' waaj by beginning its preparation and having her mother or mother-in-law taste it and make suggestions throughout the process: "Put a little salt." Many of my young female in-formants (those in their twenties and younger, married and unmarried) profess little ability to cook well. As in the past, they largely rely on the culinary skills of female elders in their extended household and typically share kitchens with in-laws until they and their husbands have the funds to build separate homes. Mothers-in-law are often feared culinary critics; it is perhaps for this reason and the demands of rais-ing small children that many younger women choose to eat meals cooked by their mothers-in-law.

When it comes to meat, highly seasonal dishes, or special-occasion foods, older women are the authority. Younger and middle-aged women take care to invite fe-male relatives in their fifties and older to supervise the preparation of these foods on a regular basis. These women determine when a dish is sufficiently salty, spicy, or sweet; they cut the best pieces of meat and stuff the sausage; and their criticisms, small and large, are accepted without argument. There even exists a more formal role for culinary supervision within the Catholic community: a *x-k'uus* is a woman, usu-ally in her forties or older, who is invited to oversee food preparation and distribu-tion.[5] Generally, the more important the event, the further outside of a woman's kin network she might go in order to procure a x-k'uus. In exchange for the lending of her knowledge and skills at a wedding or saint's day affair, a x-k'uus receives more food to bring home than would the average female guest who patted out some tortillas or cut onions.

The Nature of Culinary Knowledge and Practice

The acquisition of culinary knowledge in rural Yucatan has historically been a gradual process that accelerates with marriage and upholds established ties between knowledge and advanced age. Culinary authority is based upon the mastery of a large but discrete repertoire of established dishes. This emphasis on repetition and mastery is central to the process by which rural Yucatecan cuisine is produced and reproduced, and the highly standardized nature of the preparation of the new foods that I will discuss in this chapter is representative of the larger cuisine of rural Yu-catan. In her study of one Yucatecan community, Kray (1997) writes, "Consensus is so highly valued that each prepared dish is considered to have one single recipe, and the best cook is the one who can master that recipe, rather than adding a unique, creative, or experimental twist" (82). In Juubche, families may claim different styles of cooking, but there is general agreement about which women possess the most impressive culinary skills.

Adults may have some dislikes, but they usually enjoy the range of dishes prepared on a regular basis in the village.[6] It is unacceptable not to eat at least a little at any social gathering, so adults tolerate all special-occasion dishes (though they may decline leftovers to take home). Most eaters develop finely tuned tastes that are largely in sync with the tastes of others; typically, eaters are in agreement as to whether a dish is too *ch'óoch'* (salty), *paj* (sour), *ch'ujuk* (sweet), or *páap* (spicy), among other taste categories. Children learn to identify these tastes by observing and mimicking the frequent commentaries of adults. While older women have the final say at special-occasion events, individuals of all ages, male or female, may issue criticisms or compliments. These actions rarely go unnoticed by the cook. In one instance, I observed collective criticisms of one of the community's most revered dishes. During a meal of *relleno negro* (pork or turkey in a blackened chili sauce, served during the annual fiesta and other important events), I heard first the quiet whispers of "jach páap [very spicy]" by younger and middle-aged women and then the more confident, louder "jach páap" declarations by female elders. The faces of the hostess and her mother looked stricken. In situations like this one, individual criticisms or compliments often develop into discussions on the (mis)use of ingredients or cooking techniques: Were the chilies too spicy? Was the spice mixture too coarsely ground?

Such commentaries are rarely attributed to personal tastes. Although criticisms may be challenged, they are generally trusted and, if noted by other eaters, effectively confirmed. This emphasis on standardization is evidenced by the use of the very terms for tastes. Ch'óoch' signifies "salty," but not, as the English word implies, "too salty." Rather, ch'óoch' signifies "perfectly salty"; the response to a question about whether one's food is ch'óoch' is often *tun p'iis* (to measure) or *tiibil* (proportionate). *Jach ch'óoch'* signifies "too salty," and *ma' ch'óoch'i'* literally translates to "not salty," though the implication is really "not salty enough." Other taste words function similarly: for example, *páap*. My own preference for spicy-hot foods initially led me to proclaim, with pleasure, several dishes *jach páap*. The looks of concern on cooks' faces made it evident to me that jach páap is not preferable and implicates a cook in using too much chili. Some women are known to produce ki' waaj that is ma' ch'óoch'i', which is seen not as a reflection of personal taste but rather as a mark of inferior cooking skills.

Novel Foods: Recent Additions to the Culinary Landscape

The content of what most Juubche residents eat on a daily basis is similar to that consumed several generations ago: corn tortillas, beans, eggs, chicken, or, less frequently, pork or beef, and a small but satisfying array of vegetables from cornfields or home gardens. According to residents, many of these staples are no longer produced locally, but the ways in which they are prepared are largely similar to earlier culinary practices described by my informants. Purchased snacks and drinks are crucial parts of the gastronomic landscape in this town—and they require unique sets of cultural knowledge to guide their purchase and consumption—but they do not demand preparation and, thus, no culinary expertise. The dishes in which this chapter is interested are occasionally served for everyday meals, though usually for the lighter dinner than the main meal of lunch. They are most often served for secular events such as birthdays or New Year's Eve celebrations, which have been adopted from mainstream Mexican culture in recent decades. Indeed, none of these dishes, which I will soon introduce, are ever paired with corn tortillas, a staple and nonnegotiable part of the midday meal; thus these new foods do not qualify as *janal*. Janal, though loosely translated as "food," really refers to a meal of ki' waaj with tortillas. The new foods are not what I term "well-established"; rather, these new dishes have entered into the local diet only in the last two decades, beginning with the construction of roads into town, followed by the arrival of electricity and television to most households, all of this coinciding with the development of regional tourism. Well-established foods, on the other hand, have been consumed consistently over the lifetimes of all of my informants, the oldest of whom was born in the early 1920s.

Among the most prominent of these new foods are three dishes, and I'll focus on them here. The first is *sáandwich*, or "sandwich" in English. Yet the sáandwich of Juubche is not like the sandwiches of the United States. There is no vast array of ingredients from which to choose, nor an appreciation for creative and original combinations. The Juubche sáandwich is highly standardized: white Bimbo bread (Mexico's equivalent of Wonder Bread), a thin spread of mayonnaise, shredded chicken, sliced tomato, and a few pieces of canned, pickled jalapeño. For parties, sáandwiches are often wrapped in white paper napkins to keep them clean and to make for easy distribution. The second dish is *sopa fría*. Although it translates to "cold soup," it refers in Juubche only to a pasta salad with canned pineapple chunks, bits of processed ham, canned peas, and mayonnaise. In Juubche, sopa fría is always served with soda crackers for scooping. The third dish is called *ensalada*, "salad" in English, but this recipe refers to a very specific version of potato salad, with boiled carrots, canned peas, mayonnaise, and maybe a splash of the vinegar from a can of pickled jalapeños. Like sopa fría, it is always served with soda crackers for scooping. Both sopa fría and ensalada are seasoned with salt and pepper, and are usually dished out onto small, disposable serving plates at various occasions.

In content, these dishes bear little resemblance to well-established local foods. The ingredients are almost all purchased and produced outside of the community, and few are used in everyday cooking. Only those few families with refrigerators can store the leftover ingredients for more than a day. And, since these dishes are not eaten with tortillas, women do not need to sit in front of the fire before and during a meal, nor do these dishes need to be served at a particular temperature. Practically speaking, then, these foods leave women free to socialize or attend to other hostessing duties. Because servings are generally contained—wrapped as individual portions or served as a scoop on a small plate—the thoughtful judgments regarding who gets what and how much are largely unnecessary.[7] Furthermore, these foods do not require a table on which to consume them; guests can easily eat them in a chair with a plate or, in the case of sandwich, just in their hands. Instead of being called to eat at a limited number of tables—a hierarchy that generally prioritizes men and any esteemed guests—guests are served in a simpler and more democratic fashion: the hostess(es) and helpers distribute food by moving around the space, handing food to each and every individual in an order determined only by who is sitting or standing closest.

Once distributed, these dishes are often treated differently than well-established foods. A number of older people told me that they find these foods to be *ma' ki'* (not tasty), especially sopa fría. As such, and in light of the fact that these foods are often distributed at evening festivities (usually around most residents' bedtimes), some attendees choose not to eat their helpings at the event. As with established foods, however, guests must accept a first serving, so they often choose to bring the food home with them. Ki' waaj is exchanged between families on an often-daily basis in Juubche, and it is sent home with guests at many affairs. It is considered poor form to throw any gifted ki' waaj away.[8] Sopa fría, ensalada, and sáandwich are a different matter. For most residents, these foods are acceptable to give to dogs, cats, or chickens as soon as they return from an event. While it would still not be preferable for one's host to see such behavior, it is not considered *k'eban* (sinful), as would be the tossing of ki' waaj.

With regard to taste, these foods differ greatly from the fare that most residents consume on a daily basis. While the inclusion of canned, pickled jalapeños adds heat to sáandwich, and their juices sometimes enliven ensalada, the three dishes are bland. Well-established dishes are simply prepared but marked by generous additions of lard, pickled or sautéed onions, spice marinades, or citrus juices. Blander foods are reserved for breakfast and light dinners, in the form of French bread and store-bought crackers, or for those with illness-related food restrictions. Texturally as well, sáandwich, sopa fría, and ensalada stray from the usual preferences. Variations on the *torta*, a type of sandwich common throughout Mexico, are rarely prepared at home by Juubche residents, though many residents purchase and consume them while attending school or working outside of town. Unlike sáandwich, the torta features a serving of meat on a crusty, large roll, often with some avocado, onion, chili salsa, or other garnish.[9] A torta is texturally complex and less *suave* (smooth) than sáandwich. Sopa fría and ensalada are served chilled or at room temperature, and have a creamy consistency. Puréed foods, such as *tsabi bu'ul* (literally, "fried beans," but more like soupy refried beans) and *tsabi p'aak* (literally, "fried tomato," but more of a spicy tomato sauce), are commonly consumed, but they are served warm and lack the creaminess of potatoes or pasta coated in mayonnaise. In fact, creaminess is entirely uncharacteristic of well-established foods, in which the inclusion of mayonnaise, milk, cheese, and other dairy products is rare.

Above all, what these three dishes have in common is near-absolute uniformity in their composition, much like that seen in more established foods. Not once have I witnessed anyone suggest an addition or variation to these foods. When older women question whether a particular item—pickled onions or shredded cabbage, for example— was included in sáandwiches, younger women promptly remind them of the correct ingredients. In fact, younger women are the authorities on these foods; as one woman in her seventies announced while eating a sáandwich at a birthday party, "The children really know how to make these things." In nuclear families without young women, a niece may be invited over to assist with the preparation of these foods, nearly taking on the role of the x-k'uus despite her youth. These women remind their older counterparts of the exact ingredients, the best places to purchase them, and the steps by which the dishes should be created. During the actual preparation, they oversee the assembly of sáandwiches and the mixing of ensalada and sopa fría. They usually have the final say in how much salt and pepper must be added, and how many soda crackers should be placed with each serving. When I wondered out loud to an older women about the safety of eating unrefrigerated mayonnaise the next day (thus revealing one of my own cultural anxieties about food), she quickly relayed the question to her much younger sister, who promptly assured her of its safety. Indeed, new foods require a distinct knowledge of how ch'óoch' or how páap they are, and older women rarely hold that knowledge in preparation or in taste (nor for that matter do older men). Indeed, one noticeable difference is that while new foods are being consumed, one rarely hears any commentary on the taste.

Novel Innovations

Of course, cuisine in rural Yucatan is and always has been dynamic, an amalgamation determined by availability, necessity, force, and trend. In Juubche, government-initiated cultural missions during the mid-twentieth century sent *promotoras* (outreach workers) to instruct women in the preparation of dishes not locally consumed. Some women embraced these recipes, many of which used locally produced ingredients, more than others. Doña Paola, a respected culinary authority in the community, has not worked as a x-k'uus since becoming a Jehovah's Witness a dozen years ago. However, she often prepares foods that require specialized knowledge, such as tortilla-like breads made from corn dough, sweet potato, and vanilla, or a savory version made from corn dough and *chaya*, a leafy green. Doña Paola was not alone in learning about these foods from a promotora a half-century ago, but she has had the time and interest to continue cooking them.

A few women learned to create new dishes during time spent outside of the village. Female migration from Juubche was not common during the twentieth century, but some girls were sent to work as domestic servants in Merida or Valladolid. Prior to the construction of a secondary school in town in the 1990s, poor families often struggled to feed older girls who remained unmarried and at home. Primary school teachers who developed relationships with local families would sometimes arrange domestic work for these girls. Some were instructed to prepare new foods while doing this domestic labor, while others simply observed—and consumed—the foods prepared by the household cook. Cristina, who worked as a nanny to a Valladolid family in the early 1990s, remembered, "There was a cook, too. I watched how she cooked. Because I liked cooking, I would get close and see how she made it. That's how I learned." However, she noted that she doesn't often cook these meals at home: "Foods like that require money."

In other cases, men acted as culinary conduits; having traveled to work in Cancun or other parts of the peninsula, they were often party to unfamiliar culinary practices. Don Martín, a highly inquisitive man, remembered visiting an acquaintance in the Cancun home where she worked as a domestic servant. She offered him a *refresco* (soft drink). Expecting Coca-Cola, he agreed, but she handed him a green drink. He found it tasty and inquired as to its contents. His friend told him that it was made from aloe vera juice. Upon his return home, he prepared it for his wife and children. Unimpressed by its taste, Don Martín's wife, however, was not interested in integrating the beverage into her culinary repertoire.

If residents have always been interested in trying new foods, what is new about the acquisition of culinary expertise by young women today? Despite a lack of roads and electricity until the 1980s, Juubche's residents had contact with their local schoolteachers, most of whom came from other parts of the peninsula; residents traveled to fairs and on religious pilgrimages; and men migrated to work in *chicle* camps or on archaeological excavations. During this time, women of many ages adopted new food practices, and many of these foods were easily integrated into, at the very least, dinner and secular, festive menus. Urban street foods, such as *panuchos* (thick, fried tortillas stuffed with beans and topped with meat and vegetable garnishes), used common ingredients found in cornfields and home gardens. Women did not need much cash, nor did they need to venture out of town to shop for ingredients. These foods carried with them a faint air of urban savviness, but they were also rooted in local agriculture and tastes. Other novelties, such as the aloe vera soft drink mentioned, became mere fodder for humorous anecdotes, perhaps due to the labor of preparation or to a wife's lack of interest.

Today, a much broader range of media influences the integration of new foods. Many women watch *Al sabor del chef*, a cooking show that airs on network television; the ingredients are not always familiar, but the recipes often pique interests, for good or bad. One woman told me that, while she did watch the show, she thought many of the dishes appeared ma' ki'. In one case, Elena, a young woman known for being particularly skilled in preparing new foods, explained to me that she had one cookbook, and that she used it to prepare new foods such as fajitas and hot cakes for her husband and children. Importantly, her husband Jose, a socially mobile young man, was regularly exposed to new foods at his job in Playa del Carmen. While there, he often traveled and dined with his middle-class boss, and both Jose and Elena became interested in eating such foods at home.

Indeed, one important characteristic of the young women who act as authorities on sáandwich, sopa fría, and ensalada is their exposure to regional and national culinary practices. In some senses, these resident experts are a diverse group: several are Catholic and several are Jehovah's Witnesses; a few are married, a few unmarried, and one divorced; and they participate in a range of labor activities in addition to regular housework. However, all exercise control over the money they or their husbands earn. Thanks to their own work or that of their husbands, they are at least slightly wealthier than most women their age. They have access to cars owned by their husbands or fathers, and they also own and regularly use appliances like refrigerators and stoves. For these reasons, they can easily purchase food products from outside of Juubche, as well as store and prepare those foods in ways that are not accessible to many of their fellow-residents.[10] For women with access to cars, going on day trips to nearby cities or touristic sites may also expose them to new foods. Within families in which husbands have relatively well-paying jobs (for example, as taxi drivers or waiters), the husbands themselves may have access to more than the basic fare consumed by construction workers while working on the coast. They may discover foods that they enjoy, carefully note their preparation, and suggest the dishes to their wives upon their return home. In contrast, lower-paid construction workers often rely on what they find to be less-tasty versions of the simple foods consumed at home, stocking up on cooked chicken and machine-made tortillas at Wal-Mart or a budget eatery.

However, the differences between these women and others are not just a matter of material resources. Although they have varying levels of education, they strike both me and other residents as notably intelligent and ambitious. As an older woman remarked of one of these younger women, "She learns things quickly." Another woman in her mid-twenties, who had learned new dishes from a sister-in-law from Merida, told me that her head was "smooth" and that, whatever she saw her sister-in-law make, she learned to make for herself. All of these women are highly attentive to the culinary behaviors of others—and not only those of their kin and neighbors but also of visiting tourists, and of middle- and upper-class residents of nearby cities. These women are keenly aware of the relationship between food and class on the peninsula but, rightly so, they see the boundaries between consumption practices, ethnicity, and wealth as flexible. The appeal of these new foods is not merely a product of the status one assumes through their consumption but is most certainly connected to the respect one receives as a culinary expert within this relatively small community. In fact, it is the ability to be flexible about food—to speak knowledgeably about new foods and to express a wide range of tastes—that lends these women respect and admiration. They continue to eat well-established foods and are as likely as anyone else to invite a x-k'uus to help prepare relleno negro for a special occasion.

Yet these women have a unique relationship with a category of foods that comprises local culinary luxuries, and this strips their food practices of a locally perceived link to poverty. Two young women may both eat black beans and tortillas several days a week, but the ability of one to talk knowledgeably about and skillfully prepare, say, ensalada, distinguishes her from the other.

Not of the Poor, nor of the Cornfield

The categorization of these new foods as luxurious is based on particular sociocultural understandings and bodily experiences of their material qualities, as well as on deep-rooted ideas of class and racial difference. These foods are, again, rarely everyday foods. They are, perhaps, not entirely food to begin with, at least not the food of poor farmers. Older residents often explicitly mark simple, well-established staples like beans and eggs as *u janalil otsil* (food of the poor). What is perhaps most appealing about sandwich, sopa fría, and ensalada to all is their utter frivolity. These foods are not, by local standards, the foods of poor people, nor are they valued for health or economy. The consumption of them is pleasurable to most residents not only because of the foods' tastes—or, in fact, as I point out earlier, in spite of—but because of the luxuriousness that these foods speak.

These foods are often talked about as being *fino* (fine) or smooth. These qualities are considered those required for the bodies of *ts'uulo'ob*—wealthy, ostensibly white, non-Maya speakers—whose food does not need to fuel the hard labor of planting and sowing crops.[11] These news foods are not understood to be particularly nutritious; they are never, for example, classified as *t'saak* (medicine), as some local foods are. However, they are thought to be easy on the stomach. For that reason, some socially mobile women believe them to be particularly good for children, having adopted the idea that children have distinct food needs. Older people, on the other hand, often complain that these new foods do not fill them up, that they "mu nak'tal yetel [do not get full with them]."

The new foods are largely un-integrated into the hot-cold syndrome that organizes the logic of much of everyday eating. The hot-cold syndrome, common throughout much of Latin America, classifies foods as either "hot" or "cold," sometimes based on temperature but often not (Chevalier and Sánchez Bain 2003; Foster 1994).[12] As Callahan notes (2005: 373), the system in Yucatan has come increasingly to refer to thermal temperature, though in Juubche many metaphorical classifications persist.[13] In general, balance and imbalance are produced through combinations of "heat" and "cold" found in bodies and their parts, as well as in food, drink, and natural elements; produced by activities and phases of life; and caused by emotions such as anger. For this reason, individuals must exercise great care in their contact with food. The greatest concerns in Juubche are exposure to "cold" foods and forces, such as wind and rain, while one's *óol* (center of consciousness) is "hot."[14] Such exposure can cause illnesses, infertility, and death. Don Antonio, a farmer in his sixties, explained to me, "Why do we care for ourselves like this? We're scared!" When older people express concern about eating new foods like sopa fría and sáandwich when their óol is "hot," younger people assure them that these foods are not "cold." Assurances from younger women that new foods like ensalada and sopa fría do not hold any disruptive qualities put older people at ease with foods that would otherwise be unfamiliar and anxiety inducing. Yet, in not integrating these new foods into the hot-cold syndrome, younger women are also dismantling, or at least reshaping, a cosmology in which foodstuffs, like other natural resources, are part of larger cycles of life, death, and exchange.[15] They are further marking these foods as distinct from those grown locally; without knowledge of how these new foods are produced, Juubche's residents lack at least part of the understanding with which they would categorize them into the hot-cold syndrome.

Furthermore, that younger woman do feel confident preparing these foods and introducing them to others challenges local assumptions held by older people about racial types. Over the course of my fieldwork, I noticed differences in how younger and older people referred to themselves and their fellow townspeople. As I strolled down a quiet street one afternoon, a woman in her fifties beckoned to me from her doorway, where she sat sewing. By the time I reached her front gate, she was standing outside with a gaggle of relatives: an elderly man, a couple of younger women, and a few small children. After we exchanged pleasantries, the woman asked me how I had found my way to this town of *indios* (Indians). One of the younger women quickly corrected her: "Yucatecans. We are Yucatecans." The common practice of locals to speak in the personal plural (the -*o'on* suffix in Yucatec Maya) reveals the use of a variety of terms. Those in their forties and older almost always use terms such as *mayero*, *indio*, or *otsil*, terms that connote indigeneity and poverty, while younger people refer to themselves as *Yucatecos* and, less frequently, as *Mexicanos*.[16]

Older people tend to pin dietary differences on these perceived racial distinctions, and many suggest that ts'uulo'ob are immune to the hot-cold imbalances to which they are vulnerable.[17] For older women in particular, generally the least well-traveled among residents, the categories of mayero and ts'uul align with distinct culinary patterns, influenced by the contrast between local food practices and the consumption practices of ts'uulo'ob that they have observed on television. Older women are often surprised by the breastfeeding of *xunáano'ob* (feminine equivalent of ts'uulo'ob), as infant formula is understood to be finer than breastmilk. Ts'uulo'ob do not *uk'ul* (drink) in the morning; they *desayunar* (breakfast), and they are able to eat at that time such "cold" foods as papaya, to no ill effect. While Juubche residents of all ages believe that one can sometimes *suuktal* (grow accustomed) to different foods and environments, older informants frequently impress upon me their belief that the foods that they were accustomed to eating were uniquely suited for their bodies and lifestyles.

In contrast, younger women and men usually have more contact with urban Mexicans and foreigners, giving them less essentialist understandings of food consumption. The greater willingness of younger women to experiment with new foods also provides a concrete means of testing accepted theories of difference; as they serve their children hot cakes and sáandwich to no adverse effects, they begin to question essentialist theories of food suitability. In challenging established ideas of racial difference, however, young people have actually contributed to the development of an alternate theory of bodily difference: younger generations, some elderly residents posit, are growing more like those of ts'uulo'ob. The changing lifestyles of the young, as well as selective evidence of phenotypical change, especially with regards to height and skin color, reinforce this theory for some older people. Doña Susana, a woman in her fifties, noted how her younger neighbor gave her children "cold" drinks with "hot" food in the cool evenings. Doña Susana explained that she wouldn't have dared do that with her children a few decades earlier, but then concluded that it didn't seem to do much harm to children today.

Conclusion

The repertoire of dishes that make up everyday cuisine in Juubche is the product of centuries of adaptation to topography and climate that is more Caribbean than "Mexican," of roots in Mesoamerican cosmology, and of colonial policy and religious conversion. The adoption of dishes like sáandwich, sopa fría, and ensalada by Juubche's residents is also the result of complex factors, made possible by a series of major economic and cultural shifts during the twentieth century, including the decline of agriculture, the development of tourism, and the expansion of mass media. The rapid absorption and dissemination of food-related knowledge and skills by young women are the products of sharp observations of the ways in which food is prepared and consumed on television and in urban areas. The skill-set young women demonstrate in preparing new foods embodies—for them and for their kin and neighbors—both a mastery of one culinary realm and a mastery of the art of middle-class living. They seek to broaden their food practices and knowledge as a mechanism for personal and social development.

The ways in which young women have embraced these foods have themselves been productive of social change in Juubche. There is not a systematic devaluation of established culinary knowledge in Juubche; rather the culinary culture itself is expanding, largely due to these young women. They are assuming positions of authority within a culinary culture that continues to value standardization over creativity. In this way, these women are recreating cultural emphases on consensus and collectivity, and maintaining some form of cohesion in the face of growing religious diversity and economic inequality in their community. At the same time, their knowledge of these new foods and their access to resources complicate local and regional ideologies of race, class, and biology. Sáandwich, sopa fría, and ensalada do not just require new methods of preparation and consumption but also new understandings of bodies and health. As long as these foods remain outside of the established hot–cold syndrome and the cosmology of which it is a part, they will continue to require that Juubche residents re-conceptualize the world in which they live.

For residents, there are few, if any, connections between these new foods and the hard human labor, sometimes-extreme weather, and often-fickle supernatural forces that have affected the production of food for generations. It is this radical difference that is, in fact, part of the appeal of sáandwich, sopa fría, and ensalada. These young women's acquisition of new culinary skills and the dexterity and authority with which they exercise them bring a taste of, and for, culinary luxuries to Juubche, effectively broadening the realm of pleasure within the community. The case of these young women reminds us that food, as both objects and actors in human lives, holds the potential to challenge fixed and generalized notions of identity as much, if not more so, than it does to uphold them. Perhaps more importantly, this case demonstrates that food has the remarkable ability to shake a community's view of the world while preserving some of its core values: in Juubche, a respect for knowledge, a desire for cohesion, and a commitment to eating as well as possible.

–3–

Tourism, Seafood Memories, and Identity: Lessons from Roatán, Honduras

Heather J. Sawyer

The links between food and culture have long been explored in anthropology. In the past, food was more likely to be treated as the material embodiment of culture, but in recent years food has come to be understood as a medium through which broader political-ecological processes can be explored. Food is now understood as an especially good means of identity creation and maintenance, helping to establish and keep boundaries between groups (Lentz 1999). However, one area that has received little scholarly attention in regards to food and identity is memory (Sutton 2001). Memories are not merely nostalgic moments retold, drawn from a set catalogue of events. Instead, memories are actively formed through social practice for specific reasons. Especially in need of scholarly attention is a move beyond the literal meanings portrayed in food memories towards an exploration of the dynamic ways in which food memories come about in response to broader processes affecting when, how, and why they are told.

This chapter explores this under-researched topic through an analysis of the emergence of collective seafood memories on the island of Roatán, Honduras. To understand how and why these memories are being enacted, I will explore how seafood accessibility has changed on the island since the inception of the nature-based tourism industry and the implication of these changes for islander identity. The growth of the island's nature-based tourism industry has led to changing access to seafood through both the creation of a marine protected area as well as declining environmental quality. And while conservation efforts have protected some marine species so that the island's nature-based tourism industry could continue, other factors such as an exploding population and increasing environmental pressures have created a situation where islanders find it increasingly difficult to maintain seafood as the staple of their diets. As a result, seafood is in the process of becoming a luxury item, mostly accessible to island elites and tourists.

In this chapter I argue that even though islanders consume seafood far less today than in the recent past, it still plays an integral role in islander identity through the use of seafood memories. More specifically, islanders are increasingly using the collective memory of seafood consumption as a way to differentiate themselves from ladino migrants moving to the island in search of work in the nature-based tourism industry. An exploration of seafood narratives is a valuable way to gain insights about food as more than just a material item but also a vehicle for identity maintenance. A focus on collective memories also illuminates some of the broader shifts in food and identity stemming from growing conservation and tourism efforts in Roatán. Because these efforts have been facilitated by neoliberal policies meant to spur economic development, this chapter also sheds light on the potential impacts of these types of policies for other destinations in the Caribbean using conservation and tourism as their foremost development strategies.

Part 1: An Environment of Plenty?

The telling of seafood memories in Roatán might be especially baffling to the outside observer. Most visitors can easily access seafood and the marine environment through things such as Roatán's tourist restaurants, glass-bottom boat tours, the scuba-diving industry, and charter-fishing trips. In fact, the island of Roatán is a budding tourist destination for those seeking a seemingly unspoiled tropical paradise. The island has relatively few chain restaurants, no internationally known hotel companies and offers some of the most stunning but modestly priced scuba diving in the world. A stroll down one of the main tourist areas offers the visitor a variety of beachside restaurants. For many people visiting the island, food becomes a primary medium through which local culture is experienced and consumed. And to most tourists, these beachside restaurants embody "island living." They exude a laid-back rustic charm, offer an abundance of exotic seafood dishes, and project loud reggae or American hip-hop music that spills out onto the nearby dirt road. From a diner's table, beautiful turquoise waters, white sand beaches, and coconut tress give the appearance of ecological vitality. And as an island in the Caribbean, it comes as little surprise that most restaurants' nightly specials are seafood delicacies. Restaurant chalkboards entice passers-by with promises of: "Conch ceviche tonight!" or "Fresh lobster tails." And I often hear from visitors when spending time in Roatán that they want to "eat what the locals eat" while on the island.

However, what most diners don't realize is that as they consume these delicacies they are gazing upon a marine protected area experiencing unprecedented ecological decline. Many local marine species (including those featured on restaurant chalkboards) are threatened or endangered due to overfishing, pollution, and ecosystem destruction. In combination with dwindling local marine populations, soaring food prices on the island are making locally available seafood prohibitively expensive for most island residents, dramatically decreasing the amount of islander seafood consumption over the past twenty years. So although seafood has historically played an integral role in islander identity, it is increasingly becoming a luxury item out of reach both economically and ecologically for islanders. Therefore, the everyday consuming habits surrounding seafood on the island are rapidly diverging from the ways in which islander food identity is constructed and portrayed in the islands' tourism industry. The strong place of seafood in Roatán's tourism industry (despite local scarcity and soaring seafood prices) may be explained by the role that food plays in general in tourism industries as the embodiment of authentic local culture.

Tourism and Food

One of the earliest social scientists concerned with tourism, Dean MacCannell (1989), argued that tourists are in search of so-called authentic experiences. He reasoned that in the Western world, people were so disenfranchised with their modern lives, they felt they had lost all meaning. In an attempt to find and experience authentic culture, they engaged in tourism. Importantly, MacCannell critiqued this notion of cultural authenticity and highlighted the negotiated and emergent nature of culture. One area in particular that he focused on was the staged aspect of tourism. Unbeknownst to many tourists, dances, crafts, traditions and even cuisine have been invented by many host communities to appease tourists who have little understanding of the actual lives they live. MacCannell's work was groundbreaking because he highlighted the ways in which tourism industries are constructed through these representations of culture.

In more recent years, increased attention has been paid to the power relations involved in building and maintaining tourism destinations. From this focus grew an awareness of the political-economic factors shaping and being shaped by tourism development. For example, Bruner (2004) argues that instead of focusing on whether tourism represents authentic culture or not, tourism development should be placed in its broader economic, environmental, and political contexts in order to understand its role in power production. This framework is the predominant approach used by anthropologists today to analyze the impacts of tourism development.

A particularly useful way through which the power dynamics associated with tourism can be analyzed is through food. Although tourist destinations are diverse places comprised of a variety of attractions, food has become an essential part of the tourist experience (Caldwell 2006; Hall and Mitchell 2002a, 2002b; Richards 2002). The proliferation of national cuisines has largely been propelled by a desire to grow tourism industries. And tourists expect a destination to have some sort of regional or national dish that embodies the place's identity. Recently, host communities have become more and more competitive with each other as they enter the global economy. Local cuisine is now a powerful tool through which host communities can market and brand themselves. For tourism industries, food has emerged as an object of consumption that represents place-specific differentiation in the midst of increasing globalization.

However, it is important to stress that authenticity is a complex and shifting concept, especially when applied to food. For example, anthropological studies have illuminated many critiques of the concept of authenticity when applied to food. For example, food choices should not be viewed as simply a matter of taste and preference. Van Esterik (2006) contextualizes food choices in broader economic processes. She demonstrates that many so-called traditional foods are often consumed not simply out of desire, but out of economic necessity and affordability. When applied to tourism industries, foods understood by tourists as traditional foods could very well be "hunger foods," consumed out of desperation. Additionally, Dodds (1998) illustrates the ways in which global markets affect people's relationships with food harvesting, sales, and consumption. He uses the lobster trade in Honduras to illustrate the interconnectedness of food producers in the global South with consumers in the global North. For example, while lobsters once made up a significant portion of the diet in the region where Dodds conducted his research, it is now more economically viable to sell lobsters in the global market. Due to high demand and consumption in the global North, the species now faces serious decline. And, despite the proliferation of the lobster trade, the area is still characterized by persistent poverty. Therefore, the lobster trade exemplifies broader economic problems and local marginalization for producers in the global South, while for consumers in the global North lobsters exemplify luxury and affluence. Along similar lines, Caldwell (2006) argues that food should not be viewed simply as an object that circulates between producers and consumers, but that this circulation itself is valuable in that it provides insights about global power dynamics.

In a similarly critical vein, while the popularity and necessity of site-specific local cuisine has grown in tourism industries, many anthropologists have questioned the construction of these dishes. Anthropologist Richard Wilk (1999, 2006a) has explored the emergence of Belizean cuisine, tracing its history and highlighting the ways in which it has been largely invented to appeal to tourists. He argues that while the outside observer perceives Belizean national cuisine as representative of authentic local culture, in reality, transnational flows of people, goods, and capital have come together to produce these dishes. For example, when Belize obtained its independence from Britain in the mid-nineteenth century, a small group of foreign trained intellectuals pushed for the development of a Belizean national culture. By the late 1990s, many dishes that were associated with poverty in the country became reappropriated as so-called national dishes. Therefore, Wilk argues that the formulation of Belizean national cuisine and culture have actually been the result of complex intermingling factors from foreigners, expatriates, tourists, and emigrants who largely populate the country.

An analysis of food in tourism industries can illuminate broader processes at work. For example, Milne and Ateljevic (2001) argue, it is essential to look carefully at how interactions between the global and the local shape development outcomes for individuals, households, communities and regions. Tourism, in simple terms, must be viewed as a transactional process which is at once driven by the global priorities of multi-national corporations, geo-political forces, and broader forces of economic change, and the complexities of the local. (371–72)

Especially in Roatán, understanding shifting seafood availability sheds much light on the relationships between a variety of local, regional, and global actors, who shape development outcomes. In order to illuminate the complex factors affecting tourism development outcomes, I will provide a brief background on Roatán, its residents, and the proliferation of tourism development on the island.

Changing Regional Economy

The push to promote tourism in Roatán was part of a larger regional trend towards tourism and conservation growth in Latin America and the Caribbean. Over the past twenty to twenty-five years, Latin America and the Caribbean have established large amounts of protected areas and today have more land area conserved than anywhere else in the world (Moreno 2005; Zimmerer and Carter 2002). The increase in protected areas is linked to a regional change in approach towards economic development. This approach can broadly be labeled neoliberalism. However, I must warn that the term has been used widely in recent years to refer to economic development efforts spanning the entire globe and encompassing a wide variety of projects and policies. Therefore, when using the term it is important to define it and how it applies to specific cases.

For the purposes of this chapter, neoliberalism refers generally to deregulated markets, a decreased role of the state with increased privatization of services, intense competition between economic actors, and an emphasis on private property rights (Ferguson 2006; Harvey 2005; Peet and Hartwick 1999). While proponents of neoliberalism claim that increased trade and decreased regulation facilitates greater market participation, resulting in decreased poverty, critics argue that the theoretical underpinnings of neoliberalism are often at odds with its actual outcomes (Ferguson 2006; Harvey 2005; Larner 2000; Wade 2006). Instead, neoliberalism is attributed to increased economic marginalization and vulnerability for the poor.

A somewhat unexpected area of study that has recently been linked to neoliberalism is conservation. Fueled by neoliberal tenets and an effort to generate more sustainable forms of economic growth, conservation has been often been paired with tourism development as an ideal way to guard against the unsavory environmental, social, and economic impacts of development. However, Zimmerer and Carter (2002) argue that the push for protected areas is not a radical departure from neoliberal approaches to development, but has been fueled by them. Similarly, Igoe and Brockington (2007) argue that conservation is the latest manifestation of neoliberal development, spreading its breadth to the commodification of so-called protected resources. Conservation areas are required to become economically self-sufficient in order to pay for patrolling and management, essentially turning conserved areas into businesses. This creates new human-environment relationships as even protected resources become objects to manage and control, facilitating new forms of governmentality. For those individuals with enough capital to maintain businesses that profit from protected areas (such as scuba companies or eco-tours), the vast majority of people in these areas have been relegated to low-paying service work with limited subsistence options. Therefore, while conservation is assumed to automatically benefit local people, Igoe and Brockington argue that its theoretical tenets must be followed through to its actual outcomes in order to assess its viability.

The Growth of Roatán's Tourism Industry

In the early 1980s the Honduran government made the decision that tourism would be the country's primary economic development strategy. Roatán was one of the key places in which conservation and tourism were married in an attempt to foster sustainable economic growth. By the mid 1990s, the Honduran government declared Roatán an official tourism area and took measures to ensure its economic development through the enactment of several pieces of legislation. These initiatives followed a neoliberal agenda, encouraging deregulation, privatization, increased trade, and intensified competition. For example, the government of Honduras established special economic zones, which gave incentives to foreign investors. Benefits included: the ability to obtain 100 percent foreign ownership of land, the right to operate businesses without paying federal and municipal taxes, and exemption from duties or taxes on any imports or equipment used in developing the tourism industry. Foreign investors also had access to financing through the Foundation for Investment and Development (FIDE), a para-statal organization (Stonich 1998). These initiatives were successful in encouraging economic development, and today tourism is the primary economic force in Roatán. The most popular tourist activity is scuba-diving, followed by relaxing on beaches, dining, snorkeling, and fishing.

By the late 1990s, after fervent construction and a boom in tourist visitor numbers, the integrity of the Bay Islands' natural resources were recognized to be at risk from increased development. Deforestation, sedimentation, loss of mangroves, and diminishing quantities of fish were among the most pressing issues. In an attempt to protect the natural and marine resources of Roatán and nearby islands, in 1997, the Bay Islands National Marine Park was established and integrated into Honduras's National System of Protected Areas. The establishment of the marine protected area was meant to fulfill several objectives. According to the national government, the major goal was "to promote economic development through the rational exploitation of renewable and nonrenewable resources, especially through the least destructive means, tourism and recreation" (Stonich 2000: 92).

However, despite the seeming innocuousness of nature-based tourism development, the environmental quality of the island has continued to decline. For example, the island continues to suffer from the same ecological problems as before, but now it is also experiencing pollution of waters surrounding the island, increased generation of garbage, a lack of potable water for residents, and a growth in the amount of raw sewage without proper treatment facilities. Unfortunately, conservation initiatives on the island have not circumvented the deleterious impacts of economic growth. This paradox of simultaneous conservation coupled with ecological destruction is explained as resulting from what Carrier and Macleod (2005) term an "ecotourism bubble." They argue that the use of protected areas do not guard against the infrastructural demands of tourism industries (such as hotels, airports, roads, etc.). So while nature-based tourism is ecologically sustainable within park boundaries, the broader impacts of tourism industries continue to degrade surrounding ecosystems.

This explanation holds true for Roatán as well. For example, the conservation areas established in Roatán protect very specific places, but the infrastructure required to support the growing number of tourists on the island (stemming from road construction, dredging for resorts, increased flights, increased plastic bottle use with no recycling program, etc.) have resulted in a massive deterioration of the local ecosystem as a whole. The establishment of the marine protected area, coupled with ecological decline has also limited livelihood options for many residents who once used the waters for activities such as subsistence fishing. Especially due to neoliberal legislation that favored foreign investment, the tourism industry has resulted in economic polarization on the island between island elites and the remaining vast majority of residents. In theory, the trade-off for diminished seafood access via environmental protection laws would be compensated for by adequate paying jobs in the tourism industry. However, most locals have been relegated to low paying service jobs that devalue their labor. In addition, most forms of available employment have not been adequate in generating enough income to provide residents with food security. Taken as a whole, the proliferation of tourism development in Roatán has resulted in a situation where income levels from the tourism industry do not provide enough for a comfortable living, yet subsistence procurement from seafood is not a viable, long-term solution either.

Part 2

The first part of this chapter illuminated the changes in seafood accessibility on the island since the inception of the nature-based tourism industry. This explained how tourism development, coupled with conservation initiatives, have changed the ecological and economic terrain in Roatán and have resulted in decreased seafood access for the majority of the island's residents. The second part of this chapter explores the historical development of islander identity and the implications of decreased seafood accessibility for their unique identity. The first part of the chapter combined with the second part help to facilitate a critical examination of the island's nature-based tourism industry and the impacts it has had on seafood access and identity.

Islander History

Although Roatán is formally owned by Honduras, the island's inhabitants feel a strong sense of cultural, linguistic, and historical distinctness from mainland residents (Currin 2005; Stonich 1998, 2000). Many Honduran mainlanders conceptualize islander identity as occupying an odd ethnic category that is different from mainland ladinos but is also not indigenous either. During colonial times, a series of violent conflicts and removals eradicated indigenous groups from the island. Subsequently, over a 150-year period, Britain and Spain fought for strategic control of the island. Eventually, Britain established the first European settlement on the island. After the abolition of slavery in the Caribbean, freed slaves of African descent and former white slave owners settled on the island from other parts of the English-speaking Caribbean. Through a legal technicality, Britain ceded ownership of Roatán to Spain and in 1859 Spain gave the island to Honduras through the Wykes-Cruz Treaty (Stonich 2000).

The formal concession of the Bay Islands to the Honduran government stirred much controversy and opposition from island residents because of longstanding trade and linguistic ties with other English-speaking enclaves in the Caribbean and the United States. Many felt betrayed by Britain and refused to accept Honduran nationality. Since that time, the Honduran national government has made several attempts to "hispanicize" the island, resulting in ongoing tensions that persist even today. The importance of this history lies in the pattern of opposition and conflict between the English-speaking island and Spanish-speaking mainland, which continues today to define much of islander identity.

These tensions are now exacerbated on the island due to a significant population growth over the past twenty-five years. Since the construction of the international airport in Roatán in 1988 and the subsequent growth in the tourism industry, the island has also undergone rapid and significant population growth from around 20,000 residents to an estimated 65,000 today (Stonich 2000; Tomczyk 2004). In addition to a growing number of ex-pats residing on the island, many poor Spanish-speaking ladinos from the Honduran mainland have migrated to Roatán in search of work in the tourism industry. While ladinos have historically made up a miniscule percentage of the population, current estimates indicate that Spanish-speaking ladinos now comprise at least half of the island's population. These new migrants move to the island in search of what they refer to as "the good life." On the mainland, rumors abound that Roatán is a beacon of hope for poor families, with an abundance of good paying jobs. However, while wages are often higher on the island than the mainland, living expenses are too. Unfortunately, many mainlanders move to the island with high hopes of upward mobility but are disappointed to find sparse employment with very high living costs.

Islander Diets

One major difference islanders are now confronted with since the boom in tourism is a proliferation of imported foods. Today, over 70 percent of food on supermarket shelves is imported from the United States (Stonich 2000). Foods that were unheard of on the island just twenty years ago, such as fresh milk, lettuce, carrots, onions, and tomatoes are now available. Conversely, traditional island foods such as seafood soup, conch, lobster, and iguana have greatly declined due to environmental pressures (McDonald 2006). And ironically, today most seafood sold in Roatán is harvested in another part of the Caribbean, approximately 300 miles away and shipped to the island. Much of this seafood arrives frozen and is sold either in local markets or directly to restaurants. So although an abundance of seafood is available to purchase on the island (in tourism restaurants and from street vendors), it is now prohibitively expensive for most residents.

Food security is now a primary concern for both islanders and ladinos alike (Stonich 2000). However, before the boom in Roatán's tourism industry, residents had little problem obtaining food. Mangos, avocados, coconuts, and limes grow naturally on the island and conch, lobster, iguana, turtle, and fish were in such abundance it took very little effort to find enough to feed a family. Today, this has all changed.

The Emergence of Seafood Memories

Charlie, a fifty-six-year-old man who has lived the majority of his life in Roatán, explained the changes in seafood accessibility over his lifetime. He said that up until the past twenty years or so, food was in great abundance on the island. For example, during holidays or special occasions, islanders often walked to a nearby beach called West Bay to have a meal together. There was no need to bring any food from home, because it was possible to collect or catch as much food as needed to feed a large group of people along the way. Today, ecological conditions are vastly different. West Bay is now the premier tourist beach, lined with all-inclusive dive resorts and high-end luxury condos. This area's waters are filled with swimmers, snorkelers, and yachts. Very few islanders live in this area because living costs are among the most expensive on the island. Locals who do visit the beach are now primarily there to try to make some money in the tourism industry. Islander women offer to braid tourists' hair for a few dollars and men try to sell charter-fishing trips. And although the beach is still breathtakingly beautiful with its white sand beaches and palm trees, Charley told me: "people say to me 'West Bay is dying . . . The reefs are dying!' To me, West Bay is already dead. It's dead" (personal correspondence, July 2011). Although to many tourists Roatán offers some of the best snorkeling and scuba-diving in the world, to many islanders the marine ecosystem of the region today is only a fraction of the ecological vitality present merely twenty years ago.

Similarly, a middle-aged islander named Jenny told me that when she was a young woman, it was possible to ask her husband for fish just fifteen minutes before she wanted to cook dinner. She and her husband live in a home that has been in his family for generations and is only steps from the sea. Before the boom in the tourism industry, Jenny's husband could walk out into the waters in front of their home and easily catch as much seafood as they needed to feed their whole family. Today, due to diminished fish populations this is not possible. If Jenny wanted to harvest fish in front of her home, her husband would have to venture much further away from shore to find adequate populations. And if seafood was found, due to over-fishing species are likely to be very young and small. As a result, if islanders want to eat fish today much of it must be purchased from seafood distributors. However, to my surprise, when I asked Jenny how often she eats seafood, she told me: "I eat it every day. Islanders . . . we eat it every day" (personal correspondence, March 2011). But, after spending a few weeks with her I noticed this did not seem to be the case. She was far more likely to eat things like bread with honey for lunch and chicken and rice for dinner. Seafood did not seem to be a staple in her diet. Additionally, her husband told me that the family consumes far less seafood today than they did even a few years ago. Jenny reporting that islanders eat seafood every day seems to indicate that the realties surrounding seafood consumption are rapidly changing.

When I asked a construction foreman named Tony who grew up in Roatán how important seafood is to him, he told me: "it's part of who we [islanders] are. We eat seafood every day. They [ladino migrants] don't need it like we do. They could just eat a little rice and beans and tortilla and they're fine. Not me. I *need* fish." In this way, seafood is used to demarcate social boundaries and define group identity. In contrast to ladino migrants, islanders view seafood as an integral part of their identity and consumptive habits. The memory of seafood consumption as a marker of identity on the island is becoming a key way for islanders to distinguish themselves from recently migrated ladinos. For now, it seems there is a lag between islander food identity and the actual consumption of seafood as a result of rapid economic and ecological changes on the island. Due to this relatively recent phenomenon of seafood inaccessibility on the island, it is yet unknown what impact this will have for future and current generations of islanders and their identities. However, a focus on the process of seafood memory formation is an important analytic tool.

Discussion/Conclusion

Social memory is a topic that is growing in relevance as a way for anthropologists to better understand the relationships between the past and present (Borgstede 2010). More specifically, an investigation of social memory is useful analytically because it illuminates the links between narratives and local, national, regional, or even global processes. And since these memories must be enacted through social performance, or storytelling, food memories offer an important way for anthropologists to understand the links between food and identity. In Roatán, an analysis of seafood narratives indicates broader shifts in the area's ecology and economy as a result of processes set into motion by the island's nature-based tourism industry.

Although it is not readily apparent through a perusal of the island's restaurant menus, seafood is in a state of unprecedented decline locally and in the broader Caribbean as well. However, representations of local cuisine in the tourism industry are becoming increasing divergent from the ecological reality and dietary practices of most islanders. The ability of tourists to continue purchasing seafood despite its scarcity points to growing power disparities on the island, which can be seen through the shifting and multiple meanings of food. For visitors, consuming seafood is a way to experience so-called authentic island culture. It is an integral part of the tourist experience. For local restaurants, seafood is an important product that increases their marketability. For islanders, seafood plays an integral role in their identity, especially in the midst of dramatic demographic changes. And while seafood consumption has recently declined for islanders, they continue to draw much of their identity from it—despite its inaccessibility through collective seafood memories. Importantly, these narratives reveal insights about more than just changing food practices. Instead, an exploration of shifting seafood accessibility points to growing social, ecological, and economic inequality in Roatán, set into motion by the island's budding tourism industry.

The engagement of the Honduran government with neoliberal development has succeeded in facilitating the growth of the nature-based tourism industry in Roatán, but at what cost? This economic approach has set into motion processes that have serious consequences for islander livelihood security, access to seafood, and their identity. This case study offers much in terms of revealing some of the unintended or unforeseen consequences of nature-based tourism development and the potential impacts of adopting this model of economic development around other parts of the Caribbean as well.

–4–

Versions of Dominican *Mangú*: Intersections of Gender and Nation in Caribbean Self-making

Lidia Marte

They, the most uprooted . . . always filled with a longing for flight . . . all in a state of transition.

—Fernando Ortiz

Mangú's origins and histories—through ingredients such as plantains—have always been global and diasporic. Since its early origins in the 1500s Caribbean, this dish of boiled and mashed plantains—usually served with some protein—has remained a major food staple for the majority of Dominicans in the Dominican Republic and in the U.S. diaspora. Dominican foodways, like many other Caribbean cuisines, carries within the marks of slave, proletariat, and creole cooking syncretisms rather than being representative of an elite lifestyle (Mintz 1996; Veloz Maggiolo and Tolentino Dipp 2007; Wilk 1999). Mangú, a good example of such humble staples, has not been claimed openly in the Dominican Republic as "national," yet it is now a prominent site of self-representation for Dominicans in New York City.

I suggest that a focus on a low prestige staple allows us to examine strategic self-making (Allen 2007; Hall 1994) roles that food is made to perform in Dominican identity politics (Mohanty 2003). Food is a significant area of research to explore the formation and shifts of Caribbean and Afro-diasporic identities. The exploitative gender, class, and racial systems, which were organized during colonization, used the Caribbean as a testing ground for what would become the global social formations (Omi and Winant 1986), which created conditions of marginalization for the majority of global south populations until today. Hence these axes of identity point to historical contexts, to specific lived experiences, and to the cultural histories of those who cook and eat mangú in the Dominican Republic and its diaspora, as well as how they are "seasoned" (Marte 2008), that is, socialized through their economic conditions of survival into a sense of belonging to the Dominican nation.

Two main concerns motivate this mangú exploration: (1) how a staple dish so linked to oppression came to stand for freedom, creativity, and a rooted sense of community and belonging to the land; and (2) how such cultural practice could be invested with such powerful "commemorative vigilance" (Bardenstein 1999: 148) to make it worthy of preparing after migration. By examining three mangú preparations and the associated narratives I hope to share some insights about the intersections of gender, class, and race in the power maneuvers that migrants use to affirm and to resist Dominican narratives of national belonging. The discussion is based on archival and ethnographic materials collected over the last five years, mostly within communities in New York City, Puerto Rico, and the Dominican Republic. In New York City, food preparations were documented in seven households, with especial attention to the frequency of cooking Dominican dishes, how ingredients were procured, how migrants earned their income, as well as what food-related narratives came up while documenting their food practices. Visual data, hand-drawn maps, oral histories, and audio recordings of spontaneous storytelling were collected while I accompanied collaborators in their kitchens and during shopping trips as well as to community events and job sites in order to experience how they earned their living and how food routes helped them navigate the city. Participants responded orally to a food socialization profile in order to gather more consistent data across the group.

The fragments of narratives discussed come from three collaborators: Elsa, Rafa, and Bienve, all Dominican immigrants in their mid-fifties living in different boroughs of New York City. They self-identified as immigrants, working-class, and heterosexual, and all of them had a basic primary education. When I asked about national identity and ethnicity, the most common form of self-identification was Dominican or Hispanic, rarely Latino. When I asked further about racial identification, the Trujillo's era labels—such as *indio claro* and *indio ocuro* (dark or light Indian), or *café con leche* (coffee with milk) and *achocolatado* (coffee with chocolate)— were still used to designate racial identity. Rafa was the only one who identified as Afro-Latino or Afro-Dominican, indicating an emergent reclamation of *mulataje* and blackness in the diaspora.

Throughout my analysis I use a framing of identity based on "social locations," which takes into account the many intersecting axes of social categories imposed on individuals by society and which generates particular forms of privilege and marginalization. Social categories are, however, interpreted and contested by individuals, and hence a concept of "subjectivity" is useful as well to examine how social locations are actually negotiated in the "micro-politics of everyday life" (Scott 1990: 65) and in the context of specific places and historical times. This approach is informed by postcolonial, black feminist and critical race theory (Collins 1991; Crenshaw 1991; Mohanty 2003), which recognizes the centrality of power/agency in human interactions and offers a way to avoid assuming essentialized and static identities.

I suggest examining *food relations* from the grounded perspective of particular individuals—in this case, cooks—rather than food and identity in the abstract, since this approach helps us unravel the shifting meanings of foods and the identities they index. A second grounding of my theoretical interpretations is through a critical de-coding of domestic versions of a staple, questioning how private meanings estab-lish a conversation with public representations of national cuisine and the wider ethnohistorical contexts that frame it. This is why the migrant histories and social locations of who cooks, serves, eats, and speaks of mangú are a crucial grounding of my analysis. In tracing a meal from the personal and situated history of particular versions as prepared by a specific person, we avoid taking for granted its meaning as a representation of "national" or "ethnic" cuisine, and instead read it as a kind of cultural map that speaks of where, when, and by whom it is prepared.

Like Caribbean cuisines and identities, the historical sources about Dominican foods are fragmentary, revealing once again the global and multilingual routes of the region and its historiography (Trouillot 1995; Wilk 1999). Eclectic as well are the mix of theoretical tools that helped me compose this academic narrative of mangú. These interpretations are also influenced by my own social locations in the United States as a Dominican migrant who has tasted and witnessed the cooking of mangú throughout my life. I contribute these reflections to help open more critical this criti-cal research and dialogues about the poetics and politics of food in the Caribbean and about its social justice implications.

Roots and Routes: Emergence and Reversals of Mangú

Mangú is one of the oldest Dominican staple dishes. It is speculated that the first green plantains, which originated somewhere in Asia, came to Hispaniola early in the 1500s via the Canary Islands, and from there it spread to the rest of the Carib-bean (Ortiz-Cuadra 2006). Root crops (known as *víveres* in the Dominican Republic) grow very well in the tropical Caribbean. Large green plantains (*Musa* spp.), once introduced in the Caribbean food systems, also grew easily and became plentiful in food production (together with the more well known sweet yellow bananas). Yet the way green plantains were consumed early on in Hispaniola and other Hispanic Caribbean islands can not be precisely stated; hence, mangú's genesis as a kind of meal of boiled and mashed plantains prepared by enslaved population is uncertain. The origins and exact meanings of the word mangú are also uncertain, but popular literature and cookbooks suggest that the word is of possible *Azande* African origin, meaning power or spirit (Nina 2007).[1]

What is certain is that green plantains were the central food given to slaves (Veloz Maggiolo and Tolentino Dipp 2007; Nina 2004), and they were even called *pan de negros* (bread of blacks). Some masters specified, in their administrative guide for plantations, even the number of plantains to be given per day to each adult slave; six to eight plantains served as ready, easily stored, easily prepared, and inexpensive nu-trition for slaves in the plantation economy (Ortiz-Cuadra 2006). Because plantains can easily be prepared in large batches, they may have been used to more easily serve great quantities of slaves, as well as free laborers, the overseers, and masters. Since these earlier times, plantains continue to be an essential part of all Caribbean Creole cuisines. Mashed plantains are well known in Puerto Rico as *mofongo* (prepared today as a delicacy, in very elaborate ways with garlic, pork rinds and sometimes other meat or sea food, and served with a chicken broth). In Cuba, a dish similar to Dominican mangú is called *fufú de plátano*. The very names used to designate these preparations point to New World slave seasonings of both food and language (Marte 2008; Abarca 2006; Brian Stross, personal communication, May 2012), as the dishes are part of the reclamations of flavors and freedom that Mintz (1996) speaks of in the emergence of a syncretic regional cuisine produced by African-descended populations in the Caribbean.[2]

Green plantains for mangú are inexpensive and plentiful in New York City (sometimes specials are offered of fifteen plantains for one dollar) at Dominican supermarkets. In the Dominican Republic over the last decade, fluctuations of basic foodstuff prices have made traditional foods difficult to procure for the poorest households. Plantains, previously thought of as democratic foods available to the majority of the population, are at risk of becoming luxury items. Similarly, over the last decade *bacalao* (cod fish), which used to be a low-prestige food for poor households, has become more expensive than chicken, a middle-class food item (Veloz Maggiolo and Tolentino Dipp 2007). However, the place and meaning of plantains in the Dominican diet is so strong that many protests and national strikes have demanded price stabilization (Red Dominicana 2007). In all Dominican restaurants that I visited in New York City, mangú is a common fare across boroughs. A popular diaspora version is offered in a combo called *lo tré golpe*—"the three strikes"—served with eggs, fried cheese, and salami, and has become well known in Washington Heights. Other Latino immigrants, African Americans, and some Anglo-Americans that work or reside in the area consume it. Dominican mangú preparation and meanings are transforming among the Dominican diaspora in New York City, in the context of wider culinary changes. Mangú is a clearer representation of Dominican migrant experiences than *la bandera* (the flag), a dish of rice, beans, and meat, which is too generic and requires expensive meats to complete, a fact which appears to index the ruptures and failures of the Dominican state.[3]

To contextualize mangú within the Dominican cooking repertoire, let's consider the national *triunvirato* of Dominican staples, usually thought of by immigrants as traditional foods: *la bandera*, *sancocho* (a kind of roots and meat stew),[4] and mangú. In New York City, the prominence and prestige of mangú (and plantains more broadly) unmistakably points to a Dominican cultural difference outweighing both la bandera and sancocho. Yet, in the Dominican Republic, mangú is still a fare of working-class kitchens, and it is not usually claimed as a main national dish in public culture or at touristic sites. Mangú has become an index of Dominicanness not only in New York City. *La mancha del plátano* (the stain of the plantain) identifies

Dominican immigrants racially and culturally in Puerto Rico, Miami, and other areas of the United States, and probably in Spain and Italy as well, which are more recent routes of migration.

The prominence of these main staples in the public culture of Dominicans both in the Dominican Republic and New York City serves to explore contested narratives showing the regional experience of each cook, and reveal the marks that economic struggles left in their migrant histories. Private versions of those dishes offer a contrast to the official definitions (circulated through public media and Internet sites). Dominican migrants have a keen awareness of the ironic representations of la bandera that many were not able to complete in the concreteness of their plates. For example, my collaborators related how they could afford to cook rice and beans, but instead of serving it with meat they had to eat it plain, or if available with a substitute of eggplant or other stewed vegetables. During campaign season, Joaquin Balaguer's government (1960–1980s) would distribute food bags in poor neighborhoods and in rural areas (probably food shipments they got from international relief agencies). The irony of distributing to a forgotten majority precisely the ingredients to prepare la bandera, a symbol of supposed unity and the health of the nation, was not lost on many people. Whose bandera this dish represents is still a contested proposal even today in the Dominican Republic, and I suggest even in New York City. The presence itself of these Dominican immigrants in the United States points to the failure of a national flag (of a national project to address poverty, repression, and trauma suffered during and after Trujillo's dictatorship). They could only complete the dish by leaving their birthplaces, the very land and society indexed by this dish. Such contested versions of a plate have left traumatic and critical traces in the personal and collective memory-histories of these individuals and their communities.

The continuum of significance of mangú in the big history of African diasporas, a Dominican nation to a private migrant plate on someone's table is useful to contrast matters of scale and context in how individuals and groups negotiate cultural changes while they are busy making their histories, but also in terms of scales of values of traveling, home and nation as nostalgic dichotomies of the "miniature and the gigantic" (Stewart 1993) positing oppositions between past-present, here-there, but also implicit valorizations of male-female, public-private, political-poetic, and so on. In the interest of preserving this counterpoint between these scales of significance, I chose to focus on private versions of mangú as prepared from particular kitchens in New York City.

Diasporic Versions of Mangú in New York City

Departing from a generic plate of mangú as an index of Dominican national cuisine, we can detour to specific preparations to further unravel intersecting axes of gender, class, and race as Dominicans read themselves inside and outside of the nation. The

Figure 4.1 Views of versions of mangú in New York City; a private version, from a Brooklyn household, and a public version from a Manhattan restaurant. Photos by the author, 2006.

ways in which domestic versions of mangú are prepared is crucial for our exploration; the choice of ingredients and tools to mash, the order of the steps, as well as the precautions they take to avoid the stains. These details act as fragments of narratives during the preparation and serving of mangú, and are important for examining changes in cooking practices after migration (for example, the shift from using half a plantain to a metal tool). Such emphasis on cooking strategies to achieve a culturally appropriate meal points further to diverse responses to the process of gendered socialization, and insinuate a critical dialogue with Dominican cooking conventions and food politics.

In this section I offer an analysis of versions of mangú through three different preparations by my fieldwork collaborators in New York City. The preparations and narratives come from Fifa, Rafa, and Elsa, Dominican immigrants in their mid-fifties living in different boroughs of the city. I use short passages from narratives that arose during mangú preparation to address both the practice and its perceived meanings according to each unique history of the migrant cook.

Fifa's Version of Mangú, from Washington Heights in Manhattan

Fifa is an immigrant woman in her fifties who has been cooking for others for a long time, and also comes from a family of professional cooks. Fifa works now in New York City seven days a week, approximately twelve hours per day, at her cooking job, and then many more hours preparing food at home to have ready to bring to work next day.

> Yes, here the situation is like that, working even on Sundays, seven days without rest . . . I earn a living as a cook for a food vendor truck in Washington Heights, in Manhattan . . . and on the side I prepare wedding and birthday cakes by the order . . . I learned to make cakes here . . . I bought all my [cake-making] tools.

Even though Fifa said she rarely cooked mangú, I got to document and enjoy a beautiful version she insisted on preparing one night, finishing almost at 11:00 P.M. It is ironic to eat it at night since mangú is generally prepared as a breakfast meal, which reveals how Fifa's foodmaps are constrained by her undocumented immigrant job options. Unlike the other cooks, Fifa cooks in silence unless someone asks her something. She adds one ripened plantain to her mangú, and says so with a certain pride:

> I ate so much mangú in DR that here I don't cook it much; my mother used to make it for us, to spoil us . . . I mix in a fully ripe plantain into my mangú to give it a little sweetness . . . I serve my mangú with salted pork, I add oregano for the magic touch . . . I serve it with white frying cheese called "The Traveler," and salted pork meat, when is available, or only with cheese . . . I don't like salami . . . they used to make it with dog meat in DR, and the sardines? Some said they were made of cardboard at one time.

Fifa takes great aesthetic care in serving her mangú; she asks who does not want onions and asks us to choose a plate we like, offering her best plates. First, she serves a few plates, and then counts how many people there are (that night there were five of us). After this gesture, she begins taking out portions from each plate to make up an additional serving, making sure each person gets a similar amount. To my facial reactions, she responds: "No, no te apure, ello alcansa, le saco un chin a cada plato" (No, don't worry, it is enough, I just need to take a bit out from each plate). Each of us gets plenty of mangú, a piece of pork and cheese, and a helping of red onions. Fifa serves herself last—and less—while saying *buen provecho a todo* (bon appetit everyone).

To contextualize Fifa's mangú version it is important to understand her marginalized experiences as a dark-skinned, poor woman in both the Dominican Republic and the United States. She is a descendant from *cocolos*, an English-speaking people originally from the lesser Antilles who came to the Dominican Republic as labor immigrants in the nineteenth and twentieth centuries (Pichardo 2007). In spite of these communities' hard work and fast integration into the country, including the loss of their original language, and the harvest of prominent artists and intellectuals, they have remained at the margins of the nation, and their contribution is invoked almost exclusively through participation in annual carnivals or through the folkloric use of their music and traditional foods such as *yaniqueques* (Johnny cakes) around touristic resorts. As an undocumented black immigrant woman with no mastery of English—ironic considering that her father's first language was English—Fifa's living conditions in New York City seem harsher than in the Dominican Republic, as additional axes of identity keep placing her into more intersecting conditions of marginalization. Fifa migrated to New York City from Pueblo Nuevo in 1993. The specific circumstances are difficult to reconstruct since her undocumented status is a sensitive subject about which she gave me only few details.

> My father was English from the Islands; he left his family there and never spoke a word of English again, he never taught us his language . . . my father? He was the best father in the world, he used to take us to outings, he was a man of his house . . . there (DR) we did not go hungry often thanks god, we were the ones helping others . . . my mother used to do everything at home, she cooked so tasty . . . after she died . . . I was nineteen, we (the daughters) had to grab the kitchen and learn fast to replace her.

Fifa has worked as a cook since she was very young, and comes from a family of women that cook for hire. As it seems to have been usual for her generation and in her family trajectory, she *had* to learn how to cook, not only as unpaid-domestic labor but also as a skill to bring income into the household. In New York City, Fifa is the food preparer for a street food truck that sells *chimichurri*, *kipe*, and other Dominican fast foods. The conditions and pay are substandard, but she cannot afford to complain. Fifa also makes Dominican cakes, which she prepares at home after working all day at the van, to sell to grocery stores, restaurants, and individual clients for special occasions such as weddings and birthdays. Her specialties include leftovers, such as chimichurri sandwiches, inspired by Argentinean street food and very common in poor urban neighborhoods in the Dominican Republic, and kipes, a filling Lebanese/Middle East-inspired finger food made of bulgur wheat, which she stuffs with salted pork. These foods do not figure prominently in Dominican national cuisine representations, but they are regional foods that are appreciated in Pueblo Nuevo, Santiago, from where Fifa migrated. They are racially marked as low-prestige both in the Dominican Republic and New York City, where they are referred to as "food of cocolos," or fast street foods for workers on the go and for hangovers.

In spite of all her struggles, Fifa articulates the importance of cooking for herself and her family whenever she can, preparing for them special dishes from her home region in Santiago. She also expresses an awareness of the forced gendered socialization of having to learn how to cook at an early age.

> I still cook these foods because this is the best, to eat what is your own culture . . . I cook because it reminds me of my land. . . . I have cooked for so long I don't even know when that happened . . . me and my sisters, we learned how to cook on our own, I learned alone to cook and peel plantains by watching, or if not I invent it . . . the kipes I learned from watching my sister there (DR), she also cooks for sale . . . Oh yes, the women in my family used to make a lot of food for the neighborhood, especially cooking for funerals (nine days of prayers), so many people eating.

Fifa's jobs seem to consume all of her time and energy, but they are also her source of income and this kind of work has played an important role in her personal history. In spite of her narratives about her father being a good provider, it seems that the women in her family had either the need or desire to earn their own contribution to the household, judging by how early they were cooking for sale. Fifa's foodmaps describe very localized movements in Washington Heights, where she works, lives and gets all her food supplies. Yet even in such a familiar landscape she does not seem to participate fully due to her seven days (approximately twelve hours a day) job schedule.

> My situation has not changed much here . . . I am in the same scarcity because I load my-self with my family problems in DR, I have to send a monthly support to them . . . NYC is a difficult place . . . I want to leave already, I am tired of working . . . but I also I like it here, there is electricity, and one feels one can go anywhere at any hour . . . I came following my partner, I was not that interested in the beginning, now he is gone, and I am still here.

Rafa's Version of Mangú, from the South Bronx, New York City

Rafa learned to cook mangú this way—adding raw onions and herb—from his grandmother in the Dominican Republic and he seems proud to prepare and serve it to his own family.

> Mangú is puree of plantain . . . even though [it] is common in DR, here [it] is a food and a symbol, even the Dominican youth born here assume the label of *platanito* . . . the drink "to die dreaming" and the sweet beans are almost as characteristic [ally] Dominican as mangú . . . here they are prepared throughout the year . . . I make my mangú with *recaito*, oregano, and raw pieces of onion, my grandma used to do it like that . . . the oregano is sent to us by [a] family from Villa Jaragua . . . In my maternal home they served mangú with eggs and onions, in times of scarcity with onions only, or just plain . . . my grandma used to say that one should test the mangú with the fingers . . . add a bit of cold water from the refrigerator to the plantains as you mash so it won't get hard . . . mangú has an individual property, each person makes it more, or less soft, with different texture . . . my daughter says I make an ecological mangú because I prepare it with herbs.

Rafa's choices of ingredients for his mangú preparation connect food paths along Dominican landmarks in the city, evidencing social networks that help sustain an economy based in the neighborhood through support of Dominican food businesses.

> We buy the plantains in a supermarket called "My Country" in Upper Manhattan, they have good prices, besides [it] is a way to support community business . . . we have to wash everything here before we cook, to compete with the roaches, which are the great owners of this city.

Rafa was the only male cook that collaborated in my fieldwork. Rafa is the main cook in his household. Rafa's gendered food socialization is uncommon in the Do-minican Republic, at least for older generations of males that grew up in the fifties, sixties, and seventies. His wife shares the expenses for the household; she works at a local Dominican women's organization agency that receives city funding. She is also a writer and an activist rarely at home because of her many commitments.

I am the main cook of the family because my wife has a day work schedule outside the home, and since I gained gender consciousness . . . In my house we were more males than females, my mother taught us how to cook so we did not have to depend on a woman to eat . . . My father cooked also on Saturdays, and we helped him . . . He used to say that to be a complete man one should know how to cook . . . When I came [to NYC] my sister in-law used to cook for me, but I was ashamed (I had not found work) so I started cooking . . . later when my wife came I kept cooking, she found a job and began taking English classes . . . My schedule is more flexible at the building . . . We cook one day and re-heat what was left the next day. She cooks only on weekends . . . the kids are learning how to cook, and we have also assigned days for kitchen and domestic chores cleaning.

Rafa got the chance to finish high school and take some classes at the Universidad Autónoma de Santo Domingo (UASD), and was very active in the student movement before he emigrated. He worked at low-paying temporary jobs as a construction worker, and as a summer substitute teacher in his neighborhood public schools. Presently in New York City he does not seem to experience the same kind of marginalization due to his job that some of the other cooks expressed.

I work helping the super, as a porter cleaning in a building in Chinatown, and I am a freelance photographer . . . but the small photo jobs are not sufficient . . . I don't mind working on whatever I find . . . one thing is to earn your plantain, but the solidarity work with the community is the important commitment.

Rafa's preparation of his version of mangú was sprinkled with very detailed explanations for each step and he shared some memories of his related food experiences in New York City, sometimes presenting explicit proposals for mangú's significance.

Mangú in NYC is for Dominicans a food and a symbol of resistance . . . platanito was an insult that we turned around into a tool for unity[,] especially among Dominican youth; it is used in demands for rights in schools, and in marches against police brutality . . . When someone in a march lifts a plátano, we said "Follow the person with the plantain!"

Among Rafa's Dominican progressive communities, this poetic/political expressive use of plantains has become common, but also as he points out, it is used among high school age Dominican youth in negotiating public space with heavy policing by city institutions.

In NYC Dominicans associate marches and parades with the plantain, they carry plantains with their little flags, and it is used by the tigers (young males) like a cell phone (indicating we are calling for reinforcements) to bother the police during the marches. Even the police themselves during the Dominican parades have attempted to use this symbol, but it doesn't work for them . . . the plantain is now a sign of resistance . . . It is a way to revalorize Dominicanness . . . There [in the DR] it is not so. It is only here that plantains have been used that way . . . When the police killed a Dominican boy, pushing him down from the 5th floor in Washington Heights, the people threw plantains at the police from every apartment, as a protest against what they did . . . at an upstate jail the Dominican inmates went on strike to demand they be served *sancocho* at least once a month, and students in the Washington Heights schools protested in order to have Dominican foods served at the school cafeteria.

Evident in this narrative of Rafa's relation to plantains is an explicitly instrumental and expressive poetics of food as a tool for political action (Bentley 1998). Such use of food seems to me also present in the other collaborators' relationship to Dominican foods, but in more implicit ways. Rafa seems to understand the poetic and political power of food in his family, community life, and in Hispaniola history.

I cook these foods, even though sometimes it is a sacrifice, because I have a moral commitment to the health of our children, and this way we also support the small merchants, our community . . . to cook is a way to give love, to strengthen our family's internal culture, and besides food is a form of resistance.

Rafa's family travel to the Dominican Republic to visit family in Villa Mella and Villa Jaragua in Santo Domingo (the nation's capital). He and his wife express a desire to return to the Dominican Republic someday, but like many other migrant families the new generations have other plans as parents age and their urgency fades. His choice of cooking Dominican foods is part of this wider conscious effort to maintain recognizable Dominican practices, histories, and meanings.

Here in the Bronx there are a lot of Dominicans, but the ambiance is not the same . . . here in this building you know who is Dominican, Dominicans try to find someone to offer coffee to, or a plate of food or a sweet . . . in this building you can smell the seasonings; garlic, pepper, oregano, for the way they season their foods . . . When Dominicans are cooking they open the door so the smell comes out, that way the neighbors know what they are cooking . . . Dominicanness is not lost because of distance, but with economic class . . . some here progress, earn a lot and they lose their Dominicanness (if they go to DR they stay at hotels and resorts) and they see our culture as vulgar . . . those people have assumed new symbols.

Rafa and his family are active participants in their local and translocal communities. They also have family meetings to discuss and solve problems, as Rafa said this is a "democratic home" within a larger "progressive" community. The family self-identify as Afro-Dominican and recognizes a shared history with Haiti. This racial awareness and their critique of the Dominican Republic's treatment of Haitians is a rarity among Dominicans. He seems very interested in food politics in the Dominican Republic, as well as identity politics among Dominicans in New York City.

Here we belong to a community, to a sub-class of poor, but we are part of a left-wing and revolutionary Christian sector that work with culture, we oppose the racism and sexism among Dominicans, and we oppose the mistreatment of Haitians in DR, we are also in solidarity with other peoples' struggles like Palestine, against police brutality and domestic violence . . . I think we are a larger sector than you think, and a very creative one . . . The other sub-classes are the ones that go dancing to clubs. To be able to go dancing and drinking three times a week you need money and time; you can't be working in a factory, so many sell drugs, but they are the small fish, the ones that spend all their earnings and then either go to jail or are sent to DR in a casket . . . There are only few, and they purchase mansions in DR (the government there knows but they don't do anything) . . . Another sub-class is the "culture of fear," [who] prefer not to get involved in [order] not to get in[to] trouble. They work, watch TV, consume, and some think they can become Americans.

In a way Rafa and his family's version of "Dominicaness" is part of a wider alternative culture of the Latin American "left" that spread more visibly during the 1960s, but the roots of which go back to the movements for independence in the region in the nineteenth century. All Dominican home-maps are sprinkled with these diverse influences of Latin American commonalities, yet not every Dominican becomes aware of the presence and significance of such shared routes.

Elsa's Version of Mangú, from the Bronx, 168th Street

Elsa migrated from Pueblo Nuevo in the province of Santiago in the Dominican Republic to New York City in 1988. I gather through her stories that she grew up in a loving home, with plenty of food, except for a few years where they experienced scarcity.

Yes, I missed the three meals a day, but at least we had one a day for sure . . . when things were bad my father and brother sold home-made ices and coconut sweets, and my mother used to sell *empanadas* in another neighborhood . . . I was left with a panic that we may be hungry again . . . now I make a lot of food, just in case someone may visit and they may be hungry; I come from that tradition in my house . . . here one does not go hungry, but when things are bad here it has a repercussion there [in DR] . . . here in New York it is obscene the abundance of food.

Elsa was one of the collaborators that prepared mangú almost daily; her experience of mangú seems to express a more instrumental use for her cooking, based on her concerns with feeding many and fast.

No, mangú is no work, I can make it even with my eyes closed, in less than half an hour . . . It is good to prepare it when you have a lot of hungry people to feed, [and] it stretches. It helps one to serve everyone enough and fast . . . that is what my mother used to do.

Elsa's version of mangú, follows the usual steps: peeling, boiling the green large plantains, mashing them until soft, then serving with a side dish. For her *compaña* (side dish), she uses fried cheese with lots of fried white onions. She talks as she peels, all the time looking at the plantains, as stories come and go, sometimes including evaluative narrative memories of her survival in New York City and the Dominican Republic. Mashing plantains seems to require both muscle strength and dedication. Elsa mashes the plantains with the bottom part of a vinegar bottle, and alternates this with a fork to fine tune the mush and make it softer. She, like all the other collaborators, emphasized three aspects of plantain preparation: how to make sure the mush stays soft the longest, the choice of traditional or new tools to mash plantains (in her case a bottle instead of half a plantain), and how to avoid *la mancha del plátano*, the stain-traces of peeling plantains.

> My mother used to say that when you mash mangú with the end of a bottle it feeds more people instead of using half-a-plantain . . . look carefully, I am trying to get the stains of plantain out, if you peel them under hot water it won't stain later, but I forgot for being in a rush.

Currently Elsa earns her "plátano" as a certified child attendant. During my visits I got to experience firsthand the atmosphere of her work-home site where she cooks and cares for seven children of various ages, colors, and nationalities, including Dominican, African (from Togo), African American, and mixed Latinos. She communicates the best she can with the parents and children who do not speak Spanish, and sometimes they have to call someone to translate. Elsa wakes up early, before 7:00 A.M.; children start arriving around 8:00 A.M. The shift is supposed to finish at around 6:00 P.M. Even though she has some strict guidelines from the childcare agency in terms of diet, she usually cooks Dominican food for the children since she has calculated that the food she makes contains all the recommended food groups.

> These kids eat as if their mothers don't feed them, they probably don't cook at home . . . I give them food, so now the women tell me they ask for Dominican foods at home . . . here one way or the other one suffers hunger if one does not manage to eat on time . . . here one can't be spoiled or finicky, there is no time.

She proposes that eating Dominican foods help them grow healthy and strong, and most importantly, they get the pleasure of tasting "real" food. The children have learned to love these foods; they seem to be also hungry for affection, which she dispenses by taking turns, depending on the loudness of their requests. Through her job Elsa's household has become a site of cultural transformation; the young ones she cares for have been weaned on these foods, as she has cared for them while they were learning to walk and attempted to communicate in a sort of Esperanto-like mix of languages with a hint of Dominican accent (for example: *Dame le toy que'tá en la blue cosa*).

The day Elsa prepared the version discussed here, the children she cares for were out of control. Everyone was screaming, asking for food, hugs, or toys. I tried to help but also wanted to record what Elsa was doing. She took breaks between each step to calm some of the children down, while I distracted others. She said the plantains might get too hard to mash if one does not attend to them right after taking them out of the hot water. In spite of the interruptions she came back, mashed the plantains almost to puree, and beamed with pride. We both were amazed it came out not only okay, but delicious! Elsa summarized at one point her definition of mangú:

> Mangú was born with us . . . We prepare it in different ways but arrive at the same objective, which is mashed plantains . . . in NYC once you ask, "Give me Mangú with the three strikes," (egg, salami, fried cheese) you are already Dominican . . . once you said mangú they know you are Dominican.

Here a translocal connotation of mangú is proposed by Elsa, as both a foundational Dominican meal ("was born with us") and as an index of Dominicanness in New York City ("you only need to say *mangú* and you are Dominican"). These two fragments illustrate the reversal of mangú, at least among working-class women immigrants. The ritual practice of cooking, serving, and eating also reveal the gendered, class, and racial socialization of the cooks in the Dominican Republic, as well as the family-community histories from the regions where they migrated and the decade they migrated into the United States (in this case most participants arrived to New York City in the 1980s during the Reagan administration and the rise of neoliberal policies).

Mangú is held in great esteem among the participants, yet not all of them could cook it regularly; rather they only cooked it for special occasions, or when their families requested it as an *antojo* (a craving). These differences may be due to the fact that when they lived in the Dominican Republic they did not cook it themselves since their mothers prepared it for them. These, and other versions of mangú that I have witnessed during fieldwork and throughout my life, exhibit remarkable consistency in the preparation, in the adding of cold water (from the last touch to the mashing) to keep it soft (which many of the cooks thought of as their own secret knowledge), even when they learned how to prepare it in different regions. As I hope it became clear in the above discussion, each cook nevertheless has a different approach with at least one ingredient or step that makes his or her own mangú as unique as the personal histories that shaped their relation to food and that generated specific narrative memories.

What Are These Private Versions of Mangú Saying about Dominican Identity?

These private routes of mangú hint at the public and collective routes of a Dominican state and national project that have failed to fulfill basic needs—such as food, housing, health, and education—which prompted many to migrate, as well as to a lack of inclusion in democratic participation and fulfillment of social equality. As food is not only a marker of identity but of social action and cultural work (Abarca 2006; Bentley 1998; Williams-Forson 2006), it reveals strategic political choices, about who to feed and how, and about self-worth and cultural memory (Marte 2008).

Rafa's version and narratives of mangú show a reversal in the meanings and political uses of mangú shaped by the immigrant experiences in New York City. Fifa's version exposes the impossibility for some of integration into either the Dominican Republic or U.S. society due to their race and origins as cocola,[5] and their illegal status in New York City. For Elsa, cooking mangú to "feed many" seems to be an act of memory to safeguard a familiar thread of continuity of activist struggles in the Dominican Republic that have not translated to her life in the United States. In a sense, these versions of mangú hint at the version of gendered Dominicanness that these cooks have according to each of their migrant seasonings; this is according to their survival aspirations in both sending and receiving societies, and to the concrete life conditions they have confronted in bringing about (or not) these life projects to fruition.

Peeling plantains and the whole preparation of mangú is not only a skill but an art form and a gendered cultural performance. Mangú does require time, energy, strength, and dedication, in spite of some of the cooks considering it to be a simple dish. It seems to me one needs mighty good reasons to mash a food that could be eaten other ways, especially considering what this investment means for overworked immigrants surviving with an income below the poverty level. As Luis—another fieldwork collaborator—pointed out, while he and I ate a delicious public version from a restaurant called *Mi Nagua* in Mangú City (Washington Heights): "Mangú is special breakfast, because you don't mash plantains for everybody . . . it reminds me of my grandma, she used to mash my plantains." Mashing or not, plantains are used among Dominicans to deliver in the Dominican Republic and in New York City a sure message concerning gendered tensions or conflicts occurring in household relations between women and men as well as parents and offspring; but they also express the power negotiations outside the household in reclamations of inclusion within the Dominican Republic and the United States.

Plantains and mangú have clear gendered connotations in their social, cultural, and historical production. In the Dominican Republic, men cultivate plantains in grand scale, while women do so in small subsistence plots. Plantain shape, texture, and the perception of this fruit as a strong food to restore labor energy is perceived as a masculine index (besides the more obvious anatomical connotations). Yet the conversion of such raw produce into culturally and physically digestible food happens almost exclusively through its preparation as a meal by women's domestic labor. The cooked mashed plantains as mangú is indexical of female labor and cultural knowledge. There is an interesting, if unclear, parallelism between the degree of *softness* of the mashed plantains and its consumption as a nutritive dish to enhance the *hard* bodies of workers. This is a reversal of Lévi-Strauss's dichotomy that locates women at the "nature" end of the nature-culture continuum, and men at the "culture" end (Lévi-Strauss 1968; Ortner 1974). Extending this reversal, a masculine "hard" nation (*patria viril, de pelo en pecho*, a masculine father land with hair on his chest), erect like a plantain, is yet produced culturally through the "soft" labor and alchemical transformations by women feeding their foods and very bodies to sustain homes and communities.

In terms of class and race, the majority of dark-skinned working classes, who are (in terms of national projects and public representations) almost "invisible," have been historically burdened with hard manual work, while a small elite group—claiming a Hispanic whiteness not always translated in their very skins—profits from their labor. Mangú has come to play a prominent role in race-place politics of Dominican immigrants, especially in Washington Heights. Within the self-making strategies of new generations of Dominican-Americans, a plantain is a political symbol not so much of nation but of a minority claiming their place in the U.S. nation. Yet in doing so, and due to the relations between Dominica Republic populations and the diaspora, these alternative forms of darker Dominicanness might be influential.

In seasoning their mangú, lives, and identities in New York City, Dominican immigrants keep reimagining spaces for their survival following their long history of cimarron struggles in the Antilles (Benitez-Rojo 1992). In regards to this shared Caribbean identity, the Cuban anthropologist Fernando Ortiz proposed the concept of "transculturation"—a dialectical process of biocultural mixing, most visible among meztizo and mulatto populations—as indispensable to understanding the history of Cuba and even of America more generally (Ortiz 1995: 102). At the core of this usage is a critical recognition of the diverse negotiations that occur in the process of migration, and of making place and reinventing identities when integrating into a new society. This new vision of cultural change and historical production opens a critical space for taking into account the creative agency of Caribbean subjects, and to the wider historical interactions needed to produced the Caribbean as a fertile ground for forms of transculturation never before witnessed.

Conclusion: *La Mancha Del Plátano*

Jewels brought from bondage.

—Paul Gilroy

I have suggested that critical readings of ordinary Caribbean staples could serve as a "tangential entry," as suggested by Michel-Rolph Trouillot, to expose the global power matrix that shaped the colonial histories of Haiti, the Dominican Republic, and other Caribbean countries, and the ways in which, under neoliberal agendas, they continue to do so today. But in exposing such tangled webs there are many perspectives to consider, and many experiences of resistance from diverse groups in those societies. Dominican national belonging has always been diverse; the nation is never experienced as a whole, but as an "imagined community" (Anderson 1991: 34) in need of constant re-negotiation, perilously glued by historically specific domestication strategies and ideologies through state agencies, schools, family, food, media and other social institutions.

Mangú is significant in Dominican history and foodways as it points to the very formation of the Dominican eco-material realities but also holds power because of what represents in terms of the cultural resilience and creative agency of millions that have survived on this humble fare. Focusing on how food helps create alliances and conflicts between and within social groups, we could more easily shed light on microhistories, ordinary forms of self-making among Dominican working-class immigrants—which are crucial for creating and sustaining new forms of community in a new society—as well as healthy workers who could continue paying with remittances for the plantains needed by those left in the Dominican Republic. Cooking and eating mangú on a regular basis points to strategies of self-making, indexing the historical imagination that allows individuals to continue finding meaning in familiar meals, heal the ruptures of migration, and go on one more day.

But what kinds of Caribbean subjects are made through mangú? *Comedores de mangu*, or *maguseros* (eaters of mangú), are indexed by and index *la mancha del plátano* (the stain of plantains) wherever they go. The cooking of plantains, which entails peeling the fruit and staining the hands, represents a racial mark of "Dominicanness" for outsiders, but such stains are also reappropriated by Dominicans as a sign of direct and indirect resistance to discrimination. This points to intersecting locations of class, race, color, and gender marginalization endured in the Dominican Republic, as well as to a conflictive neocolonial history that resulted in forms of forced economic migration to the United States. The history of displacement and marginalization created by colonial regimes, within which both mangú and Dominicans emerged, has resonance in current neoliberal projects confronted and experienced now by Dominican immigrants cooking their mangú in winter in given neighborhoods in New York City. Mangú, as an index of a doubly diasporic experience, evidence a neocolonial contested nation most evident since the mass Dominican migrations to the United States during the 1970s.

Mangú among Dominicans represents the global break that gave birth to Caribbean society and the transculturation (Ortiz 1995: 98) processes that gave rise to a mostly mulatto society. From the available national assimilation models in the Dominican Republic and the United States, meztisaje, Hispanophilia, or the dichotomies of the White-Anglo-assimilation model, mangú's proposal seems to be *mulataje* or *cimarronaje* (see Andújar 2006). This proposal points to how a meal meant to deny the humanity of slaves—since it was considered fit only for animals—was reinvented and "reseasoned" such that it came to be considered not only good cuisine but an emblem of the slaves' longing for freedom, and how it continues today to fulfill such a role for their descendants as labor immigrants cooking and struggling for a dignified survival in diverse geographies.

As Gilroy has proposed for African American music and dance, mangú is like a "jewel brought from bondage." Memories of struggles and scarcity get invested with the pleasures of cooking and eating. In this marvelous feat and feast of reappropriation and reversals, of "trans-coding" (Hall 1996: 48), mangú, through the "potency of the negative" (Gilroy 1993: 196), goes from a memory of slavery that some might wish to forget to become reinvested with survival capital, becoming an act of poetic justice from "those that were not meant to survive" (Alexander 2005: 46). Resistance does not need to be proven or openly claimed to be recognized as an exercise of agency, especially among marginalized communities (Scott 1990). Choosing to cook particular meals—considering the resources and efforts needed—furthers the self-making capital potential of foodways as practices and as sites of expressions of resistance, or at the very least as a basic claim to our humanity. I suggest that mangú represents a food site of multiple historical oppressions but also of multiple forms of creative self-making among marginalized Dominicans. The re-valorization of mangú in the diaspora, and its influence in how it is now perceived in the Dominican Republic, reverses a history of exploitation into cultural affirmation and resilience. As found by Psyche Williams-Forson (2006) in relation to African American women and chicken, certain foods are marked as both a site of oppression but also of agency. Mangú seems to be worthy of "commemorative vigilance" (Bardensten 1999: 152) through the deliberate choice of preparing it; this vigilance might not be motivated necessarily by long-buried collective memory of oppression but rather by more recent history of embodied marginalizations of class, gender and immigration status. Choosing to cook mangú, given the time, labor, and emotional investment require to prepare in New York City, becomes hence cultural and survival capital for future self-making practices and memorializations for new generations of Dominican-Americans in New York City. This cultural legacy could at times function as tiny liberated territories of resistance (Kelly and Lamelle 1984), gendered spaces of pleasure and self-affirmation that acts of cooking and remembering provide.

It is from place-specific relations and *through* everyday survival that individuals are truly seasoned into any nation—through particular communities, aspirations, and sentiments, but also disappointments and distances. Examining intersecting locations of gender, class, and race is helpful to place through food the diversity of embodied conflicts, alliances, and pleasures of consuming and being consumed in the Dominican experience. Which takes me back to my own locations. In closing, I confess that this chapter has become *un mangú machacao*, a lumpy, lightly mashed meal, so far from the purée which is required to pass as *culturally appropriate*, properly served food. I offer humbly this virtual mangú, as homage to the memory of my mother; in gratitude for the delicious *manguses* she prepared for us and for the struggles she endured to earn her plantains.

The Intersections of "Guyanese Food" and Constructions of Gender, Race, and Nationhood

Gillian Richards-Greaves

The term "Guyanese food" encompasses a large body of cuisines that are directly influenced by the diverse racial heritages of the Guyanese people, the conditions surrounding their migration, their subsequent interactions with racial and ethnic "Others" in the New World, and sociohistorical developments in Guyana, such as the African Guyanese's mass exodus from sugar plantations and the ban on certain food products instituted by President Burnham in the 1980s.[1] Through cooking and eating, Guyanese people affirm, contest, and display gendered, racial, and national boundaries and identities, as well as underlying social values inherent in food production and consumption. For Guyanese in Guyana, New York City, and in diasporic communities in other regions of the world, "Guyanese food" constitutes an instrument that is skillfully manipulated to "exclude, include, reject, accept and otherwise influence each other" (Bower 2007: 8). By cooking and eating specific cuisines in particular contexts, Guyanese solidify that bond that binds them to their group while also highlighting they ways they are different from other Guyanese. More than just a biological substance that provides calories or nourishment for the body, scholars argue, food signifies who we are or who we perceive ourselves to be (Belasco 2008: 15; see also Counihan 1999; Wilk 1999). Murcott (1983: 1) asserts, "what and how people eat or drink may usefully be understood in terms of a system whose coherence is afforded by the social and cultural organisation [*sic*] with which it is associated."

Guyana's population, economy, and culture principally emerged within the context of food, and specifically, sugar production, and continue to be influenced and often defined by agriculture, cooking, and eating (Mintz [1974]1989).[2] I was born in Guyana and lived there for the first seventeen years of my life. It was there that I learned to cook and to judge Guyanese food, as well as to understand the cultural nuances inherent in cooking and eating in the Guyanese community. After I migrated to New York City, I became immersed in large and vibrant Caribbean (West Indian) community, where foods, similar to those prepared in Guyana, feature one of the central themes of everyday discussions, disagreements, and policing of ethnic boundaries. I later conducted a multi-sited, comparative dissertation research project in New York City (2005–2008) and Guyana (2008–2010), where I examined religious influences on *kweh-kweh* ritual performances and identity negotiations amongst African Guyanese in the two communities.[3] Because food is such a crucial aspect of Guyanese culture, it was imperative that I further explore its role in the kweh-kweh ritual, as well as in the larger Guyanese community.[4]

In this chapter, I discuss the role of food in Guyanese constructions of identity by exploring the influences and intersections of race and gender embedded within communal processes of cooking and eating that are part and parcel of the creation of distinctively Guyanese cuisines.

To explore racialized connections inherent in processes of cooking and eating, I ground my analysis in a historical demography of the Guyanese foodscape, linking the geographic origin(s) of each cuisine with Guyanese perceptions of the specific food's racialized place in the Guyanese community. I then address the ways that "Guyanese food" indexes a particular racial identity by briefly discussing methods of preparation and contexts of consumption for two of the most prominent cuisines associated with each demographic group. In each case, I posit the origination of possible changes to cuisines due to commonly shared experiences of slavery, indentured servitude, cultural exchange, and key sociopolitical developments in Guyana. Gender serves as an alternative lens through which I briefly explore the implications of food culture upon Guyanese men and women. Finally, I discuss the ways that Guyanese in New York City deliberately modify Guyanese cuisines in order to accommodate newer living arrangements and to assert a shared yet fragile national identity. By articulating the ways Guyanese draw from a diverse body of foods to construct collective and differential identities, I effectively demonstrate how food, a seemingly ephemeral substance, proves to be a durable marker of identity over time in spite of significant environmental, cultural, and gastronomical changes in a deeply pluralized society. This chapter specifically reveals how the cuisines of individual Guyanese races are used in specific contexts to highlight those racial differences, while in other settings they are regarded as a collective entity ("Guyanese food"), which is manipulated to celebrate group or national identities.

Historical Demography of the Guyanese Foodscape

Guyana is located in the northeastern region of South America, with a population of less than one million.[5] Despite being surrounded by Dutch-speaking Suriname to its southeast, Spanish-speaking Venezuela to the northwest, Portuguese-speaking Brazil to its southwest and south, and French Guiana being in close proximity, Guyana is the only English-speaking sovereign state in South America. This is due to the fact that the country's final colonizer, England, was also responsible for its racial composition and current sociopolitical climate.

Guyanese frequently refer to Guyana as "The Land of Six Races" as a way of compositionally indexing the nation's racially diverse population. Europeans brought Africans to Guyana en masse during the Atlantic Slave Trade to work on sugar plantations; later, after emancipation, East Indian indentured laborers replaced the African labor force who abandoned the plantations for cities. While Chinese and Portuguese also migrated as indentured servants, they did not face the same degree of oppression as Africans or East Indians. The results of colonization and migration is an identifiably diverse society comprised of Africans, Amerindians (First Guyanese), East Indians (South Asians), Europeans (including Portuguese), Chinese, and people of mixed race commonly called "Douglas."[6]

While racial diversity lends to a particular richness to the Guyana cultural fabric, it is also often the source of bitter conflict and violence amongst Guyanese (Gibson 2003; Rabe 2005; Williams 1991). Since becoming an independent nation in 1966, Guyana has undergone numerous socioeconomic struggles that were, and still are, complicated by a pivotal and indivisible triad of powerful forces: politics, race, and religion. The extant East Indian majority generally self-identifies as Hindu and support the Peoples Progressive Party (PPP), while African Guyanese, who comprise the second largest demographic group, are overwhelmingly Christians and members of the Peoples National Congress (PNC).

Food has been, and continues to be, a powerful weapon in the ongoing negotiation for national political control among the racial groups that comprise Guyanese society. For instance, the GRDB (Guyana Rice Development Board) as well as GuySuCo (Guyana Sugar Cooperation), Guyana's main export companies, are both predominantly staffed by East Indians, who are principal rice and sugar farmers as well as members of the PPP. More recently, President Bharrat Jagdeo initiated the Grow More Food Campaign (GMFC) to persuade Guyanese to increase production of homegrown foods, in order to secure Guyana's place in the region and increase the financial capabilities of its farmers. Many African Guyanese lament the fact that GMFC, often regarded as "the Jagdeo Initiative," is nothing more than a racially motivated reproduction of the late President L.F.S. Burnham's genius.

Consider too that during the early 1980s the late President Burnham, in an attempt to compel the Guyanese populace to embrace homegrown foods and live more independently of imported goods, instituted an era of increased agricultural production, during which he gave the Guyanese people the ultimatum—"Produce or Perish." During this period, flour, peas, canned foods, and other imported goods were banned. This resulted in gross modifications and a significant decline in Guyanese cuisines that were prepared with these goods. While many Guyanese stood in long lines to purchase rationed amounts of machine-made bread from bakeries and shopping complexes, others resorted to purchasing flour on the black market. Often, flour purchased on the black market was contaminated and buyers also faced legal repercussions if they were caught purchasing or possessing these contraband items. Barrels shipped to Guyana by expatriate Guyanese in the United States and other countries were routinely searched, and food items, such as flour and peas, were confiscated.

Thus, Guyanese frantically devised ingenious ways to continue eating the cuisines they had grown accustomed to. Many ground rice to create rice flour, which they substituted for wheat flour; others resorted to preparing more meals with "ground provisions," such as plantains, eddoes, cassava, yams, and other tubers. To aid Guyanese with the transition from imported to homegrown foods, members of the Women Revolutionary Socialist Movement (WRSM), a female arm of the PNC, of which President Burnham was a political leader, held workshops around the country, where they provided the Guyanese populace with various recipes for rice flour and ground provisions. "Cassava lick-down," and "rice flour bakes" were two such cuisines that were added to Guyana's foodscape, while *rice pap* (rice porridge) and *chunkay* (stewed) provisions experienced increased popularity (Momsen 1993: 117).[7] Although this period began to wane by the early 1990s, today Guyanese continue to prepare much of those culinary inventions, though to a lesser extent than more so-called traditional meals.

Consequently, as the PNC and PPP political parties take turns in monopolizing political control, thus polarizing the country as well as impacting the ways in which the nation eats, the remaining racial groups are compelled either to take sides, to join an increasing number of racially diverse yet powerless political parties, or to forego participation in the political process altogether. This generalized segmentation of the Guyanese community is then further exacerbated by maintenance of cultural celebrations—such as African Emancipation Day and East Indian Arrival Day—which generally serve to highlight the achievements, cultures, and histories of specific racial groups. As I have discussed elsewhere (Richards-Greaves 2012), it is during such cultural celebrations that "Guyanese food" is segmented into its individual racial components, and each microcuisine then manipulated to highlight the uniqueness of each race while also reaffirming racial differences and boundaries.

Raw Foods: The Source of Guyanese Cuisines

The importance of food in the Guyanese community is not only observable at cultural events, but in every aspect of Guyanese daily experiences. It is important to note that most of the raw food items that Guyanese use to prepare meals are cultivated in Guyana by local and commercial farmers, who sell their produce to market vendors, or travel from house to house selling their produce in their local community. Itinerant vendors often referred to as "the banana man," "the fish truck," or "the vegetable van," provide a reliable source of inexpensive rations for wealthy Guyanese as well as those who purchase on credit. Many Guyanese also cultivate kitchen gardens, where they plant their favorite vegetables, which they later use to prepare meals or sell to friends and neighbors. While these raw food items are used in individual homes to prepare a diverse body of cuisines, "Guyanese food" is also cooked and sold in various restaurants, at snackettes (food shops), in tiny shops on street corners, and in schools throughout the country. Although Guyanese collectively refer to the plethora of cuisines they eat in these various outlets as "Guyanese food," they are inherently aware of the specific racial tag associated with each meal. For example, Guyanese may say that their curry chicken is more delicious than those of other Caribbean nations, or even more than India, but they also know that curry is "Indian food." Knowledge about the racialized heritages of "Guyanese food" is widely propagated by parents in individual homes, through various forms of media, such as *Stabroek News* (Sunday), and through public school textbooks, where teachers use Guyanese cuisines to educate students about Guyana's history and culture (Greene and Emanuel 2001).

Guyanese cuisines may be racially tagged but the raw food products used to prepare the cuisines are generally the same. Most of Guyanese cuisines are prepared with home grown produce, although imported foods, such as sardines, corn beef, spam, liquid and powdered milk, and other pre-cooked food items are also used. In this chapter, I have divided the raw food items Guyanese use to prepare meals into three overarching categories: starches, proteins, and vegetables. It is these three food groups that I later draw on in this chapter to discuss cuisines that are associated with each race. Despite the racial origin or association of "Guyanese foods," the manner in which they are prepared varies from one household to the next. While personal choice implicitly affects those variations, the financial capabilities of the cook, as well as sociopolitical developments extant within and without Guyana, are also crucial determining factors in the nature of Guyanese cuisines.

Starchy Staples

Most of Guyanese daily meals consist of some type of starchy staple coupled with some type of vegetable stew with or without meat. The starchy foods found in Guyanese cuisines can be classified into three basic groups: naturally occurring, processed, and refined. Natural starches include plantains, and "ground provisions" such as cassava "yuka," yams, eddoes, and other types of tubers, which are harvested locally in kitchen gardens as well as commercially.[8] Ground provisions are not only used to prepare "heavy" main course meals but are also included in stews and other cuisines to add body to the meal. Eddoes, for instance, are often added to curries to thicken them. Some ground provisions, such as green and turning (half-ripe) plantains and cassava are often sliced thinly, fried, and salted to make chips, which Guyanese of all ages snack on. Cassava and plantain are also made into a powder, or grated and boiled to make thick porridges, which are said to be particularly crucial to the development and virulence of babies and men respectively.

Lightly processed starches are those that must undergo some degree of factory processing before they can be consumed. Rice is a cereal and one such lightly processed starch that Guyanese consume on daily basis. Before it is ready for human consumption, it must be harvested, shelled from a paddy, and dried. Rice cultivation is a unique example of the ways that African Guyanese continued to produce foods they ate in West Africa. Although Indians are the principal rice farmers in Guyana today, rice was first cultivated in West Africa and later brought to Guyana and other parts of the New World during the Atlantic Slave Trade (Carney 2001; Littlefield 1981; McGowan, Rose, and David 2009). During slavery, Africans in Guyanese continued to cultivate rice, though on a much smaller scale than it is today. In addition to working long hours on plantations, many slaves cultivated kitchen gardens, as well as larger plots of land in backdams (Carney and Rosomoff 2009; Whit 2007: 48–49).[9] This enabled them to supplement their food source, and increase income.

Rice and stew meal, which seems to have an ambiguous racial origin, is one of the most common meals consumed during lunchtime in Guyana. African Guyanese who grew up in villages are said to be especially fond of rice, and in particular during breakfast meals where rice is not considered to be appropriate. Nearly all Guyanese eat rice but the manner in which they prepare it often signals specific racial identities. Very often, "plain," "bare," or "white" rice is eaten with stews made from greens or vegetables, such as cabbage, eddoes, callaloo (the leaves of the eddo or dasheen root), or eggplant. Sometimes Guyanese use rice to prepare "shine rice," a dish made with rice, coconut milk and other condiments (and sometimes vegetables). More widespread and central to Guyanese cuisines is cookup rice, which is made with rice, peas, or beans, coconut milk or cream, meats, and various spices (Richards-Greaves 2012). Other popular cuisines made with rice include fried rice, black and white pudding, and rice porridge often labeled "rice pap."

Like ground provisions and rice, Guyanese use wheat flour on a daily basis, and in abundance, to prepare most of their meals. Porridge, roti, and various types of bakes, such as pot bakes (like pot-roasted bread), ply-ply bakes or drop bakes (like fritters), and floats (like fried dumplings) are some of the breakfast foods that Guyanese prepare with wheat flour. Guyanese frequently regard *metegee*, *metem*, and various kinds of soups as inauthentic or incomplete unless they contain an ample supply of dumplings ("duff" or "tiger"), which are made with flour. *Mittai* (an Indian sweet) and chicken foot, and pastries, including salara (a bread made with grated coconut dyed red), cheese rolls and patties (made with ground beef or chicken) are also made with flour. Most of the flour Guyanese use is imported from Venezuela and other neighboring countries, as well as the United States. Many Guyanese women bake homemade bread, and many bake large quantities of bread on the weekends to last the entire week. Bread and roti are two of the main breakfast and starchy foods that are prepared with flour. Burgers are gaining increased popularity as the school lunch choice for many, although meals made with rice and so-called traditional Guyanese cuisines remain prevalent.

Pivotal Proteins

Fish and beans are two of Guyana's most prevalent sources of protein. Sport fishing is virtually nonexistent and locals also spend extensive periods of time fishing for personal and communal consumption. Large quantities of a variety of fish are procured by Guyanese or preserved in special ways and stored for later use. Shark and other kinds of saltwater big fish are especially crucial in the preparation of some Guyanese dishes. Even more inexpensive sources of protein than fish are beans and peas, items that originated in various regions of the world and were brought to the New World by slaves, indentured laborers, colonialists, and others (Albala 2007). Guyanese prepare soups, stews, and cookup rice using beans and peas, such as black-eyed peas, kidney beans, and pigeon peas.[10] While most of the peas that Guyanese consume are dried peas, often purchased from markets, "wet" (or fresh) peas, such as pigeon peas, are also integral parts of their diet.

Chickens, ducks, and turkeys are the main source of meat in Guyanese cuisine. During my research tenure in Guyana (2008–2010), I observed that "meat-birds," which are chickens reared primarily for meat and not for laying eggs, had become a very popular source of steady or seasonal income for many Guyanese. It is not un-common to see a chicken coop in the yards of even the most beautiful homes in the community. Individuals often travel to the capital city, where the cost of baby chicks is generally lower; there they purchase dozens of baby chicks, which they then rear for several weeks until they are full-grown enough to be killed and sold to the public. Even very young school aged children rear chickens, which they receive as gifts or purchase with monies obtained from adults family members and friends. While rear-ing chickens (and other animals) provide the primary income for some households, others engage in the practice to bring in extra money during the Christmas season and other holidays in order to defray the cost of such celebrations.

Guyanese also rear cows, pigs, sheep and other domesticated animals, which they use for meat and, in the case of cows and goats, milk. During Christmas, weddings, and other special events, animals are slaughtered en masse to provide meat. Wild animals constitute a source of meat that most Guyanese tap into at least once during the course of their lifetime. "Wild meat," or "bush meat," refers to the meat of animals that are gener-ally undomesticated. Deer, labba (*agouti paca*, a member of the rodent family), monkey, rabbit, alligator, and other lizards generally fall into this category. Due to religious stipu-lations, some Guyanese avoid many or all of the meats discussed here. Thus, observing Muslims do not eat pork, wild animals, and other meats that are not considered *halal* (permissible) according to Islamic law; Seventh Day Adventists avoid pork, which, in their sect of Christianity is regarded as unclean; and Hindus generally do not consume beef, due to religious proscriptions. In some instances meat consumption is further pro-hibited by special holidays and holy days, such as the Christians' Easter, the Hindus' Diwali ("festival of lights"), and during the fasting days of the Muslims' Ramadan.

Vegetal Variations

Vegetables are a crucial and relatively inexpensive component of Guyanese daily meals. A brief examination of the stalls in the open markets or "market squares" in Guyana would seem to attest to the importance of vegetables in Guyanese diet, as countless venders line the streets and alleyways surrounding the markets with displays of large quantities and varieties of vegetables and other rations. As potential customers pass by, vendors would call out their produce and respective prices, often in a ritualized and musical manner akin to street calls. Squashes, including pumpkin and zucchini; roots or tubers, such as eddoes, dasheen and cassava, which Guyanese refer to as provisions; green leafy vegetables, such as eddo-leaf callaloo (leaves of the eddo root), dasheen leaves, bok choy, cabbage, and spinach; eggplant or *boulanger* (pronounced bu-lan-jay); okra, a green edible seed pod; bitter melon, which Guyanese label *corilla* (pronounced co-rye-luh); and legumes, such as the bora bean (long, whip-like string bean), and same (a flat string bean), are some of the vegetables that Guyanese consume on regular basis.[11] Many of these vegetables are prepared with fish, shrimps, or various kinds of meats to make the stews that Guyanese regularly consume with rice during lunchtime. Vegetable stews are also eaten with ground provisions and roti, although these pairings occur more frequently during breakfast and dinnertime. Guyanese also prepare soups, metemgee, cookup rice, and other meals with vegetables, which add color and texture to the dish, as well as important nutrients to their diet. Like Guyana's diverse population, the plethora of vegetables that Guyanese consume can be traced to various regions of Africa, Asia, Europe, and South America.

Microcuisines of Guyana's Racialized Foodscape

Just as vegetables, ground provisions, and other raw foods that Guyanese use to cook with can be traced to the original homelands of the Guyanese people, so can many of the cuisines they collectively label "Guyanese food." While many of these cuisines have changed over time as a result of culture contact and other factors, key characteristics and contexts of consumption can be used to link them to their initial creators or at least to the racial groups predominantly responsible for their presence on Guyana's foodscape. Also of importance is the fact that gendered divisions in cooking persist across racial lines, with women being principally responsible for preparing meals. Below, I discuss two of the most prominent cuisines associated with each racial group in Guyana and a brief description of processes of preparation and contexts of consumption. In doing so, I demonstrate the diversity inherent in the term "Guyanese food" and the ways that Guyanese also draw on the cuisines to create group solidarity.

African: Fufu and Metegee/Metemgee/Metem

Guyanese use ground provisions to prepare a plethora of meals, but *fufu* and metemgee are two cuisines that are principally regarded as African in origin.[12] Fufu is a starchy meal that is made from cassavas, plantains, yams, or other types of tubers (ground provisions). The tuber is boiled until cooked, and then pounded in mortar, using a pestle, until it achieves a rubbery dough-like constitution, much like Play-Doh.[13] Fufu is one of Guyana's cuisines that can be directly traced to its original homeland, West Africa, where it is prepared with cocoyam, cornmeal, or starchy foods, and features in a principal main course meal (Hall 2007: 19). Although slavery proved disruptive to many African cultural practices, African Guyanese and the populations of the "Black Atlantic" in general, were able to maintain much of their food values based on memory and improvisation. More importantly, slave masters as well as slaves brought seeds, roots, foods, and the necessary agriculture skills crucial to harvesting them in the New World, making it possible for the slaves to continue cooking and eating the way they did in West Africa (Hall 2007: 21). Thus, for instance, African Guyanese may have been deprived of cocoyam with which they historically prepared fufu, but they continued to prepare fufu using green plantains, cassava, and other starchy tubers they planted in Guyana. African Guyanese often openly and proudly recite such sayings as "plantain and duff mek Blackman tuff," to reference the commonly held notion that African Guyanese, and black people in general, possess high degrees of physical strength, due to diets rich in ground provisions and other earthy or energy-giving foods. Nowadays, many Africans make fufu with powdered versions of cocoyam and other tubers, which are sold in stores all over the world.

Like West Africans, who eat fufu with stews, such as igusi soup, okra soup, and pepper soup, Guyanese generally eat their fufu with various types of stews, such as chicken stew and vegetable stews. As is the practice in West Africa, Guyanese use their bare hands to eat fufu, which they pinch and roll into little balls and use to scoop up the stews. Although there is no stipulation in the Guyanese society as to which hand can be used to eat fufu, or any other hand-eaten meal, it is generally a rule in many African societies that the left hand must never be used to eat such meals.[14] Some scholars argue that fufu and similar hand-eaten cuisines are the result of the lack of eating utensils during slavery and in African cultures during the time in which they develop. Some scholars suggest that African diasporic cuisines that are eaten with the bare hands, such as fufu, as well as "one-pot" meals, where all of the ingredients are cooked up together, were directly influenced by the paucity of cooking and eating utensils when the cuisines were developed in Africa and during the period of slavery (Whit 2007: 53). So, while some aspects of African traditions were eradicated during slavery, some persist unchanged, while others were modified.

Metemgee, also referred to as "metegee" or "metem," is one of those "one-pot" meals that Guyanese also regard as African in origin. Metemgee is made with ground provisions, which are boiled in coconut milk, along with various types of meats, vegetables, spices, and *duff* (large fluffy dumplings made of wheat flour). Though cooked with various types of meats, it is customary for fried fish or salt fish to be included as a side dish that is enjoyed with the metemgee. The quantities and types of meats and other ingredients included in metemgee is generally influenced by the financial capabilities or preference of the cook and audience. Frequently referred to as "dry food," as it is boiled down until very little coconut milk is left, metemgee is especially coveted by men, who regard it as a unique source of physical strength and virility. Although metemgee can be eaten at any period throughout the day, Guyanese often enjoy this heavy meal during lunchtime. For many Guyanese, and particularly those in countryside, metemgee is that special meal that is reserved for Sundays and other special days. When flour was banned and increasing number of Guyanese reported eating metemgee and other foods made with provisions, for breakfast and dinner. Today, Guyanese continue to regard metemgee as a robust and fulfilling meal but due to financial opulence, health concerns, and a range of other factors, many modify the ingredients included in the meal.

Amerindians: Cassava Bread and Pepperpot

Like African Guyanese, Amerindians also use ground provisions to prepare special meals, such as cassava bread and pepperpot. Cassava bread is made from bitter cassava, as opposed to the "sweet" cassava, which is used in metem and everyday meals. Bitter cassava is said to have a high cyanide concentration, and must be processed extensively before it can be useful for human consumption. When processing bitter cassava, adults would sternly warn children and novices to refrain from eating it, since it can "cause your belly to swell." To make cassava bread, Amerindians would grate the cassava and extract the poisonous juices using their native *matapee*, a long woven strainer, made from reeds. The cassava husks would then be molded into flat, round cakes, which are then sun baked on flat, aluminum surfaces until they are solid and crisp. The bitter cassava juice extract is not discarded but further processed to create *cassereep*, a thick, brown sauce. Cassereep is a key component in pepperpot, an Amerindian dish, and Guyana's national dish. Cassereep gives pepperpot its rich brown color and unique taste and is often used to color and flavor other Guyanese stews.

Pepperpot is a thick, dark-brown, stew-like dish that is made with various types of meats, and boiled in cassava cassereep with various spices. Guyanese often assert that "pepperpot don't spoil," alluding to the fact that this dish is generally not refrigerated, but kept on the pot on the stove or fireside and brought to a boil each day (Whit 2007: 49). Many Guyanese also assert that the older the pepperpot, the tastier it is, as emphasized by the phrase, "some like it in the pot nine days old," from a famous Guyanese poem, "Pepperpot." Although Guyanese eat pepperpot with rice or bread, convention holds that pepperpot and cassava bread are the perfect or natural pair, since that is the way that Amerindians ate and continue to eat pepperpot. Many Guyanese Christians consider pepperpot (with bread) the ultimate Christmas breakfast. Even non-Christians ritualistically consume pepperpot and dense homemade bread on Christmas morning, and throughout the Christmas season.

Chinese: Chow Mein and Fried Rice

Guyanese from all racial groups prepare "Guyanese Chinese" in their individual homes, but it is the Chinese restaurants throughout Guyana that serve as the principal sources of Chinese cuisines. These restaurants are frequently two-story buildings with a restaurant on the lower flat and the owner's residence above. Chinese restaurants are key watering holes for Guyanese and "foreigners" alike, who desire a break from the daily grind of home-cooking or to enjoy Guyanese Chinese.[15] Ranging from two-story buildings, such as Red Bud in Linden, to grand edifices like New Thriving in the capital city of Georgetown, Chinese restaurants provide their patrons with their interpretations of Chinese food. On the menus there is a wide variety of Chinese cuisines, such as wonton soups, sweet and sour chicken, but fried rice seems to be the choice of most Guyanese who eat at these establishments.

Fried rice is made with parboiled rice, which is then colored, seasoned, and stir-fried, and is often served with fried chicken, beef, pork, or customized to suit the patron's desires. For some, Chinese fried rice is a meal to be eaten only on weekends or other special occasions, while others eat it more indiscriminately. Many expatriate Guyanese often lament the loss of Guyanese Chinese and would rectify the situation once they return home. In addition to consuming large amounts of the dish, they also purchase large quantities of fried rice, freeze it, and pack it with their luggage so they can enjoy it once they return overseas. It is important to note, however, that many Guyanese also cook fried rice in their homes, and do not depend entirely on Chinese restaurants.

Chow mein—the name of the yellow noodle and the meal it is used to prepare—features another common Chinese dish that Guyanese cook on a regular basis and regard as crucial to the fabric of "Guyanese food." Chow mein is generally prepared by boiling the chow mein noodle, and after it is strained, stewing it up with meats, vegetables, and other seasonings to achieve a unique taste. The chow mein noodle is manufactured and distributed worldwide by companies in Guyana, as well as companies abroad, such as Robert Products in Toronto, Canada. However, many Guyanese who live in rural areas, or where Guyanese chow mein is not sold, are compelled to modify the frequency or quality of their chow men to accommodate such lack.

Guyanese in Atlanta, Georgia, and New York City, for example, are able to purchase "Guyanese chow mein" from "Chinese stores," which are open markets that sell a large variety of fruits, vegetables, and ethnic foods. Whenever I travel to New York City, for instance, I usually stock up on an ample supply of chow mein and other "Guyanese foods," which I cannot easily obtain in the Midwest. Like me, countless Guyanese, who reside in various parts of the United States, converge on New York City and other metropolitan areas over the Labor Day weekend and other holidays to celebrate cultural events and also to replenish their ethnic food supplies. Although many Guyanese have various other types of noodles at their disposals, including non-Guyanese chow mein, many of them extend themselves to obtain Guyanese chow mein, as a means of achieving and maintaining some semblance of authenticity, taste, and identity. When they are unable to physically travel to purchase desired food items, many Guyanese enlist the help of relatives and friends, who mail the food items to them. Although various kinds of Chinese noodles are sold all over the world, Guyanese go to great lengths to obtain "real" chow mein noodles to cook their "authentic" Guyanese chow mein.

European: Black Pudding and Souse

European cuisines, such as black pudding and souse, do not seem to have the same degree of direct and overt racial connections as most Guyanese cuisines. This is possible due to the relatively small European population (less than one percent) in Guyana or to prevailing Guyanese attitudes of European culinary deficiency. Nevertheless, both black pudding and souse are Guyanese delicacies that are often consumed in large quantities, although they are not main course meals.

Black pudding is a sausage-like Guyanese dish that does not always experience widespread appeal. Black pudding is made with pig intestines, which are carefully cleaned, and then stuffed with a concoction made of rice, cow's blood, and various seasonings. After the ends of the newly stuffed intestines are tied off to prevent the rice from escaping, they are then boiled for several minutes until the blood is completely cooked, and the contents are a solid cake-like substance. This cooking takes place in a relatively quiet environment as noise is said to cause the trotters to rupture. As delicious as black pudding is to some Guyanese, it is repulsive to others. Some Christians, Rastafarians, and others, constrained by religious beliefs, frown upon the idea of "eating blood," animal intestines, or pigs, which they regard it as "unclean" or unholy, based on Old Testament scriptures (Lev. 7:27, 17:10, 19:26). While some shun black pudding altogether, others settle for white pudding, which is made with the same ingredients as black pudding, excluding animal blood. Still, there are Christians and other Guyanese who may verbally and openly disparage black pudding, but also consume the dish in more private settings, away from the watchful eyes of their colleagues or brethren.

Like black pudding, souse is enjoyed by many Guyanese but also often occupies a controversial place amongst some Guyanese. Made with parts of cows and pigs, souse is sometimes derided as "po-man food" by Guyanese of the upper crust, or unclean, by those with religious beliefs that are oppose the consumption of pigs.[16] This pickled meat dish is prepared by boiling ears, face, feet, tongues, and other body parts of cows and pigs with vinegar and other seasonings, until it becomes a sort of spicy aspic. Souse is commonly cooked during the Christmas holidays and Old Year's Night (New Year's Eve), when many people butcher large numbers of domestic animals to provide meat for the season's festivities. While many enjoy the sticky constitution of souse made from beef and pork, an increasingly common and less expensive trend is souse made with chicken feet.

East Indian: Curry and Roti

East Indians suffered greatly under indentured servitude, and sometimes, in ways akin to slavery; however, the degree of destruction to cultural and religious practices was not the same for East Indians as it was for Africans (Gibson 2003; Moore 2009; Williams 1991). Although, in a sense, the degree of the marginalization that Indians experience was a deliberate choice on their part. By refusing to convert to Christianity, they were often compelled to forego academic and employment opportunities, which were generally connected to the Church of England. Many who converted to Christianity did not entirely discard their "native" religions, but instead fabricated a syncretic existence that was most beneficial to them (Gibson 2003; da Costa 1994: 77). Because their families and communities were not deliberately and systematically destroyed by colonialism, as was the case with African Guyanese, East Indians were able to sustain a greater degree of their cultural practices and values. Thus, much of East Indian cuisines in Guyana can often be mapped directly to those in India and other parts of Asia. It is important to note, however, that sustained cultural interactions with other races in Guyana (and the Caribbean) has resulted in unique interpretations of those cuisines. Curries, roti, dahl (lentil soup), and other Indian cuisines in Guyana and the larger Caribbean often have different spices and flavors than those from Asia. This difference is also compounded amongst different races in Guyana, and from one home to the next. It is not uncommon to hear Guyanese talking about *their* curry, *their* cookup, *their* dahl, compared with those of other races.

Roti (often pronounced "rooti") is a popular food made with flour and enjoyed by Guyanese of all walks of life. Roti is a type of flat bread that is made with flour, baking powder, oil and water, and baked on a roti pan called a *tava*. Some roti are made soft and cloth-like, while others like *sada roti* are tougher, like bakes. Another type of roti, *alu* (potato) roti is stuffed and cooked made with potatoes and eddoes that were boiled, mashed and seasoned, while *dahl pori* is made with ground and seasoned split peas. Roti is eaten with any type of stew, but Guyanese regard curry (stew) as the natural partner of this food. From a tender age, women, and particularly East Indian women, are taught to "clap roti," with the ultimate goal of achieving the right constitution, shape, and taste. Women frequently tell stories of being teased relentlessly by family members and friends, or conked (generally pronounced, "counced") on the head by their mothers, who used various kitchen utensils to express their disapproval of their daughters' roti, which was tough like bake or resembled the "Guyana map" (that is, not round but, rather, ill-shapen).

Curry is a very popular cuisine amongst Guyanese of all ages and races. Guyanese are known to "curry" (used as a verb) just about any food item, such as fish (and seafood), meats, including those wild animals, and vegetables. Curries originated in Southern Asia and were transported to Guyana with East Indians who migrated as indentured laborers in the early nineteenth century. Although there are various types of curries of different colors and tastes, Guyanese generally regard the yellow powder, which principally contains turmeric, coriander, and cumin, among other spices. Yellow Guyana curry is produced in Guyana by companies such as Hindi Madras and also imported from India and other regions of the world. The flavor of curry powder is generally consistent, although some include varying amounts of pepper and other condiments. While curry can be consumed with rice or other starchy staples, Guyanese regard roti as its natural culinary partner.

Guyanese: Cookup Rice

Unlike most Guyanese foods, which have definitive and traceable racial origins, cookup rice often occupies an ambiguous place within Guyana's foodscape (Richards-Greaves 2012). Cookup rice is prepared by boiling rice, peas, meats, vegetables, and spices with coconut milk. Cookup is an everyday meal, as well as a dish consumed on special occasions, such as Old Year's Night (New Year's Eve), kweh-kweh rituals, and other African-centered cultural events. African Guyanese often argue that this one-pot dish, prepared with coconut milk, and frequently with black-eyed peas, is an African construct that was that later modified by slaves in the New World (Albala 2007: 117–26; Henderson 2007; Witt 1999). Other Guyanese regard poverty, not race, as *the* determining factor in cookup's origin. Thus, cookup creates a unique platform for Guyanese to celebrate some semblance of unity and to focus on more pervasive underlying Guyanese values.

"Bring in the Bacon," "Wife Material," and "Frock Tail"

Despite the racial labels attached to Guyanese cuisines, issues of gender consistently underscore each act of food production and consumption in the Guyanese community. Through cooking and eating, Guyanese create a unique space within which Guyanese affirm, construct, and contest the nature of social relationships, and particularly gendered values (Counihan 1999: 13). In a society that is generally divided along male-female gendered lines, who cooks, who eats, who evaluates food, and who is evaluated are all factors influenced by existing gendered expectations in the Guyanese society. Men and women who do not adhere to gendered culinary expectations, or who deviate too far from the norms, are regarded as social misfits who threaten the authenticity, viability, and security of the opposite sex, as well as the community at large. Very often the value of a man or woman is intricately linked to the process of cooking and eating. From the time children are very young, mothers begin teaching them the appropriate steps of the food dance, which is crucial to proper adult socialization in the Guyanese community.

Young women are taught how to prepare simple and complex Guyanese cuisines by spending extended periods of time in the kitchen with mothers, older siblings, and other community members. To be able to cook, and to do so well, is one of the truest markers of a well-adjusted Guyanese woman. Guyanese, and particularly men, often refer to young women who are excellent cooks as "wife material," as a way of highlighting the fact that they have demonstrated their ability to "feed" a husband and children. In addition to establishing or elevating self-worth amongst her peers and in the larger community, a woman who is "marriage material" has also proven her own mother's good work and value as a woman. These expectations of women transcend racial boundaries and can therefore be regarded as "Guyanese values."

Mothers are generally the primary caretakers of children, who are tasked with instilling proper "home-training" in them, and thus, are often the principal recipients of praise for well-adjusted children, or ridicule for social misfits (DeVault 1997: 184). For this reason, women who marry before mastering the art of cooking are said to bring shame to their mothers (Richards-Greaves 2012). In times past, this shame was compounded and exposed when husbands physically abused their wives or sent them back to their natal homes. The importance of gendered food values are often reaffirmed in folk songs, such as "Pack she back to she ma" and "Send she back to she muddah" (send her back to her mother), which cite domestic offenses for which a woman can be "put away." Children learn to sing these songs from the time they are very young, and understand the importance of appropriate gender-specific behaviors associated with food preparation and consumption in the Guyanese community. Even in today's society, where women frequently work outside of the home, they are still expected to "guard" their homes by cooking and taking care of other domestic responsibilities. It is important to note, however, that an increasing number of women are utilizing higher levels of academic training and financial affluence to consistently negotiate their stance in romantic relationships and their community. The constant negotiation of power and gendered culinary space facilitates variations in cuisines, and threatens what many Guyanese regard as traditional Guyanese food. Although "Guyanese food" is always in a state of flux, Guyanese are constantly policing the boundaries of authenticity of their cuisines, and women are principally tasked with this responsibility.

While women are expected to be good cooks, among other things, men are required to "bring in the bacon." Although an increasing number of women are ensuring that their sons are self-sufficient in the kitchen, the expectations are not the same for men as they are for women. In fact, boys who spend too much time in the kitchen under their mother's "frock tail" are generally frowned upon. This is particularly so when said boys forego other, so-called manly activities, such as sporting events, to engage in kitchen matters. Although many young men living with mothers who are single parents often assist with cooking and other household chores, the community also expects them to demonstrate their manliness in other areas of their lives or risk being labeled "anti-man," or other pejorative terms. Even when men are excellent cooks or own restaurants and other establishments that sell food, women are usually the ones responsible for the cooking or, at least, presented as the face of the kitchen.

The food a man eats is equally important as the person who prepared it and the manner in which it was prepared. His status in his home, his actions, and even his self-worth as a man are evaluated based on the quantity and quality of food he consumes (Kahn 1986). As the head of his home a man is expected, and in some instances, entitled to "eat good," that is, to consume foods that are both delicious and nourishing. Some foods are said to strengthen a man's back (make him virile) and are thus coveted by most men. Barley, sago, and various porridges; "ground food" (foods made with provisions), such as metegee; broth (often pronounced "broff"), made with large fish head; thick soups, such as cow heel soup, with split peas, various types of meats, and duff (large dumplings sometimes called "tiger"); custards; and sea moss represent a sample of the "good food" Guyanese men, and Guyanese in general, crave. A man who is married to or cohabits with a woman who has a reputation as an excellent cook is often praised or tantalized for his perceived physical strength, sexual prowess, and elevated status in his home and community.

Many Guyanese regard "good food" as an anchor that keeps many a philandering man in his home. It is not surprising then that bad cooking is one of the frequently cited reasons for a man cheating on or leaving his wife. Poor cooking or the lack of food is also one of the excuses men provide for emotional, physical, and verbal abuse against women (Ellis 1983). Sometimes the simple act of eating at another woman's house, and particularly at the expense of his wife's cooking, is regarded as a direct attack or insult against his wife. Similarly, women often accuse each other of stealing each other's men using food.

While men exact revenge against women for poor or inadequate food by infidelity, neglect, and abuse, women also use food to exact revenge. While some women punish men by refusing to cook or to serve food to their mate, or by cooking unpalatable food, others use *obeah* (witchcraft) to "catch, to keep or to harm their mates—or other people in their lives" (Counihan 2004: 1). Very often, men who are not openly unfaithful to their mates are said to get "do" (bewitched). It is not uncommon to hear people say, "She mussee do he" (she must have bewitched him) to refer to a woman who is perceived to exert undue influence over her mate (Behar 1989: 180).

Diet, Migration, and the Reconstruction of Segmented Nationalism

When Guyanese migrate to other regions of the world, such as New York City, they draw on food-related experiences in Guyana to construct and police the boundaries that demarcate what is and what isn't "Guyanese," and to forge newer ethnic and national identities (Royce 1982: 40). In New York City, for instance, Guyanese comprise a large community of more than 130,000 nationals, where African Guyanese primarily reside in Brooklyn, and East Indian Guyanese in Queens (New York City Department of City Planning 2000). The Guyanese population is, however, only a fraction of a much larger and vibrant Caribbean (West Indian) community, whose members consistently and strategically demonstrate national identities (Jackson and Cothran 2003). During the West American Day Carnival (Labor Day Parade) and other smaller scale cultural events, Caribbean groups display their cultural differences by showing their "national colors," embodied in such symbols as flags, music, and most notably, cuisines.

While pan-Caribbean events such as these allow for exhibitions of diverse aspects of "Caribbean culture," it is during daily interactions with each other that Caribbeans regulate the boundaries that distinguish them from cultural and national "Others" (Brown and Mussell 1984: 5). For Guyanese in New York City, one of the most visible symbols of their national identity turn out to be the very "Guyanese food" they use back home to mark their heritage and to distinguish themselves from other Guyanese (Fischler 1988: 275). Although other Caribbean communities, such as Barbados, Jamaica, and Trinidad, cook similar cuisines, such as cookup rice (a rice and peas dish), Guyanese often claim that, due to the combination of spices they use, their culinary skills, and other factors, their cuisines are different or "sweeter" (more delicious) than those of their Caribbean neighbors (Richards-Greaves 2012).

To ensure that the cuisines maintain a certain degree of so-called authenticity, Guyanese often use homegrown and homemade Guyanese seasonings, which they include with their luggage or have family members ship to them from Guyana. Ground peppers, *achar* (an Indian pickle), cassareep, dried fine-leaf thyme, and *marri'd man poke* (basil) are some of the condiments "from home," which Guyanese use in their New York cuisines (Ray 2004: 1). Although Guyanese in New York City can rarely trace the origin of the raw foods they purchase, as they did in Guyana, they ultimately judge the authenticity of the cuisines they consume based on taste (Wilk 2006b). When they consume "Guyanese food" they judge each cuisine based on their past experiences with it. When the foods meet or exceed the standard of deliciousness of "real Guyanese food," Guyanese would, for example, exclaim that it "tastes more-ish" or "sweet bad" (extremely delicious). At a kweh-kweh I attended in New York City, one participant asked the server to return with the *poluri* platter because "the polouri talkin' to me" (were extremely delicious). On the contrary, Guyanese express their displeasure for foods they regard as different or inauthentic by adding labels to them, such as "cookup's friend, cookup's cousin or cookup's in-law" (Richards-Greaves 2012). This is not to suggest that prepackaged foods, such as canned coconut milk, are used indiscriminately, but that taste and context of consumption determines authenticity.

While New York Guyanese may differ on what constitutes authentic Guyanese food, there seems to be a general consensus that "Guyanese food," with all of its racial parts unites them when they are physically displaced from their homeland

(Sutton 2001: 9). Food allows them to relive particular experiences, to be symbolically transplanted to specific areas "back home," and to relive the memories that were systematically constructed through acts of cooking and eating (Douglas 1971: 67; Kalcik 1984: 48; Mintz 2003; Sutton 2009). While they continue to grapple with racial tensions and political divisions amongst themselves, through food they maintain the boundaries, a consumptive act that also distinguishes them from other races and ethnicities in New York City.

Conclusion

Amongst Guyanese, food constitutes a ready and visible marker of Guyaneseness. Through food, Guyanese mark their place in time by referencing, recreating, and repeating culinary interpretations they perceive to be inherently their own (Mintz 2003). Food, therefore, does not only signify a people but also their unique origins in their original homelands, their journey across the Atlantic, and the complex of their experiences in the New World. Not surprisingly, in a country that emerged as a result of colonialism, slavery, and indentured servitude, food features as a sociohistorical marker of the overarching experiences of each race, while also featuring a symbolic boundary that marks the "Other."

Food is a particularly unique symbol of the racial identities, since most of the cuisines housed under the umbrella label of "Guyanese food" can be directly traced to a specific geographic region of the world and racial group in Guyana. While food does serve to highlight specific races, a specific dish is not always a rigid representation of a singular racial group because of "blending," "mixing," and "borrowing" over time; similarities abound across cultures.

While underlying gendered values associated with cooking and eating are constantly policed by men, women, and the larger community, changes to food preparation and consumption continue to take place in Guyanese society. As more women work outside of the home and as American culture and discourse regarding marriage—specifically domestic abuse and women's rights—gain momentum, men and women are relinquishing their holds on traditional spaces in the home, and specifically, in the kitchen. These changes are particularly evident when Guyanese migrate to places like the United States, and are faced with insurmountable ethnic difference and gender education.

Whether they reside in Guyana or the United States, "Guyanese food" is regarded as a distinctive culinary entity that continues to be a crucial symbol of collective national Guyanese identity (Ray 2004: 126). The body of microcuisines, each with its perceived unique blend of herbs and spices, serve to representatively unite Guyanese people as one nation. As they consume "Guyanese food," they are keenly aware of the symbolic strife and history they jointly share. Yet, it is also "Guyanese food"

Figure 5.1   Traditional pepperpot served with bread. Photo by Gillian Richards-Greaves.

upon which they draw to celebrate and consume the colorfulness, the deliciousness, and the difference that is characteristic of Guyana as a nation, albeit a fragmented one (Adair 1986: 50).

Pepperpot Recipe

(Guyana's national dish)

Ingredients:

1 lb. beef
1 lb. pork, trotters/tripe (or cow's heels)
1/2 lb. pigtail (optional)
1 cup cassava cassareep (or to taste)
1 red hot pepper
1 cinnamon stick
1 ounce brown sugar (or to taste)
1 pinch of salt (or to taste)

2 stalks basil (marri'd man poke)
1 bunch fine-leaf thyme
1 large onion (finely chopped)
3 garlic (finely chopped)
4 cloves

Directions:

1. Soak pigtails in hot water; scrape to remove hair and grime.
2. Boil pigtail until partially tender.
3. Boil or pressure cow heel and/or tripe in separate saucepans.
4. Skim sediment and discard.
5. When all meats are partially tender, combine them into one pot.
6. Add cassareep and other ingredients to pot with meats.
7. Simmer on low fire for an hour (or until meats are fully cooked).
8. Add salt and sugar to achieve desired flavor.

Important: Pepperpot does not need to be refrigerated. Bring to a boil every day to intensify flavors and to prevent from spoiling.

Enjoy with cassava bread, solid homemade bread, or rice.

–6–

Cooking Cubanidad: Food Importation and Cuban Identity in Santiago de Cuba

Hanna Garth

Fernando Ortiz, a Cuban folklorist who wrote about twentieth-century Cuban society, used a Cuban stew—the *ajiaco*[1]—as a metaphor to define Cuban culture as an ongoing identity process "open to hybridity, heterogeneity and hyphenation" (Pérez Firmat 1987: 14). In his 1940 essay, Ortiz defined the ajiaco as a native dish, a renewable Cuban stew consisting of different ingredients that combined to symbolize the Cuban people (Ortiz [1940]1963). According to Ortiz, the Amerindians supplied the corn, potatoes, taro, sweet potatoes, yams, and peppers. The Spaniards added squash and other tubers, while the Chinese added "Oriental" spices, and enslaved Africans contributed *ñame*, a tuber similar to a yam, along with their culinary taste. The Cuban ajiaco is made by simmering starchy root vegetables until they soften, then adding meat, usually pork, seasoned with a *sofrito*—a sauté of onion, garlic, peppers, cilantro, cumin, and oregano. The analogy represents the coming together of natives, Africans, and Spanish people, among others, to create Cuban society today. The key to the ajiaco metaphor is that as the ingredients are brought together to make the soup, they do not lose their original identity, but mix together to create something with a new and different flavor; new ingredients can always be added.[2] Ortiz suggested that Cubans are "a *mestizaje*[3] of kitchens, a *mestizaje* of races, a *mestizaje* of cultures, a dense broth of civilization that bubbles on the stove of the Caribbean."[4]

The ajiaco metaphor was used to illuminate Ortiz's notion of "transculturation," which he developed to refine the notion of "acculturation," an identity theory developed by Herskovitz, as discussed in the introduction to this volume. Ortiz felt that the term acculturation was an insufficient concept for Cuban mestizaje because it emphasizes the newcomer or outsider taking on the culture of the Other. His concept of transculturation includes the process of "deculturation," the shedding of the outsider's culture of origin; "acculturation," the incorporation of certain aspects of a new culture; and "neoculturation," the mixture of parts of the old and new culture (Ortiz [1940]1963; Pérez Firmat 1987: 135). For Ortiz, one important aspect of the ajiaco metaphor is that the ingredients do not lose their original form; they come together with others but maintain their own distinction.

Figure 6.1 Making ajiaco in Santiago de Cuba. Photo by Hanna Garth.

The ajiaco is also symbolic of Ortiz's ([1940]1963) understanding of *Cubanidad* (Cubanness), which he defines as "the quality of that which is Cuban, in other words, a way of being, their character, their nature, their distinctive conditions, their individuation within the universal" (166). Cubanidad, a term that denotes general and uniform "Cubanness" rather than individual identity, is the most commonly used expression for Cuban identity (Hernandez-Reguant 2009b; Pérez Firmat 1997). For Pérez Firmat (1997: 3), the concept of Cubanidad is critically linked to the state, nationality, and citizenship. It has been used since the Cuban independence struggle to denote a sense of nationalism that emphasizes unity, homogeneity, and solidarity. What it means to be Cuban, like what is considered to be Cuban food, is not always static; elements of these forms of identity may undergo reconsideration, refining, and change.

Understanding Cubanidad through Cuban Meals

This chapter explores present-day culinary practices through the lens of Cuban history. Two of the dishes featured in this chapter, *spaghetti con picadillo* (spaghetti with ground meat) and *arroz con pollo* (rice with chicken), are commonly consumed in everyday Cuban households, but they are not infused with the same sense of cultural identity as other dishes consumed in Cuba, such as rice and beans (or *congris*), or *hal-*

laca (a local version of tamales sometimes spelled *ayaca*). Through an investigation of Cubans' everyday experiences of their food system, this chapter shows how changes in access to certain foods transforms everyday eating and in turn expands local understanding of what is considered to be Cuban food. This project focuses on Santiago de Cuba, Cuba's second largest city, located in the southeastern part of the island. The data for this project were collected over a fifteen-month period between 2008 and 2011.

In Cuba, nationalized, state-level food acquisition has historically involved a diverse mixture of imports. Local food acquisition and consumption processes reflect the importance of Cuba's continuing participation in the global food trade. In this case, globalization is not a situation of disrepair, disruption of tradition, or homogenization of culture, but rather part of a history of food importation that has long shaped Cuban cuisine. Whereas many Caribbean nations' traditional cuisines have been altered due to increased international media, marketing, and the success of international food chains, Cuba has experienced relatively few overt international influences of media and corporations. Some food scholars have proposed that this type of neoliberal influence accelerates change, fosters homogenization, and leads to loss of cultural identity (Appadurai 1988, 1996; Friedman 1994). However, I argue here that in the case of Cuba local identities are strengthened despite the integration of "foreign" foods and new technologies into Cuban cuisine. I build upon Ortiz's work, showing that the history of importation and mestizaje in the Caribbean allows for new foods to be readily integrated into Cuban cuisine without leading to a sense of identity loss. However, as I will show, not everything is integrated into Cuban identity, and there are clear ways that Cubans distinguish themselves and their culinary practices from others.

Although seasonings and preparation practices have varied over time, the foods that my research participants connect with Cuban identity have been in place for several generations. Rice remains at the center of the Cuban plate; it has long been the most important staple in Cuban food consumption. Following rice, beans, *viandas* (tubers), and pork are all absolutely essential to Cuban cuisine, both in terms of the calories people actually consume and their prevalence on the imagined plate. However, the families in my study often ate meals that did not consist of any of these foods. After rice, beans, pork, and viandas, my data show that among households in Santiago de Cuba pasta and pizza[5] are the second most commonly consumed dishes. Many of my research participants distinguish Cuban pizza and Cuban pasta from any other kind, noting that it is the way in which these ingredients come together that makes them Cuban.

Background

Under the Cuban socialist state, a food rationing system was established in 1962. It is referred to locally as *la libreta*, a reference to the ration cards administered to all Cuban citizens for the purchase of basic food items (Benjamin, Collins, and Scott

1984; Garth 2009). The items available in the ration have slowly changed over the last fifty years. During my fieldwork, the monthly ration per person included five pounds of white rice, ten ounces of beans, three pounds of refined sugar, one pound of raw sugar, one kilogram of salt, four ounces of coffee, and 250 milliliters of oil allocated monthly, as well as a roll of bread per day.[6] Meat products included six ounces of chicken, eleven ounces of fish, ten eggs, and eight ounces of ground meat mixed with soy.[7] If there is a national shortage at any given time, some of these meat products are substituted with pork-based sausages, other processed meats, or extra chicken. All of these items together cost the consumer about twenty-five national pesos a month.[8] This ration is essential for making ends meet in most Santiago households.

The present food system is a product not just of the 1959 socialist revolution but also of a long history of flows of goods to and from the island, a process that has given rise to certain tastes in the Cuban palate. Spanish colonists first arrived on the eastern part of the island in the late 1400s. Under Spanish colonial rule, most foods were imported from Spain,[9] and the local economy was based on agricultural production for export. In the early 1500s Spanish governor Diego Velázquez de Cuéllar moved the island's capital from Baracoa to Santiago de Cuba, and the first African slaves were brought to Cuba from Hispañola. Slaves were brought to the region to work sugar and coffee plantations. Spanish customs and traditions prevailed among the colonists in Santiago until the early 1800s when, in the years after the Haitian Revolution, French and Haitian foods became an integral part of Cuban cuisine.[10] In addition to Spanish, French, and African influences, Chinese immigrants have also added culinary tastes to the Cuban palate. There have been many other migratory influences in Santiago de Cuba, including the influence of North Americans in the nineteenth and twentieth century and the continued influence of the Cuban-American diaspora. By the 1870s, products from the United States accounted for the majority of Cuban imports (Pérez 2003). This influence continued through the 1940s and 1950s, when Cuba's most popular magazine, *Bohemia*, was filled with ads for Kellogg's Corn Flakes, Heinz Ketchup, Quaker Instant Oats, and other American products.

Many recent ethnographic accounts of Cuba analyze the ways in which institutional changes after the collapse of the Soviet Union have affected everyday life on the island (Brotherton 2005, 2008; Hernandez-Reguant 2005, 2009a). What is striking for many ethnographers is the fact that many social services and state programs remain in place and continue to provide assistance, while at the same time the population calls out for more. As state services are contracted, my research participants note their frustration with increased household expenses without an increase in salary. The Cuban food system is no different; the state continues to provide basic food staples at extremely low prices through the food rationing system, but as the food available in the ration diminishes and the prices for additional foods elevate, complaints increase. Many Santiagueros say that the transition to state control over food production caused a great shift in the everyday eating habits of a typical Cuban household, yet when asked what typical Cuban meals consisted of before the revolution, most respond that the standard foods—rice, beans, and tubers—have in fact not changed. It is true, however, that for many people the *acquisition* of these essential ingredients has become increasingly difficult. Food acquisition shifted radically from a system where a wide variety of foods, from cheap to luxury goods, were easily accessible in various types of markets, to a system where fewer and fewer things were available in markets, prices rose, and the process of food acquisition involved going further and further from home, spending more time and money to acquire less food than they had before (cf. Garth 2009).

In most Santiago households, domestic work is carried out by women. This work includes: the planning, preparation, and serving of meals; cleaning and laundry; ensuring that bills are paid; and that the house runs smoothly (Garth 2010). The traditional notion of the *calle/casa* divide remains prominent in Santiago; women belong in the home and men in the streets. The *calle/casa* division of gendered spaces has persisted since Cuba's independence from Spain (Garth 2010; Pertierra 2008; Smith and Padula 1996; Stoner 1991). This gendered division of labor was very common in my sample, though there were a few exceptions where men occasionally cooked, or were always in charge of one aspect of household food practices, usually food acquisition. This approach to women's place in the world is often linked to white bourgeois Spanish thinking, however it is still seen today across racial and socioeconomic lines. In the following sections, I describe the typical daily process of food acquisition and household meal planning in Santiago households where women do the work of planning, acquiring, preparing, and serving meals. These ethnographic vignettes show the daily processes of food acquisition and how this process relates to food consumption choices over the course of a typical day in two different Santiago households.

A Day in the Life of Pati and Susi

Pati lives in a two-bedroom house in the heart of downtown Santiago with her five-year-old son, Gorgi, her mother, Susi, and her father and brother. Pati's grandfather first moved into the house in the 1920s, and her mother was born there, as was Pati. Pati works as a secretary for state legal services, her father works in construction, and her brother is in school studying to be a dentist. Her mother stays at home with Gorgi and does most of the household food preparation. The fact that Pati's mother stays home to maintain their large, centrally located household, and that she, her brother and father are all studying or working during a period of widespread unemployment in Cuba, is typical for a relatively well-off urban household in Cuba.

For breakfast, the family starts off the day around 6:00 A.M. with strong Cuban coffee made with lots of sugar and served without milk. Little Gorgi drinks powdered milk instead of coffee for breakfast. Each family member also eats half of a roll of bread that they either dip in the coffee or eat with homemade jam made with seasonal fruits that they get from their relatives in the countryside. This is the typical morning meal, though every once in a while breakfast may include an egg and fresh-made juice as well.

After breakfast Pati and her father head off to work, her brother goes to school, and Susi will take Gorgi out to pick up the ingredients for the day's food. First, they will stop at the ration station to pick up any dry goods, such as beans, rice, or sugar. Then they will go to the *carniceria*, or butcher, where they pick up the meat products and eggs distributed via the ration card. On this particular day there is only *picadillo* (ground meat) in the ration.

At both of the ration pick-ups, they may have to wait in line for up to an hour. Then Susi will head to the state market to pick up nationally grown onions, garlic, and any other fresh herbs, vegetables, and fruit that they may need. Susi will buy whichever products are inexpensive, and she will have to just buy whatever is in stock, since there is not often much variety. On the particular day that I observe her food-acquisition processes, Susi picks up some spaghetti noodles since she has pica-dillo and hopes to make spaghetti with meat sauce for lunch that day. She is about to head into the hard currency or "CUC" store when she notices that a man sitting on the curb up the street is selling a few things he has placed on the ground next to him.[11] He has three bags of spaghetti for sale at about 70 percent of the price in the store. He is able to undercut the store price because the spaghetti is stolen from ware-houses or stores and then resold to him, which he then sells in the street. She buys all three packages and is very happy to save the money. She is about to go into the store to buy canned tomato sauce but counts the few CUC that she has and decides to buy the thinner tomato sauce that her neighbor makes at home. On the way back to the house she stops and buys two cups of tomato sauce through her neighbor's window for twenty cents. She will use the onions, garlic, and oil to make a sofrito that will help stretch the picadillo and tomato sauce so that it can serve the whole family.

Susi prepares lunch for her husband and Gorgi, but Pati and her brother do not come home for lunch because they eat a free meal at their workplace cafeteria. Pati receives a small cardboard box with about a cup of rice and beans, some fried plan-tains, and a tiny piece of pork. Her brother eats a sandwich with a ham spread and mayonnaise on it. Knowing how little they eat for lunch, Susi tries to save them a portion of the spaghetti from lunch to eat when they get home from work in the evening. On top of adding extra oil so that the meat sauce will be enough to coat everyone's noodles, Susi overcooks the noodles so that they are thick and sticky, an-other trick to make the food stretch to serve more people. Although Cubans usually prefer to have liberal amounts of cheese in their spaghetti, Susi doesn't have enough money to purchase cheese so she sprinkles on some Maggi-brand *Sazon Completo* for flavoring. She wishes she could use natural spices but it is much cheaper to use Sazon Completo to get the same level of flavor.

For the evening meal, Pati and her brother will eat a plate of spaghetti. Susi, her husband, and Gorgi will have a roll of bread with butter or mayonnaise and a glass of juice or soda. They will eat this around 8:00 P.M. as they are winding down their day and getting ready for bed.

Elvira's Kitchen: A Second Case

Elvira, the head of another typical middle-class family living in downtown Santiago, wakes up everyday at 4:30 A.M. to clean her house and prepare breakfast and lunch for the family. Elvira's family is similar to Pati's in many ways except that in this case Elvira does all of the household labor on top of working outside the home and is not able to rely on her parents, who live with her, for household help. Because of this, Elvira has created routines and household practices that allow her to manage all of her household labor and work outside the home. For instance, she prepares twice as much food for lunch and they eat leftovers from lunch for dinner. She spends four to five hours cleaning, cooking, and getting showered and dressed for the day each morning. After she completes her morning housework she goes out to buy ingredients for the following day, returns home, and gets ready to head to her office job on the other side of the city. Because she works full time and is in charge of all of the domestic labor in her house as well, her life requires a rigid schedule, planning, and constant foresight. As she gets ready she serves her husband, son, and two elderly parents their breakfasts. Like Pati's family they each have a roll of bread with coffee; however in Elvira's case, her eight-year-old son has a yogurt and fruit smoothie rather than milk for breakfast.

Elvira had left out chicken to defrost when she went to bed the night before. The chicken quarters, always a leg and a thigh, are available once a month in the ration, but Elvira accesses more because her son has access to a special "underweight child diet" that she got by paying a doctor to falsify a medical order. The chicken quarters are Tyson brand, raised and processed in the United States and imported to Cuba. (Since 2000, agricultural and medical products have been exempted from the U.S. trade embargo.) She decides to make *arroz con pollo*.[12] After she removes the skin from the chicken quarter, she measures out eight cups of rice, the most that her state-issued rice cooker will fit and just enough for lunch and a light dinner for her family. She obtained the rice from the ration station earlier that week; this particular batch of rice was imported to Cuba from Vietnam. Once the rice is clean she begins to peel garlic, and cut onions and peppers. She pours about one fourth of a cup of oil into the bottom of the rice cooker, and after it heats she adds the garlic, onions, and peppers and to make a sofrito. Again, in this case, the garlic, onions, and peppers are grown in Cuba; though they are not original plant species to the island, they are considered an essential part of Cuban cuisine. She adds the cleaned rice and stirs, letting the grains open up a bit before she adds the water. She adds extra water so that the rice "grows more" and she drops in a cube of Maggi chicken-flavored bouillon. She drops in the chicken quarter, covers the rice cooker and continues with her daily house cleaning routine.

At midday, Elvira's family members will serve themselves from the rice cooker, which she leaves on the "warm setting" all day. Since the state eliminated her free lunch at work and she does not trust "street food," she does not eat at all during the workday. She told me on several occasions how awful she felt during her commute home from work because she was so hungry having just consumed coffee and a roll all day, but she was unwilling to eat street food as a snack on her way home. When she arrives home from work around 5:00 P.M. she will serve everyone another portion of the same meal. She usually makes a homemade juice to go along with the evening meal, which everyone eats in the living room in front of the television.

Another Kind of Cuisine

Pati, Susi, and Elvira's daily food acquisition, preparation, and consumption practices are representative of the middle-class families in my study of Santiago de Cuba. The meals featured above are extremely common. However, these meals are not referred to as specifically Cuban, but rather as Cuban versions of a more general cuisine. This section outlines dishes that stand in contrast to those featured above as more explicitly linked to Cuban identity. In many of my interviews, participants brought up foods that they thought of as specifically linked to Cuban identity. As fifty-eight-year-old Omaro put it:

> Well if you are studying food in Cuba—Cuban food that is . . . all you need to know about is rice and beans—what we call here *congris*—and then pork and *viandas* that's all we eat because that is *our* food. What the Cuban people live, our way of living is congris, pork and viandas.

The notion of a specifically Cuban diet was continually reified by many of my research participants in comments similar to those made by Omaro. Similar to the ways in which the Makushi of Guyana designate certain foods as "we food" (Schacht, this volume), some participants specifically emphasized a sense of ownership and identification with certain foods both on a national and a local level. When I asked her to tell me about what kinds of foods her family usually eats at home, Maria Isabel explained her view of the Santiaguero struggle to maintain local food traditions:

> For example, we have another dish that we have tried so hard to preserve it as it is—the *hallaca*—in the west [part of the island] they call it *tamal,* but we have to maintain our hallaca. So we have entered into a state of a lot of energy and effort around this, we keep trying to find a way to overcome these difficulties, to continue living our way of life.

Maria Isabel specifically ties this dish to local Santiaguero identity and way of life. She is quick to note the importance of preserving a distinct Santiago dish. Later in the interview she elaborates that this is about more than just a difference of labels between *hallaca* and *tamal,* explaining that:

> What is most important is that our food is grown here on the *Oriente* soil, which is so fertile with a history—with our history—of the blood and the *lucha* of our African, French-Haitian and Cuban ancestors and years of lucha and victory that give the corn grown in the region with a sweeter flavor and juicier kernels. And also the people who sell corn here in Santiago they still grind the corn by hand for hallaca, and this gives it the flavor that makes it special to us.

While her sentiments reveal a highly romanticized view of the relationship between the history of Eastern Cuba and contemporary Cuban foods, Maria Isabel communicates here how much she values particular aspects of food cultivation and preparation for their connections to her Santiaguera identity. She clearly prefers foods grown not only on Cuban land, but on local *Oriente* land as not only better tasting but as morally laden with Santiaguero work ethics and values. She casts the preservation of regional dishes as a type of struggle that she continues to put energy into despite difficulties (Garth 2009, forthcoming). Maria Isabel's focus on a dish that is not an everyday food and does not use the typical staple ingredients of Cuban cuisine was also quite common. Because of changes in the Cuban food system, many of the foods that are linked to identity are increasingly difficult to acquire. Other foods, like those made by Susi and Elvira, are much more common for everyday consumption.

Although there are some Santiagueros who uphold the view that Cubans eat and should eat foods that are "traditionally Cuban," there are still many who note that Cubans do not always eat this way and that this view has become increasingly romanticized as foods thought of as traditionally Cuban become more scarce or difficult to make. For example, during one of my interviews I asked a young man named Martin what his favorite meal was. He smiled and replied that his preferred meal was: "*Congri* [White rice and black beans], yuca, *tostones* [deep fried mashed tubers], and pork with seasonal vegetables, of course." When I naively responded with the statement, "like every Santiguero," Martin quickly corrected my assumption. He pointed out that now, with the influence of tourists, television, and fancy CUC restaurants throughout Cuba, many Santiagueros want to "change what they eat," and that although many cannot afford to eat in the tourist restaurants they try to replicate this foreign way of eating in their homes, as part of what he observes as an increasing desire for the Euro-American aesthetic, not only with regard to food, but in dress, music choice, and attitude. He pointed out that although people eat these types of foods:

These foods are not our way of eating. The Cuban body wants our traditional food. That is what we have to eat. People eating these foreign foods and chemical foods that is why there is so much sickness, so much cancer. We have to eat our own foods to maintain our health.

Martin's comments about what he perceives as an increase in the consumption of "foreign" foods may illustrate a discrepancy between how Santiagueros actually eat in practice versus the foods that they think of as being traditional Cuban foods. While Martin perceives the shift away from consuming traditional foods as the result of tourism and media, other research participants have noted the ways in which the state and changes in the Cuban food system create barriers to accessing traditional foods. Along similar lines, in response to a question regarding how she felt about the Cuban government adding soy to the ground beef in the rations, Carolina explained that:

Soy is very aggressive for the Cuban body, for the stomach, it's very hot and since the climate here is so hot our bodies are not adjusted to such hot foods. Not all bodies are the same, no? Some people, like from northern climates can eat soy, but not Cubans.

Both Martin and Carolina allude to the notion that the Cuban body best suited to certain kinds of foods. Carolina's classification of soy as a food that is too hot for Cuban bodies, a humoral pathology reference,[13] again asserts the idea that Cuban bodies were made to consume certain "Cuban foods" that stand in contrast to "new" foreign foods. Soy is mixed into the rationed ground beef because pure ground beef is too expensive for the state to include in the ration. For Carolina and many other Cubans, they feel as though they are forced to eat soy even though it is not a part of "their" cuisine.

What Makes These Meals "Cuban" Food?

For Ortiz's ajiaco, the origins of the ingredients matched the ancestry of the majority of Cubans. Many of my research participants were unaware of or uninterested in the origins of the foods that they eat in Cuba today. Some thought that all of the foods that they ate were cultivated on the island, and only a few were aware of the fact that Cuba imports most foods. The majority of my participants make decisions about what they are going to eat based on what foods are most available and accessible (cf. Garth 2009). For instance, Susi decides to make this dish because of the availability of picadillo in the ration; for most Cubans, ground meat is usually paired with spaghetti. Many years ago picadillo was made of 100 percent ground beef; today increasing amounts of soy are added to the ground beef. The portion of the picadillo that consists of beef is likely to come from the United States (USDA 2008). Most of the soy products consumed in Cuba are processed on the island but the soy is likely to be imported from Brazil and the United States.[14] Similarly the pasta was probably processed on the island with imported raw materials.[15] The Maggi-brand Sazon Completo is imported; the Maggi Corporation has offices all over the world and their products come from dozens of countries across the globe. Based on my interviews, Cubans tend to think that their Sazon Completo comes from Venezuela.[16] The garlic and onions added to flavor and stretch the meat are grown on the island for domestic consumption, and the homemade tomato sauce is made from tomatoes grown in Cuba. For this meal, the onions, garlic, and tomatoes may be the only things that are arguably 100 percent Cuban, and even they are not native species to the island.

Unlike in Ortiz's ajiaco, the ingredients for these meals do neatly match with the ancestral origins of Cubans; they come from all over the world and sometimes it is not even possible to pinpoint where they come from at all. But to the people that are eating these meals, the food is still "Cuban food." The ways in which they come together is what makes them Cuban. Both Pati and Susi use the sofrito as a base for their meals. The sofrito is analogous to the ajiaco, in that when you slowly cook the onion, garlic, and oil, the flavor that results is not simply a combination of the three ingredients; when they come together in a particular way, their flavor is unique and different.

Spaghetti con picadillo and arroz con pollo are not dishes that have historically resonated with the national myth of mestizaje, yet their contemporary popularity reveals some important connections between Cuban food and identity. In the case of these meals, it is the particular combination of ingredients that makes them "Cuban" versions of a more generalized cuisine. Cuba's history of importation and mestizaje is precisely what allows for "new foods" to be readily integrated into Cuban cuisine. In the case of these dishes, the origins of the ingredients are less critical to what makes them a part of Cuban cuisine—rice, pasta, and even meat are imported from across the globe—than the particular way of bringing them together. These dishes are not seen as completely foreign because they have been modified to be "Cuban." However, such foods do not carry the same sense of Cuban identity as the foods discussed in the section above—congris, the hallaca, and other dishes thought of as specifically Cuban.

The foods outlined in this chapter that participants demarcate as specifically Cuban, as "our" food, incorporate a conscious reflection on how these foods relate to Cubanidad. In the case of Cuban food, the dishes that are seen as specifically Cuban are not unique to Cuba—we find rice and beans, tamales, tubers, and pork dishes all over the Caribbean and much of Latin America. In the case of these dishes as well, it is the particular combination of ingredients that makes them Cuban, and their long history as a central part of Cuban food that ties them so closely to Cuban identity.

However, not everything is integrated into Cubanidad or Cuban cuisine; there are clear ways in which Cubans distinguish themselves and their culinary practices from others. Although ground beef mixed with soy is readily consumed in Cuba, it is consumed because there are not many alternatives. Like Carolina, many of my research participants were very upset about the addition of soy to their ground meat; they were also upset about the addition of soy to yogurt and other dairy products—though less upset than in the case of meat. Carolina constructs a specific argument that soy is hard for Cuban bodies to digest; others argue that they simply don't like the taste. This discourse indicates that although Cubans readily integrate new ingredients into their culinary repertoires, these additions must be done willfully. In some cases it appears that the rejection of certain foods or ingredients is tied to state provisioning and the lack of choice.

If we return to Ortiz and the use of food as a metaphor for Cuban identity, these examples show that, with some exceptions, Cuban cuisine and identity are indeed open to hybridity, heterogeneity, and hyphenation. In the case of all of the meals detailed here, the ingredients come together with others but maintain their own distinction—their own Cubanidad. Yet it is clear that the ajiaco metaphor does not extend to all of the food consumption practices outlined here. The foods that participants perceive to be specifically Cuban clearly resonate with a particular sense of Cuban identity that aligns with Ortiz's notion of transculturation. Although the other meals that are "Cuban" only in the sense that they have been modified from a generic meal to have a particularly Cuban flavor—because of the particular mixture of ingredients—do not have the same social meaning, their consumption does not indicate a loss of identity either. The foods that are explicitly scorned, such as soy, on the other hand, do seem to indicate a sense of lost identity and a strong rejection. As the changes in the Cuban food system shift access to particular types of so-called traditional foods, Cubans are still able to consume a type of cuisine that remains distinctly "Cuban" in their eyes, though not one that they see as their own.

From Colonial Dependency to Finger-lickin' Values: Food, Commoditization, and Identity in Trinidad

Marisa Wilson

Nothing in Trinidad is too sacred not to be commoditized. Even Carnival is there to sell people stuff.

—Trinidadian student in a first-year human geography class, February 2011

In a Trinidadian bar or fete, or any place where one might escape from the "pressure" of everyday life, consumer objects are often linked to status.[1] Johnny Walker Blue is better than Johnny Walker Gold, which is, in turn, socially better than Johnny Walker Black. Heineken is better than Stag or Samba (local varieties of beer). The lowest and cheapest drink on the social hierarchy is Puncheon or even the medicinal Bay Rum, either of which may or may not be linked to the petroleum industry.

Another example of this kind of consumer hierarchy is how my "Trini" students, aged eighteen to twenty-one, evaluate the retail food sector, placing "clean" and "safe" supermarkets, with all the imported tinned and packaged varieties of food, above "dirty" and "unsafe" local markets, where arguably more healthy and cheaper meat, fish, and produce is available. As one of my students said, the meat and produce market in Tunapuna[2] is "just a market," while the Hi-Lo supermarket is "an experience" (in-class interview, February 2011). Compare this statement to those of people in Oxford, United Kingdom, whom I have also interviewed: "I go to the supermarket when I do not have time to go to the farmers' market"; "I prefer to buy local."

Consumer values in Trinidad differ markedly from those in countries like the United Kingdom. In formerly colonized places like Trinidad, values for imported commodities like Kentucky Fried Chicken (KFC), and for modern experiences like shopping in an air-conditioned supermarket in a U.S.-style mall, have consistently trumped official efforts to localize food. In what Daniel Miller (1994) claims to be the first modern area of the world—the Caribbean—they correspond to one side of an oppositional value system that emerged as a consequence of slavery and its aftermath. On one side of this value system lies the view that imported foods are more civilized than local farmers' markets, while on the other are values of autonomy epitomized by official campaigns to "localize it." These contradictory values, which on a national scale correspond to what Miller (1994) calls "centripetal" and "centrifugal" tendencies for the domestic scale (for a related argument, see Wilson 1973), characterize the history of the Caribbean, and to some extent all modern societies.

Despite dominant discourses in Trinidad for a return to a so-called authentic past when Trinidadians were not so dependent on imports of food and other commodities (Miller 1994: 205), an emerging subculture of younger people, largely undeterred by ethnic (or gendered) divisions, treat the consumption of imports as essential to their very identity as Trini. To understand this cultural phenomenon, it is first important to consider the relation between centrifugal and centripetal tendencies in Caribbean history in general and in Trinidadian history in particular. In the first section I describe early dependencies and social hierarchies of consumption that developed in the Caribbean as a result of slavery, indentureship, and the plantation, patterns that led to the contradictory value system described above. Then I argue that this value system has taken particular shape in Trinidad, given its status as an oil-producing country. As I show in the second section, official plans to localize the Trinidadian food system in the post-independence era have not only ignored governmental preferences for industrial over agricultural development, but also eclipsed historical valuations of foreign commodities. In the third and final section I narrow the analysis to present-day Trinidad, revealing how modern values that emerged in Trinidadian history are reformulated by younger people who associate experiences such as Kentucky Fried Chicken with Trini identity.

The Emergence of Social Hierarchies in the Caribbean and Trinidad

A nation draws its history behind it, like the wake of a great ship. . . . [It] looks to have its destiny carved out for it in advance, as if everything before were a preparation for something still to come. (Tonkin, McDonald, and Chapman 1989: 7)

Michel-Rolph Trouillot (1992: 22) claims that no cultural or social aspect of Caribbean peoples can "be accounted for, or even described, without reference to colonialism" since "the Caribbean is nothing but contact." It therefore makes sense to start with historical patterns that have emerged in the Caribbean, which form the backdrop to present-day values for imported foodstuffs in Trinidad.

The Caribbean is a region where *pre*colonial tastes, values and ways of being were significantly lost to modern industrial practices. As Jamaican Philip Sherlock wrote: "Colonialism, however important, was an *incident* in the history of Nigeria and Ghana, Kenya or Uganda; but it is the whole story of the West Indies, and . . .

it has deeper meaning for the West Indian than for the African" (cited by Lowenthal 1974: 5, my emphasis). In a similar vein, Richard Wilk (2006a) writes: "Within 150 years of Colombus' discovery of the area, most native cultures had been swept away, and the population was replaced by a polyglot mixture of people from Europe and Africa, many torn by force from their own local traditions" (10). The region differs from all other colonized areas as it is the only place where Europeans could start afresh in a "new" world. Sidney Mintz wrote of the near-complete extermination of indigenous peoples in this region that "scourging of the human landscape enabled the Europeans to set the terms of their future colonialism in the Caribbean area in ways very different from those available to them in the densely-occupied areas of the non-Western world" (Mintz 1971: 919). Through brute force, disease, and slave labor, the histories of extant societies were eliminated along with their physical existence. Elsewhere in the former colonies, precolonial identities continued to influence thought and action. But in the plural societies of the Caribbean, values and standards that developed from institutions of slavery and the plantation became one primary measuring rod to evaluate economic and social activities such as food consumption. The importation of European food was essential for the colonial project, as human factors like population increases from brutal forms of labor recruitment and geographical factors such as floods and droughts created scarcities (Richardson 1992: 67, 109). The kind of food imported was also part of the colonial project. Manufactures from the metropolis produced for long journeys across the ocean became staples in the Caribbean, changing the diets of both the colonizers and colonized. As Colonel Hislop, Governor of Trinidad in 1806, is claimed to have said in V. S. Naipaul's (2001) fictive history, *A Way in the World*:

> It's like living on a ship here. We've got twenty thousand Negroes working on the plantation from five in the morning to six in the evening, six days a week. But the scarcest thing here is food. All they do on the plantations is cocoa and cotton and sugar-cane and coffee . . . Nearly everything we eat here is smoked or salted and comes in a box from Canada or the United States. Beef, mackerel, salmon, cod, herring . . . Butter is orange-red with salt and costs six shillings a pound. No one thinks of churning it locally. (265)

The counter-tendency in the Caribbean was to produce indigenous and African crops like yams, sweet potatoes, and cassava for home consumption and sometimes for the local market. In countries like Jamaica and the Guianas, runaway slaves or maroons established their own methods of farming, combining indigenous and African cultivars and techniques, and marketing their produce to whites as well as Africans. Such patterns of proto-peasant "resistance" (Mintz [1974]1989) were not as prevalent in smaller islands like Trinidad, however, which was the last to adopt slavery with fewer large plantations (Miller 1994: 20). Still, slavery in all places corresponded to a dual orientation towards adaptation—or the adoption of European ways of life, and resistance—or proactive efforts towards self-sufficiency and autonomy (Mintz

[1974]1989; Olwig 1985). The value for metropolitan products like white wheat flour coexisted with tropes of resistance like stealing (Lichtenstein 1988: 414–15; Mintz 1996: 29–35). As Mintz (1971, [1974]1989) has argued, this contradiction was an essential aspect of everyday life: "The house slave who poisoned her master's family by putting ground glass in the family food had first to become the family cook" (Mintz 1971, cited by Trouillot 1992: 31).

For Mintz, the plantation was more than just an economic institution; rather, it constituted a "societal model of a kind" (Mintz 1971: 921). Slaves and their owners were interlinked economically as well as socioculturally, including the ways "luxuries" from the metropolis were valued. Those who had access to such luxuries were stratified from those who did not. Thus rations of imported commodities set the domestic or skilled slave apart from his low-caste counterpart: the lowly field slave (Knight 1990: 121–34). The chance to eat white wheat bread over plantains allowed slaves to "literally tast[e] freedom" in the modern (i.e., market economic) sense (Wilk 2006a: 61). To eat what the master (or overseer) ate, usually commodities imported from Europe or, later, the United States, was akin to "reclaim[ing their] dignity as human beings" (Wilk 2006a: 61).

Many Caribbean scholars, such as the Jamaican George Beckford (1972: 41–42) have also claimed that rivalries and hierarchies between field and house slaves emerged because of preferential access to European foods and ways of life. Like other Caribbeanists of the 1960s and 1970s (i.e., Best and Polanyi-Levitt 2009; Lowenthal 1974), Beckford understood the Caribbean as a unique grouping of plural ethnicities and classes, unified, however, by their common orientation towards economic rewards that came from outside:

> The strongest elements of social integration in plantation society are to be found in the areas of economic production and achievement motivation. Individuals in every group are bound by their dependence on each other for economic survival . . . [T]hey all want the same things in life. So they [have] common aspirations for material things associated with a Great House life style, such as housing and consumer durables. (Beckford 1972: 83)

The primary way to get such commodities was with money. So while some Afro-Caribbeans became "reconstituted peasants" (Mintz 1961a: 31–34) relatively distanced from the world of money and commodities, many others moved to urban areas to work. As Mintz has written of the period, at least in regards to Afro-Caribbean peoples: "Rising expectations influenced by external stimuli . . . creat[ed] a wage-seeking people that 'neither ha[d] nor (eventually) want[ed] land'" (cited by Richardson 1992: 188). In Trinidad, wage work and urbanization was especially prevalent, as Afro-Caribbean laborers on plantations were replaced by a wave of indentured peoples from the Indian subcontinent. As Miller (1994: 23, in reference to Macdonald 1986) suggests, Trinidad saw the rise of middle classes before most other British colonies and they set the standards for most people (just as slave owners had done previously). Indeed, despite its complicated ethnic history, which includes Africans and East Asians as well as Chinese, African Americans, Europeans, and Middle Eastern peoples, common orientation to the outside unified Trinidadian peoples, a stratified unanimity that characterizes all of the West Indies: "Differential rewards occasion much grief, but West Indians still tend to accept stratification as natural, almost inevitable. Status aspirations blunt the impetus of reform but also stitch together the social fabric" (Lowenthal 1972: 142).

Social Hierarchies of Consumption in Post-Emancipation Trinidad

In Trinidad, ties to the outside were anything but strengthened in the post-emancipation period, when people of all ethnicities (but especially Afro-Trinis) came to associate social status with modern commodities. Local food production also increased after emancipation and competed with imports until the latter half of the twentieth century. But despite some diversification efforts in the late-nineteenth and early-twentieth centuries (Brereton [1981]2009: 92–94), particularly of export crops like cocoa and citrus, the distribution of lands to Indo- and Afro-Trinidadians was hindered by strict regulations that precluded small-scale purchases (Brereton [1981]2009). After 1869, the East Asian population secured lands for wet rice and vegetable cultivation through a royal decree that allowed all male Indo-Trinidadians whose indentures had expired and who had lived in Trinidad for ten years to exchange their return passage to India for ten acres of Crown lands (Brereton [1981]2009: 107). In the twentieth century, Crown lands were increasingly bought by all ethnicities, but it was mostly East Asian smallholders who grew food for domestic consumption (Brereton [1981]2009: 95).

Though domestic production did increase in the post-emancipation period, the plantation "legacy" (Best and Polanyi-Levitt 2009) continued as most of the best agricultural lands in Trinidad were dedicated to export crops like sugar and cocoa, cultivated on larger properties usually owned by people of European origin. Public institutions such as the University of the West Indies (which was the Imperial College of Tropical Agriculture until 1960) dedicated most research and development efforts towards exports. At a national scale, credit and investment, finance and banking, labor legislation, and infrastructure were all geared towards export crops such as cocoa and sugar, and other raw material exports such as oil and bauxite.

After independence (1962), the Trinidad and Tobago government implemented a series of five-year plans to increase the domestic production of foodstuffs (Gomes 1981). The third five-year plan, spanning from 1969 to 1973, was written with the explicit aim to create a market for domestic foodstuffs by shifting Trinidadians' tastes away from imports and towards traditional crops like *sapodilla*, and to local foods like *callaloo*, a soup made with amarynth leaf (or "dasheen bush"), ochra (or "ochro"), and local spices. Government efforts to change Trinidadians' tastes for imported foods continued until the oil boom of the mid-1970s (and returned in more recent efforts to "localize it," discussed below), but the "culture of emulation"

(Miller 1994: 22) persisted. This culture had as much to do with earlier plantation patterns as with twentieth-century connections to the outside world.

During World War II, many Caribbean people had experienced other material worlds as soldiers in Europe. Along with emigration to places like Canada, which continued throughout the century, islands such as Trinidad had housed North American bases that paid in cash, bringing in American commodities and ways of life. As Lowenthal argues: "Trinidad especially was Americanized in its tempo of life, in its demands for modern consumer goods, and in its impatience with Old World forms" (Lowenthal 1972: 75). One Trinidadian recalled this era when the middle classes became a formidable role model for consumption:

> When the first set of money came in this sort of area, people started to look for the car first, and then we had this TV first and video, and when this money did start to come in those people who did have the black and white, when money started to flow people would tend to say, "me eh [don't] want black and white, I want colour." (Miller 1994: 32)

During the oil boom of the 1970s and 1980s, the first prime minister of Trinidad and Tobago, Eric Williams (1956–1981), encouraged people to spend money on consumer durables with the slogan "money is no problem." He was anything but deterred by massive increases in foreign exchange through petroleum exports and concomitant economic ties to the United States. Inflated by early (if not later) support by members of the black power movement of the 1970s, Williams's development plans were completely opposed to the concurrent plans for agricultural diversification. As one activist for the current "localize it" campaign told me: "Eric Williams did not help agriculture. Because of him agriculture continued to be the bastard child of the Caribbean."

The first prime minister followed Sir Arthur Lewis's project for "investment-by-invitation," which demonstrated in policy form the Trini sense of having "made it" according to outside rules:

> [Williams's] antagonism to local agricultural production, seem[s] to have been dictated less by economic sagacity than by the desire to assert something that had always been denied—the capacity for a developing country to manufacture materials generally associated with First World forms of industrialisation. (Miller 1994: 23)

But, as calypsonian The Mighty Sparrow sung in his 1980s song "Capitalism Gone Mad," climbing up the socioeconomic hierarchy was easier for some than others:

> You got to be in skullduggery, making your money illicitly To live like somebody in this country . . . Where you ever hear, a television for seven thousand . . . A pair of sneakers—two hundred dollars . . . Eighty, ninety thousand for motor cars . . . At last here in Trinidad, we see capitalism gone mad.

While bemoaning the reliance on money and commodities, Sparrow still claims that one cannot "be someone in this country" unless they have money to buy televisions, sneakers and motor cars. His calypso reflects internal contradictions between the "pressure" to express one's identity and increase one's social standing through material culture, on the one hand, and the reality of capitalist dependencies, on the other.

Such contradictions of modernity established what Miller (1994: 22) calls "a culture of disparagement of the powerless and emulation of the powerful." Fast-forwarding into the future, one may note this cultural tendency in some of the ways young Trinidadians explained their purchasing decisions: "You go to the grocery and the price of [New Zealand] cheese has gone up a dollar. One person walks away. He can't afford it. The other says to him: 'I can afford it!'—buying the cheese just to show that he is better than the other." Another young man said: "Once you move up, you do not want to go back to traditional lifestyle, work hard. You want an easy life and nice things. You don't want to travel no more, you want a big car. You want to eat meat all the time." And still another: "I used to go to the [local] market once a week, but now I don't because I can afford not to!"

Miller's ethnography from 1994 reveals similar thinking:

> They say Trinidadians, even if you give them a palace will always have some renovations to do, that is what they're like. I think they live to show one another—well I could do this . . . So everybody trying to make it at least slightly different from their neighbor. So most people trying to make it as different as possible. (46)

Mostly it is stuff that comes "from foreign" that symbolizes status. When I asked my students whether they preferred foreign or local food products, the former almost always surpassed the latter: "Foreign is always better and superior. [People prefer] Heinz over Matouks, Cadbury over Charles, Anchor over local cheese, imported sardines over local, imported pineapple, lettuce, bananas," "Trinis believe if its imported, its good. . . . Its ah big brand so it is quality," "You know you made it in Trinidad when you buy your groceries at Trincity mall."

Discourses of Local Food in Trinidad

In considering the admittedly narrow history of Trinidad presented above, it is clear that modern values linked to material culture emerged as part of its very social fabric, rather than from a rupture with a more "authentic" or "traditional" past. Thus Miller argues that "given the particular history of the region, [Trinidadian] people come up against the problematic of modernity with a particular jolt, having had stripped away many of the traditions and structures which would mediate this relationship elsewhere" (Miller 1994: 12). In the final section below I will argue for a wider understanding of food and values in Trinidad than that depicted by policymakers and activists who promote the localization of the Trinidadian food system. While the latter associate values for modern, imported food with negative attributes like selfishness and laziness, young people who eat KFC use similar, though positively represented aspects of Trinidadian culture to associate the fast food chain with Trini identity. Indeed, as we shall see later, the culture of Trinidadian consumption, with its strong element of class (as well as ethnic and gendered) competition, is shifting in new, "ultra-modern" directions, as imported food becomes associated with values that are just as centrifugal as centripetal.

According to his critics, the first twenty-five years under Eric Williams led people in the country to develop a "dependent mentality" or a "gimme, gimme" attitude, a sense of entitlement that made them too "lazy" to practice agriculture. As one well-off Trinidadian told me:

> When independence came and all that crap, [Eric] Williams introduced a make-work program. Agricultural workers left estates and worked for the government on road works . . . The work ethic changed. Now people have a gimme, gimme attitude . . . My father had 350 acres in Hapio, on which he grew coffee, cocoa, citrus, plantains and bananas . . . He had chickens and a pig or two for the family . . . After independence, all that went to pot.

Williams's policies not only followed outside prescriptions for industrialization, but according to many people, including the man cited above, his emphasis on urban over rural development changed the nation's work ethic. With his "make-work" program, agricultural workers left estates and worked on government road works, a pattern that persists to this day.

The post-Williams governments have also done a better job drawing workers to the manufacturing and oil sectors and to state-funded Urban Development Programs (UDPs) than to agriculture. The former types of work not only pay more (sometimes three times as much), but they are more desirable as they require fewer hours in the hot sun. Views of UDP workers are revealing: "People who work for UDP just cut that bit of grass there [weeds on sides of street] and leave at ten in the morning. They do not want to work"; "People do not want to work an eight-hour day milking cows or cultivating crops, seven days a week. They would rather cut grass for an hour."

For Trinidadians I interviewed, laziness is a Trini quality closely associated with self-interestedness. I have heard many Trinidadians speak of laziness in terms of Trinidadian history, specifically that the "gimme gimme" attitude of Trinidadians came from their smooth transition to independence: "Trinidadians have never had anything to fight for, they are lazy . . . Independence did not come with a fight, because we have always been given everything." Another way of expressing the popular self-criticism that Trinis are self-interested is the phrase "crabs in a barrel," a lyric from a calypso by The Mighty Sparrow. As one Trinidadian explained: "See all Trinis want to reap, not sow . . . There's a calypso about crabs in a barrel—everyone climbing on top of each other fighting one another. Rather than taking action . . . They crab in a barrel, all looking after their own interests!"

These popular narratives resemble the discourses of members of the Agricultural Society of Trinidad and Tobago (ASTT) in a meeting held in late 2009, which was dedicated to inspiring farmers to increase their production for local and regional markets. Leading the "rum and roti" politics[3] of ASTT's national forum was president of the organization, Mrs. Dhano Sookoo, who spoke of a need to look at food production as a sacrifice. Countering the "gimme gimme attitude" of post-independence Trinidad and Tobago citizens, Sookoo quoted John F. Kennedy, stating that it is time for farmers to "d[o] something for our country rather than our country doing something for us . . . The concept of begging must be eliminated, especially in the farming sector!"

Denigrating people who see it as "fashionable to leave half the plate," another speaker at the meeting criticized the "mafia food barons" who control both market accessibility and local demand. He countered the ideology of cheap, processed food by stating: "We don't need cheap food! A man says, 'Three dollars for a mango! I cannot pay that! Then he goes down the road and buys a five dollar beer!'" According to this activist's account, the only way to counteract the "few mafia food groups in the [Caribbean] region [who] dominate imports by killing local food production" is to create vertical linkages between farmers and the processing sector. This would not only allow for the production of what Dennis Pantin[4] called "replaceable imports" or manufactures produced with some local ingredients, but would also develop the idea of agriculture as a *business*, a key conceptual argument used in Trinidad to counteract the idea of the small farmer as poor and backward.

> We are not just poor farmers! We are agribusinessmen and women! . . . We want to see our farmers driving Mercedes Benzes too! We want them to live in big houses! We want people to recognize farmers like they do bankers! . . . Young people say there is a stigma with agriculture, but then you see them carrying chemicals on their backs up the hill to grow *other* things [marijuana]. You know, these youth make a lot of money in agriculture! It is not so backward after all!

While on the one hand, this discourse promotes the need to recognize agriculture as an essential aspect of Caribbean autonomy and self-determination, on the other, it points to the idea of "making it" as a Trini by owning things like expensive cars.

The same tension between long-term goals of localization and values for modern commodities is evident in discourses surrounding Christmas celebrations, a time of year in Trinidad when food imports are at their most abundant. Indeed, contradictions of buying "foreign" are no more evident than during the Christmas period, when the norm in Trinidad is to redecorate one's home. Trinidadian poet, Paul Keens-Douglas, expresses this tension in a poem of 1975:

> Lord Miss Julie, dis Christmas go' kill me,
> Ah don't know why dem people feel
> Dey must put up new curtain an' cushion cover
> Every Lord living Christmas . . .
> De woman cleanin' house since
> November
> Like she married to Fadder Christmas. (cited in Miller 1994: 86)

Mass consumption during the Christmas period has continued up to the present, as I have just witnessed (January 2012) when visiting newly redecorated or at least thoroughly scrubbed houses during the annual series of house parties. During Christmas it is obligatory for households to purchase imported fruits like apples and grapes, though official and media portrayals attempt to convince Trinis to go local:

> There was a desire, expressed mainly by elite groups, to localize Christmas and provide Trinidadian equivalents to imports. The media was constantly asserting the value of developing a truly Trinidadian Christmas . . . A newspaper headline advised "Pawpaw, cashew and melon rinds for Christmas fruit cake." But when I asked during the survey if people had tried or considered trying such a strategy, the result was almost entirely negative and the relevant media items were disparaged as typical "chupidness." [stupidity] (Miller 1994: 87)

As Miller has argued, discourses of localizing Christmas in Trinidad, or of returning to an "authentic" Trini Christmas, do not correspond to the way the holiday is understood and practiced by most Trinidadians. Indeed, despite persistent calls by the government and media to "localize it" during the 2011–2012 holiday period, the purchase of imported commodities such as apples and grapes continued unabatedly (interview with grocer, December 29, 2011).

Miller (1994) argues that it is the very involvement of such things that allows Trinis to celebrate Christmas "properly" (105), since such materialities as home furnishings and imported fruit make Christmas in Trinidad truly Trini: "Unlike the journalist who was concerned with the dependence upon imported symbols, for the majority of people these fruits are defined anew by their context, they become essential for this process of nostalgia in which all true Trinidadian Christmases include the symbolic tokens of their past celebration" (Miller 1994: 103).

Trini Identity and KFC

It remains to gather all the threads of the argument thus far and relate it to Kentucky Fried Chicken in Trinidad. I have argued that the history of slavery and the plantation in the Caribbean established a contradictory value system from which stratification or what I call social hierarchies developed, which associate modern and/or imported commodities with higher status. This hierarchy is certainly present in all modern societies. But as George Simmel ([1907]2004) argued for the liberating potentialities of money, the creation of identities through mass consumption may unify as well as divide.

While material culture like cars, houses, and "where you market [shop]" are attached to social hierarchies that have developed since the period of slavery, some forms of mass consumption in Trinidad unify rather than divide, as I have shown with Miller's (1993: 134–66, 1994: 82–134) example of Christmas. As Miller (1994: 82–134) argues, Christmas is a holiday that everyone celebrates in Trinidad, unlike Divali or even Carnival, which only draw in subsections of the population. Like Christmas, Kentucky Fried Chicken (KFC) embodies Trinidadian unity. For younger Trinis at least, KFC is associated with being Trinidadian: "KFC is part of our identity and to some extent it is what makes us Trinidadian"; "KFC caters to all people in Trinidad, from Carnival to Lent, to Christmas, to the simple beach lime, to family gatherings, and from vegetarians to Muslims, to the ordinary meat lover." Yet while Christmas may be associated with what Miller (1994) calls transcendent values, such as family and collective memories of past Christmases, KFC represents transient values, such as the importance of spontaneity and individual satisfaction. I will take each of these in turn.

As mentioned in the statement above, KFC is considered the ideal food for "the simple beach lime." In Trinidad, the concept of a "lime" means an off-the-cuff social gathering that usually involves consuming food and/or alcohol. While "liming" was traditionally a male activity, in recent years and especially among younger Trinis, it is practiced by both men and women. Miller (1994) writes on the subject: "The ideology of a lime is that it should be spontaneous and unlimited. During a lime, there will be many stories about how one only went to post a letter in one's slippers but then met a friend and ended up liming in the small islands for four days" (34). Impulsiveness is an important aspect of other kinds of fast food (or street food) in Trinidad, particularly the morning doubles (fried bread served with chickpea curry, most of the ingredients for which are also imported). As one Trini explained: "Eating doubles is part of being Trini. Being Trini means eating on the go." Another spoke of KFC as "food for relaxation and liming. It is easy, quick, cheap . . . Trinidadians only like convenience." In a similar vein, one of my Trinidadian friends asked me: "Do you know what KFC stands for?" Naturally, I responded, "Kentucky Fried Chicken." He said, "No. It means Cyan [can't] Fuckin Cook!"

The value of spontaneity and convenience relates to the concept of "bacchanal," epitomized by the advertising slogan for KFC during the past several Carnivals: "Food for d' road." As Miller (1994: 246) argues, bacchanal has both a positive meaning and a negative meaning. The first resembles the European sense of bacchanal, connoting sexual and other excitement arising from the shift from everyday time to chaotic time as experienced during Carnival celebrations, which is said to bring us closer to our so-called real or beastly selves (Miller 1994). The negative sense of "bacchanal" reflects a need to reestablish order, to come back to transcendental values like long-term relationships and stable institutions. Much like the contradictions of modernity, both sides of bacchanal reflect opposing moralities of life in Trinidad: "Scandal and confusion have highly ambiguous moral overtones, at once undermining patiently constructed systems of order and stability but also bringing us closer to the true nature of social being" (Miller 1994: 246–47).

While concepts like bacchanal reflect the value of spontaneity and transience, a similar quality attached to KFC is the immediate satisfaction of a craving. The psychological, if not physical, need to eat KFC was expressed by one of my students: "I often come to campus with a packed lunch, and find myself in the KFC line, almost bewitched, ready to spend money on a meal that I did not need but felt I must have." Most often, the issue of individual satisfaction is associated with taste. When addressing the subject, my students always came back to the conception of "Trini flavor." In a morning address to all its "friends" on Facebook, "KFC Trinidad and Tobago" set up a competition for the "best rhyme" about KFC, the prize being an eight-piece chicken meal. One of the runners up (whom Colonel Sanders generously gave a five-piece meal) wrote: "Whenever I eat KFC I'm never disappointed itz d bess in the world possessing 'the real' taste itz not bland or tasteless like Toronto KFC. KFC chicken in Trinidad rules." The sentiment that "best KFC [is] in Trin" is not surprising, since it is widely held that the most profitable KFC in the world is the branch located in Independence Square, Port of Spain.

The transient values of spontaneity and individual satisfaction may be contrasted with transcendental values that Miller (1994: 82–134) describes for Christmas such as the "spirit" of sharing with family (though KFC has tried to use this value in its Christmas advertisements). But each also unifies Trinidadians by associating imported objects with internal values of what it means to be Trini. In this way, both Christmas and KFC represent the modern condition, a contradictory reality comprised of both internal and external forces. Centripetal tendencies meet centrifugal tendencies, and transient values become just as important a factor for identity formation as transcendental factors. Indeed, as Miller (1994) argues: "[T]he same imported commodity forms may, as acts of consumption, become the very instruments by which a culture defines itself as specific" (313).

The expression of Trini identity through modern consumption has roots in slavery, when imported products became a way to evaluate the worth of people and things. Given continuous relations with outside forces, modern commodities are now used to cancel out such cultural divisions. Yet critics of modernity do not acknowledge the positive role that "superficial" values of consumerism have for "rootedness" and identity formation (Miller 1994: 310–13). Thus, while young people in Trinidad may associate KFC with Trini values like the freedom to be spontaneous and to eat "on the go," others may condemn KFC as "lazy food," reflecting a particular nostalgia for a lost past:

> After the 1980s post-oil boom, there were more imports. People buying can of thing and can't even read the label! They don't even know how to prepare the thing! They buy KFC! . . . Trinidadians got lazy. KFC is lazy food . . . Now Trinis don't produce anything . . . Trinidadians have never had anything to fight for. We've had everything just handed to us. Before Trinidad and Tobago was the bread basket of the West Indies.

In Trinidad, reliance on imported food like KFC is condemned in both popular and official discourse. Still, those making the critique may use similar forms of categorization as the people they criticize. When an advocate of the current "localize it" campaign promotes the value of agriculture with the argument that "agrobusinessmen" drive Mercedes Benzes, he is internalizing similar contradictions of modernity. On the one hand, agrobusinessmen and women represent people who will "save" Trinidadian agriculture, returning society to a past when Trinidad was less dependent on food imports. On the other, becoming an agribusinessman is associated with a social hierarchy structured by values for modern imports like expensive cars. In making his case for local production, this activist both contradicts and conforms to the value of modern commodities that have developed in his society over time.

Conclusion

As Miller and Slater (2000) argue for the way Trinidadians use the Internet (and as Miller [1993: 134–66, 1994: 82–134] claims for Christmas), in Trinidad some very foreign things have become associated with nationalistic sentiments. Indeed, this is the very point of many of Miller's writings: "On the whole Trinidadians have found it more difficult to appropriate and render specific the discourse [against] mass consumption than the objects of mass consumption" (Miller 1994: 254). Rather than any collective shift towards a more "authentic" and centrifugal sense of locality, it is the very dichotomy between foreign and local, or centripetal and centrifugal, that is called into question in everyday Trinidadian life.

Given my own concern about food miles and uneven development, the realization that a large section of the Trini population did not consider "local" food in the same way was anything but easy to accept. Indeed, my own perspective is more aligned with the food activists and policymakers I have been discussing than with the young people in Trinidad who associate "locality with Trini flavor," regardless of the oriins of products. Yet this kind of discrepancy is necessary for the project of writing about others. For a reflexive discipline like anthropology, understanding others and understanding ourselves are two sides of the same coin.

But if we are to have political voices as well as academic voices, we must go further. Lest those who study culture rally in demonstrations with blank banners (Ardener [1989]2006: 25–26, 44), it is essential to align cultural accounts with wider structural factors like political economy (and ecology). An inordinate emphasis on political economy leads to an account of modern cultures as "alienated," but the opposite tendency risks a return to a romanticized relativism, where ethnographic details prevent one from giving due attention to structural factors like inequalities: "Just as an earlier political economy imperialistically ignored the lifeworld, it is also possible for an imperialistic culturalism to ignore systems, arguing that actors' cultural interpretations 'go all the way down'" (Sayer 2001: 693). Combining "system" and "lifeworld" (Sayer 2001) may lead to holistic solutions for Trinidad's overdependence on food imports. Indeed, such a perspective may prove more useful than surface-level changes, like the recent campaign to make KFC seem more "authentic" by offering locally made cassava fries.[5]

Peasant Resistance to Hybrid Seed in Haiti: The Implications of Agro-industrial Inputs through Humanitarian Aid on Food Security, Food Sovereignty, and Cultural Identity

John Mazzeo and Barrett P. Brenton

Anthropology, Identity, and Global Food Production Technologies

The distribution of genetically modified and hybrid seed by multinational corporations into societies that are dependent on local seed sources for food production raises questions about how this form of globalization impacts food sovereignty, food security, and cultural identity. International aid organizations responding to food security emergencies provide a mechanism by which improved seeds[1] are introduced to farmers under the rubric of agricultural development projects or humanitarian assistance. Local populations have resisted this form of agricultural production technology based on the premise that it can irreversibly damage local food production systems. This chapter explores the case of Haiti, where hybrid vegetable and maize seeds were donated by the Monsanto Corporation after the 2010 earthquake as part of an agricultural development project aimed at peasant farmers.[2] This explores how agricultural inputs are also central to identity because of its influence on the means of production, food choice, and consumption. The potential impacts of improved seed in rural Haiti can influence the connection between the peasantry and agriculture. The chapter examines attitudes held by the Haitian peasantry regarding agricultural innovations and the ways the introduction of improved seed could influence agricultural production. The factors explored in the latter part of the section emphasize the authors' experiences with livelihood systems, agriculture, and food security.

The hybrid seed project encountered resistance from an organization representing the interests of peasant farmers called MPP (*Mouvman Peyizan Papay* or the Peasant Movement of Papay). The movement's leaders were critical of Monsanto and the aid organizations involved—USAID (U.S. Agency for International Development) was the largest distributor of hybrid seed—for not considering the consequences of bypassing a traditional seed-supply chain, which includes local varieties adapted to diverse agroecological zones. MPP leaders claimed that the replacement of local varieties with hybrid forms would reduce biodiversity, disrupt local food production systems, and reduce food security. The conflict between Monsanto, USAID, and MPP, and its supporters characterizes a wider, global debate surrounding improved seed technology that has become highly polarized (Stone 2010).

Peasant farmers' resistance to the introduction of improved seed offers a case study to understand the connections between food, food production, and identity. Anthropologists highlight the critical role that food production activities have on shaping cultural identity (Messer 1984). More recently, there is the recognition that transformations in agricultural technology hold the potential not only to reshape the environment, but also to impact those cultures and populations who adapt these technologies (Stone 2010). The globalization of agricultural technologies has the potential to transform the cultural identity of peasant societies in places like Haiti and the Caribbean where peasants identify as autonomous cultivators with minimal dependence on foreign inputs (Smith 2001).

One of the central arguments against improved seed made by the MPP is that it threatens food sovereignty. A protest slogan used by this group, "*Semans Peyizan = Souvrennte alimantè*," translates as "Peasant (or local) Seeds = Food Sovereignty." Our working definition of food sovereignty encompasses the fundamental right to choose what foods are produced and consumed along with supporting structures that guarantee those rights. Food sovereignty, in the case of Haiti, rests on peasant production. The concept of food security, more commonly used by development organizations, refers to the population's ability to access sufficient safe and nutritious food that meets its dietary needs and food preferences (FAO 1996). The difference between these two is that food security approaches are concerned with the availability of sufficient quantities of food, regardless of origin, while food sovereignty focuses on the ability of domestic production, and especially the contributions of small scale producers, to meet national demand (Via Campesina 2011). Food sovereignty is also more significant to sociopolitical movements like MPP and its international ally Via Campesina, while this concept has less sway at the household level than does the promise of food security. Peasants are more concerned about their ability to access sufficient quantities of food than with the source of the food they consume. This is not to say that the two concepts are unrelated in Haiti, because improving food sovereignty would likely involve increases in peasant agricultural production, creating greater economic and food security.

Our analysis is influenced by the broader conceptual framework of "Ecohealth," or the ability to decrease health disparities and improve health conditions through mechanisms that promote sustainable ecosystems while navigating the political, economic, and sociocultural systems that maintain them (Singer 2011). For farming communities, this approach is inextricably linked to agrobiodiversity and the ways that local agricultural systems can be sustained within appropriate agroecological zones. An important goal of these approaches is advocating for community-based food systems that increase food security and sustain local livelihoods. The success of this system therefore relies on the expression of a cultural identity that can integrate food sovereignty.

In tandem with the Ecohealth model, we have proposed the concept of Dietary Biodiversity to embrace a larger paradigm of food-based rights or food justice (Brenton and Mazzeo 2009). A working definition of Dietary Biodiversity incorporates access to and consumption of a wide spectrum of food products originating from within traditional local and/or regional food environments or food systems. From this position, we argue that to obtain long-term sustainable development in rural Haiti, close attention must be paid to the maintenance and promotion of local seed varieties and traditional farming systems.

Today, many discussions of agricultural development, food insecurity, and food sovereignty end in a debate over the use of biotechnology in food crop production (Brenton 2007a, 2007b). Developing countries' resistance to adopting GMOs (genetically modified organisms) or GM (genetically modified) foods has understandably polarized the dialogue about strategies for confronting current and future food insecurity and directions for sustainable long-term development.

There are strong anti-GM positions around the globe, but these positions are not taken seriously. However, across the world people are ambivalent, cautious, or unknowledgeable about the issue. Developing nations' concerns are often dismissed as unscientific, based on the limited knowledge of decision makers, and/or under the influence of developed nations (the European Union in particular) or environmental activist groups (e.g., Friends of the Earth, Greenpeace) who have clear anti-GM agenda. The strong and often terse paternalistic tone used toward the developing world that resists GM agricultural technology rings of an unsettling neocolonial enterprise for many people in formerly colonized nations.

Similar to the reaction against hybrid seeds from Haitians, the rejection of GM food aid by the Zambian government during a food crisis between 2002 and 2003 led to a politically and economically charged debate about the potential impact GM foods could have on both people and the environment (Brenton 2011). How GMOs affect the Ecohealth and Dietary Biodiversity of recipient nations through direct food aid or agro-industrial inputs is a deep concern to small farmers worldwide. We need to better understand controversial plans for development alongside those interventions that pay attention to the shifting nature of coping mechanisms and resilience at household and community levels.

A complex interface of political, economic, social, cultural, and scientific factors contributes to views and cultural values held about GM foods. For example, since the pro-biotech Gates and Rockefeller Foundations partnered to promote AGRA (Alliance for a Green Revolution in Africa), with former UN Secretary Kofi Annan as its chief executive officer, their agenda for using biotechnology in agricultural development has drawn a great deal of controversy. Annan has suggested that the alliance will not incorporate GM food crops in their programs and will first work with traditional seeds.

Ironically, when considering the use of genetically modified and hybrid crops as a sustainable option for reducing food insecurity some seem to have forgotten the lessons of failed top-down approaches from the first round of the Green Revolution (Lansing 1991; Richards 1985; Scott 1985). Basic improvements in traditional soil and water management and equitable access to arable land will be more beneficial in the long term than any "quick fix" pest resistance or vitamin enhancement from GM food crops. At the same time, there is a need to target support that can provide both affordable and nutritionally diverse food crops toward the livelihoods of smallholder farmers. This emphasis will also aid in reducing micronutrient malnutrition and the lessening of nutrition-disease synergisms and vulnerability to food insecurity. Food security is as much a matter of food production as it is one of inequitable systems of distribution and access to markets.

In 2009, a United Nations synthesis report titled "Agriculture at a Crossroads" was prepared by IAASTD, the International Assessment of Agricultural Knowledge, Science, and Technology for Development (McIntyre et al. 2009). A five-year project involving hundreds of experts from around the world, it was the most extensively peer-reviewed and researched synthesis to date on the future of agriculture and technology; however, developed nations such as the United States did not approve of the report's conclusions. A most telling but controversial component of the report was its statement on GMOs:

> The controversy over modern biotechnology outside of containment [biosafety concerns] includes technical, social, legal, cultural, and economic arguments. The three most discussed issues on biotechnology in the IAASTD concerned: Lingering doubts about the adequacy of efficacy and safety testing, or regulatory frameworks for testing GMOs . . . Suitability of GMOs for addressing the needs of most farmers while not harming others . . . Ability of modern biotechnology to make significant contributions to the resilience of small and subsistence agricultural systems. (McIntyre et al. 2009: 40)

Independently cultivating land to earn cash and provisioning food to the household is a strong part of the cultural identity of the Haitian peasantry. This self-sufficient identity emerged alongside the end of French colonialism in Haiti in 1804; during this time, the plantation system was destroyed and land was redistributed to individual cultivators. The cultural connections between enslaved populations and agriculture are clear during the moments preceding independence:

> For the slaves of Saint-Domingue, the ideological significance of those provision grounds may have been as important as their intrinsic economic worth. In a system

that denied them the most fundamental rights, the cultivation of their grounds remained one of their few prerogatives. In a society in which they themselves were treated as property, the products from these grounds were foremost among the few things that they might control . . . That the Haitian peasant has used every means to cling to a bit of family land and the laborer's right to the product of the labor on such land were the terms under which freedom was first formulated in the history of the nation. (Trouillot 1990: 39–40)

Thus, the introduction of agro-industrial inputs in the context of rural Haiti could reshape the cultural, social, and economic identities of the peasantry. The contemporary peasant movement in Haiti is conscious of the potential impacts that a dependency on foreign agricultural inputs, including hybrid seeds, can have on local production systems. This awareness is articulated by peasant groups and translated into agricultural projects that stress a preference for using Creole or local seeds and strengthening local food systems to protect food and livelihood security.

Overall, this case reflects an emerging area for the study of food and identity that explores how agricultural inputs (agro-industrial vs. local varieties) are also central to identity in that it has real impacts on the means of production, food choice, and consumption. Resistance to agro-industrial inputs stems from the value of local varieties and perceived threats (political, cultural, social, and economic) from the non-local. The historical context of a population's experience with the introduction of new technologies and their level of acceptance ultimately raises a series of fundamental questions that need further investigation, including:

1. What role does the growing power of global agro-industry have in reshaping local forms of production and consumption in market areas that have been difficult to penetrate, such as in the developing world?
2. What is the cost and degree of access to agricultural inputs—including seed (GM/proprietary), but also fertilizers, water/irrigation systems, agricultural production techniques, knowledge, and education through extension work?
3. What is the value of these untapped markets in the continuing growth of agro-industry and the use of humanitarian aid or development aid as a mechanism for accessing these populations as potential consumers?
4. What is the impact of these interventions in terms of sustainability, food security, food sovereignty, and poverty, but also their influence on cultural identities and practices?
5. What are the potential gains and losses of introducing GMO or other agro-industrial products?
6. How do we reconsider the value of local foods/seed for sustainable production in light of the costs associated with agro-industry?
7. What is the value of local foods/seed in terms of national cultural identity/autonomy, food sovereignty, food rights, and food justice?

Haiti, Agricultural Development, and the Monsanto Controversy

Global attention to Haiti and the challenges surrounding reconstruction after the earthquake has involved renewed commitments by international development organizations to restore Haiti's ailing agricultural sector as part of a broader strategy to enhance national food production and to reduce rural poverty. Food assistance programs, such as large-scale food distributions, are reserved for emergencies but are unpopular with international donors as a model for sustainable development because they do not improve food security, and the resale of food aid undercuts local producers in the marketplace (Woodson 1997). A significant program to rebuild Haiti's agricultural sector after the earthquake is USAID's WINNER (Watershed Initiative for National Natural Environmental Resources) program, "a 5-year $126 million dollar project to build Haiti's agricultural infrastructure, capacity and productivity in a sustainable way" (USAID 2010b). One of the objectives of the project is to distribute improved maize and vegetable seed (i.e., cabbage, carrot, eggplant, melon, onion, tomato, and spinach) to farmers for the purposes of boosting crop production.[3] Non-genetically modified (non-GM), hybrid seed were donated by Monsanto. The donation was valued at four million U.S. dollars.[4]

The distribution of improved seed was met with strong resistance from farmers who viewed these seeds as a potential threat. The MPP, representing the interests of farmers near the city of Hinche, organized a march of 10,000 farmers that threatened to burn 60,000 sacks—475 tons—of "improved" seed donated by Monsanto (Bell 2010b). The reaction against Monsanto generated international support for MPP and several U.S.-based organizations that rallied to MPP's aid with parallel events (Bell 2010a). MPP differs from other peasant groups through its strong involvement with international advocacy groups such as Via Campesina, CLOC (*Coordinadora Latino Americana de las Organizaciones del Campo*), and COMPA (Convergence of the Popular Movement of the Americas). Additionally, the leader of MPP, Chavannes Jean-Baptiste, received the Goldman Environmental Prize for his grassroots environmental work. The demonstrations in Haiti constitute a carefully coordinated and calculated protest against the introduction of Monsanto's seed using arguments that reflect MPP's connection to international environmental movements. In an open email to the international community, Jean-Baptiste characterized the Monsanto donation as "a very strong attack on agriculture, on farmers, on biodiversity, on Creole seeds . . . and on what is left of our environment in Haiti" (MPP 2010, group e-mail, May 14, 2010). Furthermore, the logic behind MPP's resistance uses arguments that stress the deep connections between protecting the economic interests of the peasantry and preserving the cultural practices and values of the peasantry. According to Jean-Baptiste:

> We need to establish seed banks and have silos where we can store our Creole seeds. Local, organic seeds are part of our base of food sovereignty. We have a danger today

from countries in the Americas, especially the U.S., Brazil, and Argentina where Monsanto has already developed big farms to produce genetically modified seeds. If they start sending these seeds into Haiti, that is the death of peasants, who since independence more than 200 years ago have protected their seeds. (Bell 2010c)

Peasant Resistance and Agricultural Innovation

The introduction of improved seed is part of a strategy to strengthen Haiti's food security that recognizes the potential for biotechnology to reverse the diminishing returns peasant farmers are seeing from their agriculture investments. The vast majority of the food produced in Haiti is grown by independent peasant farmers on small, intensively cultivated parcels of land using basic technologies and a wealth of specialized indigenous knowledge sets and skills. However, Haitian peasantry, agriculture, and food security is in crisis because declining productivity since the 1950s has made provisioning sufficient quantities of food to feed the nation (SACAD and FAMV 1994) increasingly difficult. Parallel to the decline in national food production, the population of Haiti increasingly depends on cheaper, imported food. The shift away from domestically produced food and toward imported food is fueled by the inability of the Haitian peasantry to compete against multinational food corporations in the marketplace. At the same time, dependency on imported food has made consumers vulnerable to sharp fluctuations in global food commodity prices as seen in the global food crisis that emerged in 2008 (Mazzeo 2009). The unfavorable relationship between production and consumption for the peasantry contributes to rural poverty and the exodus of rural populations in search of improved livelihood to urban areas in Haiti and to other locations internationally. Technologies that increase productivity without raising the monetary costs of production could provide a much needed advantage to growers. Nevertheless, other costs must be considered.

The strong resistance to the introduction of improved seed for staple food crops suggests that the Haitian peasantry perceived that this new technology would disrupt the local agricultural systems that are foundational to their livelihoods, food security, food sovereignty, and cultural identity. Despite the clamor over Monsanto's donation of hybrid seeds, improved seed technology is not new in Haiti. Since 1988, the ORE (Organization for the Rehabilitation of the Environment), a nonprofit nongovernmental organization (NGO) operating in the south of Haiti, has offered improved seeds to farmers on credit as an incentive for soil conservation work (ORE 2011). However, efforts to introduce improved seed over the past twenty years have yielded little impact, and the use of this technology remains low. A recent study by CRS (Catholic Relief Services) of an area in southern Haiti where improved seed technology was introduced shows that although improved seed was available for purchase, only 12 percent of households planted non-local varieties of seed. This statistic includes improved seed and seed that is the result of crossbreeding local and improved varieties (Walters and Brick 2010). Similar findings by a USAID seed sector study found only 14 percent of farmers had used new or non-local varieties of seed in the past five years (USAID 2010b). In the case of Monsanto's seed, the main objections voiced by MPP regard the need to purchase hybrid seeds annually, the unsustainable cost of fertilizer and pesticides, and the potential loss of local plant varieties. Given the precarious state of agriculture, the high stakes for failure, and the tensions between peasants and outside development experts, the reaction by the peasantry to the introduction of Monsanto's improved seeds should come as no surprise.

Resistance to agricultural technologies introduced by outside agents has a long history in Haiti. The peasantry has been subject to numerous top-down projects designed to transform their agricultural practices through the adoption of new technologies. Efforts to increase the productivity of the peasantry began shortly after Haiti's independence in 1804 with the introduction of the plow under King Henri Christophe as part of a failed plan to reinstate plantation agriculture (Lundahl 1983). In retrospect, the failure of the plow can be attributed to practical constraints such as the small size of land holdings, the cultivation of land on steep slopes, and the lack of draft animals. Peasants' resistance may have been related to the cultural significance of collective work and the loss of this valuable form of socialization (Leyburn 1941). This and subsequent attempts at transforming peasant production both during and after the U.S. occupation of Haiti from 1915 to 1934 were resisted because the interventions either did not make economic sense in the short term or ran against the cultural values or core social institutions of the peasantry (Erasmus 1952). Agricultural projects under the Duvaliers (1957–1986) were managed by politically motivated community councils, were tied to expectations of political patronage, and designed to benefit the rural elite and exclude the peasant majority (Smucker 1982). Since the 1990s, scores of rural development projects aiming to introduce new technologies or techniques have not survived beyond the pilot phase and few have had any impact on influencing peasant agricultural practices (Buss 2008; Smith 2001).

It is incorrect to characterize the peasantry as uninterested in innovation; rather, the social context in which technologies are introduced makes a significant difference in how peasants perceive and respond to ideas. The peasant group (*gwoupman peyizan*) is a grassroots organization based on local cultural values of democratic representation whose leaders consist of farmers from a single locality (*abitasyon*) and whose purpose is advocating for the social, economic, and political interests of its members (Smith 2001). These groups originated out of the democratic social movements in rural Haiti during the late 1970s and have had great success in designing and implementing projects around agricultural innovation, including initiatives such as reforestation, land management, agricultural extension, labor sharing, credit, crop processing, and marketing (Locher, Smucker, and Woodson 1983; Maguire 1979; Woodson 1987). MPP, established in 1973, has been closely involved in promoting agricultural innovation within its peasant base. The movement, which includes

39 smaller peasant groups and a total membership of 50,000, has implemented projects that address reforestation, soil management, and irrigation (MPP 2010). Compared to top-down or outsider initiatives, the success of MPP and other peasant groups in promoting change can be attributed to the high levels of trust held for them, their deep cultural knowledge of the conditions surrounding local agricultural production, and the complete control members have over projects (Maguire 1984; Smucker and Noriac 1996; Smucker and Thomson 1999). In the case of USAID and Monsanto's donated seed, improving dialogue with MPP probably would have not immediately changed attitudes toward improved seed, but at the very least it would have provided an opportunity to discuss opportunities for addressing growing constraints faced by farmers in the area.

The Impact of Improved Seed on Agricultural Production and Food Security

The Haitian peasantry's decision on adopting new agricultural technology ultimately rests on the technology's economic, ecological, and cultural suitability. Assessing the potential impact that improved seed has on agricultural sustainability requires moving beyond a polarized rhetoric toward a critical examination of local food production systems and consumption practices.

Seed Access and Availability

Seed shortages and nonproductive crop varieties are not significant barriers to production, while other factors, including access to arable land, soil erosion, unfavorable market position, unpredictable rainfall, and labor bottlenecks, pose far greater challenges. Haiti does not have a formal seed sector; the majority of seed is obtained from grain vendors and is therefore subject to the same price fluctuations that food commodities experience. According to CRS, about 75 percent of all seed is sourced from the market (Walters and Brick 2010). Households unable to save enough seed to plant out of their own stores are obliged to purchase seed in the market when the crop is the most expensive. There is no distinction made by consumers between grain used as food and grain used for seed. Households will also make no distinction between grain stored for food or seed and will sort grain and select the largest, most uniform, unbroken and unwrinkled grains to use as seed. These grains are kept separate from food grains in anticipation of planting but are also consumed as food when necessary. Most farmers actually prefer to source seed in the market rather than used saved seed from their harvest since some seed, such as beans, have a short shelf life before they will no longer germinate. The vast majority of peasants do not use improved seed unless they are donated by NGOs. According to CRS, farmers did not express an interest in improved seed nor did they believe that improved seed offered any advantages over local seed (Walters and Brick 2010).

In terms of availability, both of the seed sector surveys found that seed is widely available and the vast majority of growers can meet most of their seed requirements. Farmers preferred seed from their area since these varieties are adapted to local soil and climatic conditions (Walters and Brick 2010). According to CRS, 73 percent of households reported being able to locate seed in the market and grain vendors report adequate supplies of seed (Walters and Brick 2010). Only 4 percent of households in the USAID study reported that seed availability caused a reduction in the amount of land cultivated (USAID 2010b). If seed is not available in the nearby marketplace, farmers will visit markets in neighboring areas with similar ecological conditions to find appropriate seeds (Walters and Brick 2010). In summary, seed distribution projects would not significantly improve availability or drastically change how peasants acquire seed. Additionally, greater use of hybrid seed could result in a larger proportion of grain in the marketplace that is second-generation (F2) seed. Neither vendors nor buyers would be able to distinguish F2 grain and farmers would be at greater risk for selecting less productive F2 grains for seed.[5] Thus, the long-term impact would be the contamination of the peasant's main source of seed, leaving few options other than certified seed vendors.

Access to seed, as measured by the ability of farmers to acquire what seed they need, is another issue altogether and poses a real barrier to production because of the high cost of food grains. Most seed is purchased from the marketplace and the cost of seed as a proportion of a household's income poses the greater challenge to farmers than availability. Additionally, since most households have little cash on hand, grain purchases are made on credit through personal relationships with specific vendors (*pratik*) (Mintz 1961b). The USAID study estimates that the cost of seed, on average US$60 to $70 per household per season, represents 20 percent of an annual income of US$600 to $700 (USAID 2010b).[6] This proportion does not account for interest accrued on loans if seeds are purchased using credit. Loans made by local money-lenders often have interest rates of 100 percent or more per month. The introduction of improved seed through specialized seed vendors at a subsidized rate, as proposed by USAID, may offer farmers a less expensive source of seed in the beginning, but as subsidies are gradually reduced, it is possible that the cost of improved seed could exceed the cost of seed obtained from food grain (USAID 2010b). Additionally, if peasants come to rely on improved seed for a greater proportion of their planting needs then increases in seed cost could lead to higher financial stress.

Impacts on Production Systems

Another issue when adopting improved seed is the unpredictability those new crop varieties will have on existing configurations of land, labor, and capital. Farming systems vary significantly across Haiti's diverse agroecological zones, leading to regional differences in production, harvest, and marketing strategies.[7] Several of these differences include the type of species grown, intercropping patterns, crop rotation systems, timing of cultivation across two growing seasons, and decisions on which crops to market, when to market, and what proportion should be sold (Baro 2002). Without careful consideration of these regional differences, the investment by peasants into growing improved varieties may lead to poor decisions. Individual farmers make decisions based on a deep knowledge of local crop varieties. Improved seeds, distributed with little if any information about the growing conditions, input needs, or performance of these varieties, could negate the influence of this hard-earned and long-practiced expertise (USAID 2010b). New varieties could have different growing seasons; different water, nutrient, and sunlight needs; or may be more sensitive to weeds and other crops. It is both difficult and costly to change the natural cycle of farming (Lundahl 1984). In a system where peasants base planting decisions on resource constraints over opportunities, the risks posed by unanticipated outcomes may result in losses rather than gains.

The second barrier in adopting improved seed is the indivisibility of this agricultural innovation from other sorts of inputs and technologies. Peasants will need to provide all of the inputs necessary for the successful cultivation of improved seed (Lundahl 1983). Innovations are capital-consuming and require investments in various types of capital of a certain minimum size (Lundahl 1984). Depending on the needs of a new variety, the real price of using improved seed may also include special commercial fertilizers and specific irrigation schemes. Applications of fertilizer and water will probably not increase yields for local varieties. Local seed has not been selected to take advantage of additional nutrients and water, but rather to do as well as possible in the absence of these. Additionally, some farmers do not see the lasting benefits of fertilizer. According to one study, "Farmers say if land is already fertile it does not need chemicals, and if it is not, chemicals will simply wash away" (Jaffee 1990: 136). CRS found that only 33 percent of farmers used fertilizer, and when it was used, it was not applied generally but only on higher value crops such as beans or vegetables (Walters and Brick 2010). For improved varieties to catch on, they must produce a surplus beyond what is required to carry out current production. Innovations need to take place at a pace fast enough to compensate for diminishing returns to labor and for the effects of land erosion (Lundahl 1984).

Furthermore, most peasants cultivate multiple parcels of land in a variety of tenure arrangements. A combination of rural population pressure, a shrinking arable land base, and large landholders in some parts of Haiti leaves a large number of peasants landless and completely dependent on short-term tenure arrangements (Murray 1977). It may not make sense for peasants to invest in the physical landscape of their garden (irrigation canals or terracing) at their own expense if the land they occupy is leased, sharecropped, squatted on, or shared between kin (Woodson 1990). There is also the possibility that if an improved variety proves to be highly successful, peasants could be pressured to move off the land by landowners who impose higher rent or take on cultivation themselves.

Household Food Security

Peasant households obtain most of their food from their own gardens and the local marketplace. However, peasant livelihoods are not subsistence oriented. Livelihoods are market-driven and the amount of crops the peasants retain for personal consumption are related to the price of food in the marketplace: "Haitian peasant households neither produce all they consume nor consume all they produce" (Woodson 1997: 117). The decisions about what to produce and the proportions of crops that are sold and consumed demand balancing income with expenditure. A common strategy is to grow beans and peas for market and use the cash to pay off debts, while growing a crop such as maize for subsistence because it has a low market price and does not compete well with imports (Walters and Brick 2010). The last point in this case study examines the impact that improved seed can have on the costs of production.

One of the risks a farmer assumes by adopting improved seed and the additional inputs required is that the heightened cost of production makes their food most costly. A substantial proportion of staple foods is imported from the U.S. and costs less than Haitian varieties. The market for rice, for example, is dominated by U.S. imports because the cost of U.S. rice is less than half that of locally grown rice.[8] The decision to purchase imported rice is purely financial and not a matter of preference, since most vendors and buyers in the marketplace agree that Haitian rice tastes better and provides more energy than U.S. rice. Food aid presents another source of competition for farmers because much of the food aid finds its way back into the marketplace, where it is sold at unbeatably low prices (Woodson 1997). With these market pressures working against the peasant farmers' interests, it is risky to increase the cost of production without the guarantee of substantial, long-term increases at harvest.

Following the 2010 earthquake, Haiti experienced high and widespread food insecurity. One of the patterns observed in household consumption was the shift toward less expensive foods. Despite the need to increase food production, households were also forced to reduce land under cultivation due to the relatively high cost of inputs including land, labor, and seeds. Farmers chose to cultivate crops with shorter growing seasons, such as sweet potato and short season corn, to fulfill immediate demands (Walters and Brick 2010). These adaptations suggest that to sustain production of improved varieties, farmers need strategies to keep costs of production low and flexibility to make quick decisions about choosing what varieties to plant based on the market conditions at present.

The matter of food preferences is another consideration that must be addressed. Income from market sales is a critical part of household food security and it is critical that improved varieties appeal to consumers. There has been no market research into how the organoleptic qualities of improved varieties, such as taste, texture, color, or cooking time, might influence decisions by consumers. As mentioned with rice, local varieties of some crops including vegetables and beans are preferred to imports because they offer superior taste and greater strength or vigor to consumers. In discussions with consumers, the positive taste and health benefits of local varieties are based on cultural beliefs about Haitian soil and cultivation techniques. Similarly, these types of arguments are also made about meat, especially in regards to local chicken as compared to live chickens brought over from the Dominican Republic. Without evidence that improved varieties are as desirable as local varieties to consumers, moving forward with this technology would not make sense to market-oriented peasants.

An additional concern is the potential loss of dietary biodiversity due to the infiltration of genetic material from improved varieties. The way farming is conducted in Haiti makes preventing the interbreeding of local and improved varieties impossible. The introduction of new genetic material will have a permanent impact on the availability of local varieties that are adapted to the different growing conditions across Haiti. The loss of local varieties can be compared to the eradication of the Haitian pig and its replacement with U.S. commercial pigs as part of PEPPADEP (Program for the Eradication of Porcine Swine Fever and Development of Pig Raising) in 1982. The Haitian pig played several important roles such as helping prepare soil for tilling, consuming organic matter harmful to crops, providing fertilizer, and eliminating human waste, and their symbolic use as part of religious sacrifice. These pigs were disease resistant, required little water, and consumed most anything. Most important was the use of the Haitian pig as a means for accumulating and saving wealth (Abbott 1988). Of an estimated 1.2 million pigs, 380,000 were killed and some owners were given only US$30–$40 in compensation as compared to their US$150–$250 value at market (Diederich 1985). Following the elimination campaign, commercial swine from the United States were introduced, but these pigs failed to thrive because they required special diets and housing, and overall were not well suited to the environment. The decimation of the Haitian pig was a devastating blow to household wealth. Like the Haitian pig, local seeds are well adapted to the environment and can survive under stressful ecological conditions. The introduction of improved varieties could also lead to the permanent loss or contamination of local varieties. The implications of this loss need to be considered from a food security perspective.

Separate seed sector assessments conducted by CRS and USAID after the decision to distribute Monsanto's hybrid seed provided similar recommendations on the use of improved seed in Haiti under the current emergency conditions. Three conclusions made by CRS highlight the problems of distributing improved seed in the current context and without having first invested into significant testing of new varieties. The report states:

- "Direct seed distribution should not take place given that seed is available in the local market and farmers' negative perception of external seed. This emergency is not the appropriate time to try and introduce improved varieties on anything more than a small scale for farmer evaluation" (Walters and Brick 2010: 22).
- "Efforts to improve seed quality should be undertaken through long-term investments into seed development, production, and extension systems with farmers remaining as managers of their own seed" (Walters and Brick 2010: 22).
- "If donated seed is made available, it should be made available through seed fairs or voucher systems and sold by existing seed vendors allowing farmers a choice" (Walters and Brick 2010: 22).

Several of the conclusions reached by the USAID research team suggest a similar approach to the use of improved seed:

- "Any seeds made available to farmers through aid interventions have to be shown to a) be adapted to local conditions, b) fit well with farmers' preferences, and c) be of a quality "at least as good" as what farmers normally use . . . One should *never introduce varieties in an emergency context which have not been tested in the given agroecological site and under farmers' management conditions*" (USAID 2010b: 93, emphasis in original).
- "Novel improved varieties should generally not be introduced to a broad population in the context of an emergency distribution. Rather, new varieties should be tested and promoted within the framework of a longer-term development program where technical advice and clear monitoring can be ensured" (USAID 2010b: 93).
- "If new varieties are to be distributed in a humanitarian response, better practices should be respected: a) farmers should have a choice between using the new variety or using an established one; b) small quantities should be sown; c) follow-up in the field should be scheduled—during the season and post-harvest" (USAID 2010b: 93).

The findings of both studies contradict the early decision by USAID to distribute improved seed to farmers as part of an earthquake response strategy. The reports do not support immediate seed distributions as an emergency agricultural response in Haiti. They also caution against the rapid introduction of improved varieties without considering the long-term sustainability of these inputs and their impact on local food production systems. Both reports highlight that chronic problems inherent in the seed sector predating the earthquake, and that challenges to seed access are the outcome of financial rather than market constraints. Finally, the reports do not preclude the use of improved seed and instead suggest that this type of technology may still prove to be of value to peasant farmers under the right conditions.

Conclusions

Resistance to modified seeds is not limited to MPP and its members; other peasant groups in Haiti embrace this perspective as well. The following ethnographic example is based on the work of a local organization called MODIEB (*Movement Development Integral du Borgne* [Movement for Integrated Development in Borgne]), a group with strong ties to the peasant group representing the area, KGPB (*Kotdefè Gwoupman Peyizan Borgne*). The mountains in Borgne, on the northern coast of Haiti, have become increasingly bare as trees are cut for charcoal production and lumber. According to a MODIEB member, the inspiration for their tree project came from "[l]ooking up at the mountains. We don't see any trees. Every year there are fewer trees. This project is to bring back the trees."

MODIEB's tree nursery contained 13,000 seedlings, including mahogany, papaya, orange, mango, coconut, breadfruit, and "Murray" trees—a fast and straight growing tree ideal for making wood planks that was introduced through a project in the 1970s involving an anthropologist, Gerry Murray.[9] The seedling project received no external assistance, funding, or inputs, and depended on volunteer labor, donated land, locally acquired seed and construction materials, and cash for purchasing local seed from a nearby seed vendor. MODIEB stressed that all seeds were local varieties. They explained that local seeds can grow better in local conditions and that farmers know how to grow these varieties. The decision to use local seeds was related to suitability not cost, since non-local varieties of seed are sold in nearby Cap Haitian at lower prices and with greater availability than local seed. Seeds from local trees were also collected in season and germinated in empty plastic Culligan drinking water bags recovered from the streets by school children. The groups' organizers emphasize that this project focused on providing food and helping households to build their wealth using natural resources.

Seedlings were grown under a canopy of dried palm branches that were gradually thinned out to allow more sunlight as the seedlings grew. Distribution and planting was done on June 24, the feast day of St. John the Baptist. The group's leaders explained that this saint corresponds with a Vodou spirit named Ti Jean Danto, a playful spirit who has a reputation for climbing coconut trees. It is believed that trees planted that day will bear fruit all year, or at least more frequently than other trees, and therefore vendors in the marketplace sell coconut saplings on this day only. For some households receiving the trees, the seedlings will serve as a natal tree for newborns. This ceremony involves the planting of a tree, usually a fruit-bearing tree, along with the infant's placenta in his or her home yard or the yard of a close family member. It is important that the natal tree is cared for since its fruits will be used to feed to the child and to provide cash for the child's needs. The emphasis on local varieties reflects the beliefs that not only are these varieties better suited to the environment, but that they also hold a cultural, spiritual significance.

The distribution of trees was preceded by a community meeting during which two MODIEB members trained farmers to oversee distribution and instructed them to follow up with recipients. These education sessions engaged the community in a discussion about the purpose of reforestation in combating environmental degradation and protecting household livelihoods. They talked about each of the saplings and their use—food, lumber sale, construction—and then demonstrated how to plant and care for the saplings. On the distribution day, representatives from surrounding communities arrived at sunrise with a group of twenty growers to collect saplings. The tree nursery had a long line of people carrying all sorts of receptacles full of neatly packed seedlings on their heads or loaded onto the backs of donkeys. In total, 11,730 saplings were distributed—9,000 mahogany and the remainder a variety of fruit bearing trees. Trees were planted in the yards and gardens of household compounds in order to stabilize the soil against erosion and to provide shade. MODIEB envisions two crops of saplings a year, a seed bank that stores local seed for farmers, and several new nurseries constructed in different localities to meet specific demands and growing conditions. The model of a seed bank for local seed best meets the needs among farmers for ecologically suitable and culturally valued crops. This model stands in contrast to the improved seed varieties offered by USAID and Monsanto that are imported and require additional inputs.

Promoting local agrobiodiversity is potentially an effective and sustainable alternative to the introduction of hybrid and GM crops. The world development community has been slow to realize its failure to invest in basic agricultural strategies such as water and soil management, renewable sources of fertilizer, and agrobiodiversity over the past twenty years, while investing heavily in other income generating agendas (e.g., dams). This has, in part, contributed to many failures in food production and food security.

There is a real need for food and agriculture researchers and advocates to centralize the development of applied research models (e.g., Ecohealth) that have dietary biodiversity and agrobiodiversity at their core and are guided by the overlapping of themes of human foodways, nutrition, health, and agriculture. A strong argument can be made for a diversity-based approach to food security by creating strategies for combating the rapidly emerging nutrition transition, the impact of noncommunicable chronic diseases, and the influence of multinational food and agricultural corporations on local markets (Johns and Eyzaguirre 2007). The negative impact of dietary transitions could be countered by incorporating household livelihood models that seek to enhance nutrition and subsequent health outcomes through promoting dietary biodiversity via locally improved agricultural practices while also promoting local marketing opportunities and other poverty reduction strategies.

In conclusion, this case study about the resistance by peasant farmers to the introduction of improved seed offers a perspective from which to understand the connections between food production, food security, food sovereignty, and cultural identity. The cultural identity of the Haitian peasantry is closely tied to values of independence and autonomy of production, food security, and independence from foreign inputs. Furthermore, the acceptance of hybrid seed by the peasantry is hampered by a history of exploitation by the state and the absence of tangible and lasting development by NGOs acting on the behalf of the state (Trouillot 1990). The case study also contributes to the anthropology of food and identity by demonstrating the significance of agricultural activities in peasant societies on how cultural identities are shaped and how new technologies have the potential to reshape the environment and negatively impact those populations who adapt these technologies. Finally, it brings attention to the need for greater ethical responsibility by international aid organizations when working with donors from the private sector to safeguard vulnerable populations against potential harm from solutions intended to reduce poverty and food insecurity.

Notes

Introduction: Understanding Caribbean Identity through Food

The idea for this volume came out of a panel that I organized with Jena Barchas-Lichtenstein for the 107th Annual Meeting of the American Anthropological Association, San Francisco, CA, November 19–23, 2008. I am grateful to Jena and to our discussant Robin Derby for their support in getting this off the ground. I owe a tremendous debt to Richard Wilk, and to Akhil Gupta and Sidney Mintz for their comments on this introduction and the volume as a whole. I am also grateful to Mara Buchbinder, Hadi N. Deeb, and Grete Viddal for their comments on earlier drafts of the introduction. Carole Browner, Jason Throop, and Linda Garro have all been great supporters of my work, and I thank them for it. All errors are my own.

1. Geographically, the Caribbean basin includes all the islands (Anguilla, Antigua and Barbuda, Aruba, Bahamas, Barbados, British West Indies, Virgin Islands, Cayman Islands, Cuba, Curacao, Dominica, Dominican Republic, Grenada, Guadeloupe, Haiti, Jamaica, Martinique, Montserrat, Puerto Rico, St. Kitts and Nevis, St. Lucia, St. Vincent and the Grenadines, St. Maarten, Trinidad and Tobago, and Turks and Caicos), Central America, Mexico, Columbia, Venezuela, Guyana, Suriname, and the United States. Many North American scholars focus only on the English speaking part—but this omits Cuba, the Dominican Republic, Haiti and Puerto Rico, which make up four times the population of the English speaking Caribbean.

2. Arguments have been made for dividing the Caribbean based on the country by which they were colonized. For example, Cesar Ayala (1999) asserts that the Spanish Caribbean shares a certain historical continuity that makes it appropriate to study them as a unified whole. Classification along colonization lines allows for some assumptions about intertwined history, migration between the islands, and shared aspects of economy, culture, and society. However, the largest and most populated parts of the Caribbean today were colonized by different countries, thus this type of distinction cannot provide a full picture of Caribbean life.

3. In addition to these massive migrations, there have long been intra-Caribbean migration patterns. The Haitian Revolution (1791–1803) caused hundreds of thousands of Haitians to flee Saint Domingue for other Caribbean islands.

4. For a thorough discussion of the relevance of syncretism as a theoretical approach to the Caribbean today see Apter 2004.

5. However, as Robin Moore points out, even the later opinions of Ortiz are "replete with troublesome ideological implications" about Afro-Cuban expressiveness—Ortiz works to develop an unproblematized national identity. (Moore 1997: 34, cited in Ryer 2006).

6. In Ortiz's earlier work he espoused a theory of racialized evolutionism that looked disparagingly on Caribbean people of African descent.

7. Edward Said's work *Orientalism* (1978) was highly influential in understanding the ways in which identity can be used and abused by group members and outsiders. For Said, Orientalism was a term used to encompass the ways in which Western societies had dominated Asian societies not only in terms of political and economic imperialism but in an identity-based manner as well. According to Said, European self-identity is often based on a contrastive understanding of self and the other. In this case the notion of the other was based on stereotypes of Asian individuals and groups, particularly the notions that people of the Orient were docile, unchanging, and "traditional."

8. The welfare state followed the idea that the reinvestment of profits into the economy would increase demand for goods and services, yielding greater profits that are then reinvested into the economy. Due to economic factors outside of the region, the welfare state did best in the Caribbean in the 1960s; primary and secondary education was expanded, levels of literacy were impressive, and Caribbean states invested the income derived from favorable international circumstances to improve the standard of living for and Caribbean citizens. However, as the global economic climate shifted, Caribbean nations began to shrink the role of the state by giving priority to sustaining current expenditures and cutting capital expenditures instead. As a result, maintenance has been neglected, supplies to deliver government services have been insufficient and the quality of services and infrastructure has eroded (Dominguez 2003).

9. CARICOM members include: Antigua and Barbuda, the Bahamas, Barbados, Belize, Dominica, Grenada, Guyana, Haiti, Jamaica, Montserrat, St. Kitts and Nevis, Saint Lucia, St. Vincent and the Grenadines, Suriname, and Trinidad and Tobago.

10. This body of work articulates with the literature on the loss of state sovereignty to international power structures (Agamben 1998; Escobar 1995; Gupta 1998: 60; Harvey 1989: 161; Trouillot 2001).

Chapter 2: Transformations in Body and Cuisine in Rural Yucatán, Mexico

I would like to thank, above all, the people of Juubche for sharing their lives with me. I am grateful to Judith Farquhar, Suzanne Gaskins, John Lucy, and Joseph Masco for their invaluable insight over the years. I also thank Robin Derby for her comments on some of these materials, and Justin Nevin for his support and editorial advice. Portions of this material were presented at the 107th Annual Meeting of the American Anthropological Association, San Francisco, CA, November 19–23, 2008. The research on which the chapter is based was conducted between 2005 and 2009, with the generous support of the University of Chicago's Center for Latin American Studies, the Whatcom Museum Society, and the Fulbright-Hays Doctoral Dissertation Research Abroad Fellowship. I received additional support from the Doolittle-Harrison Fellowship, the Marion R. & Adolph J. Lichtstern Fund Travel, and Mark Hanna Watkins Post-Field Fellowship. I use pseudonyms for the names of the town and all informants. Unless otherwise noted, all translations are mine. The orthography used here is explained in Blair and Vermont-Salas (1965).

1. As I discuss later in this chapter, some girls and young women worked as domestic servants in nearby cities during the twentieth century. During the middle of that century, many men left home for months at a time to extract chicle in the forests of neighboring Quintana Roo.

2. See Kintz (1990) and Re Cruz (1996) for more detailed ethnographic accounts of the decline of agriculture and the development of tourism.

3. In 2009, I estimated that the average two-person household spent about $80MXN (during the period of my research, this ranged from about US$6.00 to $7.50) on daily food expenditures. This does not include alcohol.

4. Few women drink outside of special occasions such as weddings and birthday parties; when they do so, it is rarely to excess.

5. A woman will stop her work as a x-k'uus if she converts to a non-Catholic faith. That said, older *hermanas* (non-Catholic Christian women) still hold culinary authority within their families when it comes to well-established foods.

6. However, like Castellanos (2003), I found that *gustos* (personal tastes) are encouraged in children, who often voice them from a very young age. Some mothers consider preparing separate meals for their children *tráabajo* (literally, "work," but its usage here is perhaps best translated to the colloquial English "a pain"). Nonetheless, most do accommodate their children by preparing an additional food for them to eat. This pickiness tends to subside with adulthood or, at least, it has in previous generations.

7. The distribution of well-established foods at special occasions is important work, usually left to an older woman, the hostess in consultation with an older woman, or the x-k'uus, if one has been procured. These women carefully dole out pieces of meat and broth to men, women, and children.

8. The rare exceptions are when one receives food from individuals not trusted, for example, those suspected of witchcraft or those with whom one has serious and unresolved conflict.

9. I hypothesize that tortas have not been adopted as special occasion food in Juubche for several reasons. First, a loaf of Bimbo bread is more cost efficient

than, say, ten individually purchased rolls for tortas (not to mention that such rolls are often unavailable in the village). Second, as mentioned, rolls for tortas are larger than Bimbo bread slices, thus requiring more filling. Lastly, there is far less standardization in tortas, and I suspect that this keeps residents, who are accustomed to fixed recipes, from preparing them.

10.   There are now several large, well-stocked stores in Juubche, but prices are typically higher than at stores in Valladolid. Even when required ingredients are available locally, they may be financially out of reach.

11.   *Ts'uulo'ob* is the plural form of *ts'uul.* The *–o'ob* suffix denotes the plural for nouns in Yucatec Maya.

12.   I use quotation marks where "hot" and "cold" refer to classification within the hot-cold system.

13.   However, the distinction between thermal and metaphorical may obscure other qualities that determine any given food's categorization: taste, odor, the feeling it provokes in the mouth or gut, or its growing environment.

14.   Kray describes the óol as "the emotional 'heart'" (1997: 93), while Hanks describes it as "roughly the will and the capacity for involvement and sensate experience" (1990: 87).

15.   That is not to say that this cosmology was ever seamless or that these women began the process of dismantling or reshaping it. The decline of agriculture and the development of regional tourism have certainly been significant forces. However, while these forces may have shaped change in local kitchens, they did not originate there.

16.   For older residents, *Mexico* refers to Mexico City and not to the larger nation. Thus, they do not include themselves in the category of Mexicanos.

17.   I categorize these distinctions as racial rather than ethnic because they are reliant, for my older informants, upon notions of inherent biological difference. In contrast, many younger women understand dietary differences via the more flexible categories of ethnicity.

Chapter 4: Versions of Dominican *Mangú*

Thanks to my fieldwork collaborators for permission to use their words and for sharing their foods, time and lives during fieldwork, to Hanna Garth, Brian Stross, and Dina Rivera, and anonymous reviewers for helpful suggestions to improve this chapter.

1.   The precise meaning is not of immediate concern to us for the purposes of this discussion, more important to me are narratives that offer versions of its origins by those that still prepare and eat mangú. One of my fieldwork collaborator's partners told of having overheard as a child growing up in Santiago that mangú was used to designate mashed plantains during the U.S. invasion of the DR in

1916, when an American soldier tasted the dish and said "man, good," which may have been converted to Spanish as mangú. I was told by participants in this study and by other Dominicans (residents in Puerto Rico) that the word mangú can also be used as a verb, and other types of mangús exist, such as *mangú de yautia*, de *yuca*, de *ñame* (or of any other root). Mangú of squash, a delicacy in the DR, is called *mazamorra*. In this discussion I will refer to mangú only to indicate the dish made of green plantains.

2. The fact that this staple is shared among other Caribbean cuisines does not diminish its importance as a marker of difference; it occupies a culturally privileged place among Dominicans, since mangú, unlike mofongo or fufu, remained in the DR as everyday fare for the majority of the population until today.

3. In spite of the transformations and, I suggest, precisely because of them, there are consistent efforts to preserve the diverse tastes of each cook's regional foods, and the culturally specific trajectories in each family's culinary lore. Seasoning styles, which are seen as part of a family's culinary history, are part of changing cooking practices for migrants that could eventually transform into more generalized regional "American" cuisine. In fact, as Garcia Cuevas (1999) has suggested, Dominican foods in New York City (as well as in Puerto Rico and Miami) taste more "authentic" now than in the DR, where economic fluctuations make it difficult for local people to access plantains now (Red 2007). The preservation of specific flavors may be due in part to how at the moment of migration each cook "froze" in memory a version of the meal and its preparation. It makes sense to safeguard a degree of familiarity since food flavors are not only physical but emotional responses embedded in certain landscapes and relations to past neighborhoods and past senses of self, which helps to achieve some measure of grounding and continuity. Nonetheless, over time changes in these practices are perhaps inevitable, as are strategies employed to preserve memories of the familiar in the foreign context.

4. A Dominican *sancocho* is usually defined as a thick stew composed of meats, roots, vegetables, and spices, prepared as a festive food usually on Sundays, and for family gatherings and celebrations (Rosario 2001). Sancocho, as a mélange of diverse foodstuffs, was probably one of the first vernacular meals prepared by the already Afro-diasporic inhabitants of Hispaniola. As a boiled, overcooked, and soupy preparation, it implicates "the cooked" in opposition to the "raw" polarity (as identified by Lévi-Strauss). Yet this slow simmering of flavors, fruit of many lands, domestications, journeys, and struggles, may also be considered an extreme case of cultural over-ripeness, a "house of difference" as Audre Lorde might say. Its ingredients implicate Spanish, African, Taino (and even Middle Eastern) admixtures (Veloz Maggiolo and Tolentino Dipp 2007). As was probably the case for *la bandera* and mangú, sancocho only became a "Dominican" staple when it was claimed and appropriated as a national dish between the end of the nineteenth century and in representing a coherent national project.

It is common knowledge in the DR and abroad that both mangú and sancocho are usually prepared by women. In the case of sancocho, it is a complex staple mostly associated with darker women's labor, and in some regions with the *marchantas* (merchants, Haitian or Haitian-Dominican women) street food vendors. Men are usually the consumers of such labor and flavors in their homespaces or as clients in public. As a cooked gathering of difference (that preserves certain darkness) this dish may point more clearly to the *indio oscuro* (dark indian) *mulataje* of Dominicans, opposing, in a way, a contrasting meaning to the more demarcated boundaries of la bandera as criollo, mestizo, and indigenous heritage. Such analysis of sancocho's indexical relations to Dominican racial and gendered predicaments is very productive, and will be further explored in relation to mangú.

5. *Cocolo* is also used in some cases to identify descendants from a group of African American runaway slaves granted asylum, particularly in the province of Samaná, by the Haitian state during the 1822 occupation of the full island (Nina 2004).

Chapter 5: The Intersections of "Guyanese Food" and Constructions of Gender, Race, and Nationhood

1. I use the term "racial" as opposed to "ethnic" because Guyanese create group taxonomies based principally on phenotype and use "race" rather than "ethnicity" to refer to groups.

2. The majority of the country's population migrated, forcibly or voluntarily, to provide the labor force for sugar plantations (Mintz 1989).

3. *Kweh-kweh* is an African Guyanese pre-wedding ritual that takes place on the eve of a wedding ceremony. Through music, dance, storytelling, and other performances, Guyanese praise, chide, and instruct the bride and groom about sex, gendered responsibilities, and other matters pertaining to marriage.

4. I use the term African Guyanese to be politically correct and inclusive, as I discovered during the course of research that some Guyanese find the prefix "Afro" objectionable, as it principally references a hairstyle and not people of African descent.

5. There are more Guyanese residing abroad than in the country itself.

6. Historically, Portuguese were not regarded as part of the white race; this was, and still is, reflected by Guyana's Bureau of Statistics (2002). "Douglas" historically referred to individuals of mixed African and East Indian heritage, but nowadays it describes anyone visibly biracial or multiracial, particularly when the mixing involves the black race.

7. Disgruntled Guyanese, who were forced to use rice flour and other inventions, and to drastically modify their ways of life, frequently and openly poked fun of the PNC and WRSM with statements such as, "WRSM: Women Rule Stupid Men."

8. The category "ground provisions" in the Guyanese context is similar to "viandas" in Cuba, and includes various types of tubers and plantains.

9. The backdam is the region on the outskirts of plantations, which many slaves cultivated during and after slavery. The produce from backdam supplemented daily diet as well as income. Guyanese continue to actively farm backdams even today. In the Spanish Caribbean backdams are referred to as "conucos."

10. Guyanese use the terms "beans" and "peas" interchangeably.

11. It is important to note that although Guyanese classify squashes, eggplant, tomatoes, and other foods as vegetables for cooking purposes they are botanically fruits.

12. African Guyanese also regard cookup rice, a rice-and-peas dish, as African in origin; however, unlike fufu and metemgee, this claim is sometimes disputed, as cookup rice is regarded as a Guyanese construct (Richards-Greaves 2012).

13. Fufu, including variants such as foofoo, foufou, foutou, and fufuo, is consumed in Central and West Africa and in the Caribbean. Foods similar to fufu, but with different names, are also consumed in other regions of Africa.

14. Amongst West Africans, and Africans at large, the left hand is regarded as the hand used to wipe oneself after using the toilet. Thus, using the left hand to eat fufu, or similar communal meals, is regarded as unsanitary.

15. The term "foreigner" is a term used to refer to individuals who are not Guyanese nationals, as well as Guyanese who reside outside of Guyana.

16. The concept of "po-man" food is not unique to Guyana but can be observed in other parts of the world, such as the southern United States, where African American "soul food" include animal extremities and organ meats, which were generally shunned by the mainstream society. For the people who consume them, however, these foods embody the essence of their experiences and their identity (Witt 1999; Henderson 2007).

Chapter 6: Cooking Cubanidad

I would like to acknowledge my friends in Santiago who have made this project by sharing their stories with me. In particular, I thank the Casa del Caribe, María Isabel Berbes Ribeaux, and Julio Corbea Caldazo for supporting my work. I am grateful to Mara Buchbinder, Hadi Deeb, Sara Garth, Sarah Grant, Ariana Hernandez-Reguant, and Kristina Wirtz for comments on earlier drafts. Carole Browner, Linda Garro, Jason Throop, Akhil Gupta, Robin Derby, and Christel Miller have been invaluable to this study. All errors are my own.

1. Cuban *ajiaco* is similar to a dish called *sancocho* in Columbia, Ecuador, Peru, Costa Rica, Panama, and the Dominican Republic. In Cuba, the word sancocho refers to household food scraps used as pig feed.

2. This is in contrast to the concept of the "melting pot" which Ortiz aligns with the notion of acculturation; things lose their original form and meld into something new.

3. The ideology of *mestizaje*, racial and cultural mixing, has a long history in Latin America and the Caribbean. It is loaded with colonial and contemporary aspirations to improve Caribbean society by whitening the population, with the goal to diminish Africanness in terms of phenotype as well as cultural expression, "hailing the virtues of miscegenation" (Yelvington 2001: 242). For Ariana Hernandez-Reguant, in colonial Cuba, mestizaje became "the foundational myth of the nation," which was "embraced as a positive and profound ongoing process" (2005: 287).

4. Ortiz focused on the colonial and early republican eras of nation building in Cuba when influences were largely from Europe, Africa, and the indigenous population, but his work stopped short at the American and Caribbean influences that began later in the republican era and continue today under Cuban socialism.

5. According to Cuban anthropologist Jiménez Solar, "after the Italians, today's generation of Cubans we can safely say is the second most addicted to pizza, spaghetti, and macaroni" (2008: 140).

6. As of March 2011.

7. People with certain chronic conditions, such as high cholesterol, diabetes, cancer, renal problems, etc., are able to purchase additional or different food items for their special diet restrictions.

8. This is the equivalent of about one dollar. Most Cubans make between the equivalent of twelve and twenty dollars a month.

9. Spanish colonists also introduced many European domesticated animals to the Caribbean, including cattle, sheep, pigs, goats, chickens, geese, and doves.

10. A few years after the Haitian Revolution began, between July and August 1803, Santiago went from a population of 7,779 to 29,767 as tens of thousands of Franco-Haitians migrated to the region (Orozco Melgar 1994: 51).

11. Cuba has a dual currency economy. The hard currency is known as the convertible peso or CUC. It is a close equivalent to the Euro, and the national peso is worth about four cents. Cubans get paid in the national peso.

12. *Arroz con pollo* (rice with chicken) is a popular dish historically consumed on Sundays throughout Cuba (cf. Soler Puig 1975).

13. Humoral theory as an understanding the body was made up of certain fluids, or humors. If these humors were imbalanced or came into contact with substances that were incompatible, illnesses could arise.

14. In 2008 the United States sold a record amount of food products to Cuba, totaling over $710 million. These rates declined in 2009 and 2010. Still, at the time of this research, Cuba imported over 60 percent of the food consumed domestically, and the United States was the number one country from which Cuba imported. The U.S.-Cuba agreement for food sales does not allow Cuba to make food purchases on credit; as Cuba faces financial problems the state is forced to turn to other countries such as Brazil, France, Canada, Russia, and

China, which allow them to use credit. Among other things the U.S. exports corn, wheat, chicken, soybeans, and powdered milk to Cuba (Frank 2010).

15. According to the USDA, Cuba is the largest importer of wheat and wheat products in the Caribbean, taking virtually all of its one million tons per year of imports from the European Union.

16. After Venezuelan president Hugo Chavez was elected in 1999 a significant trade relationship was established between Venezuela and Cuba. This relationship includes development aid, exchange of human resources for energy resources, joint business ventures, and increased importation/exportation.

Chapter 7: From Colonial Dependency to Finger-lickin' Values

1. Like Miller (e.g., 1994), I focus on Trinidad and not Tobago, the smaller island of the two-island state, since the latter has a very different history and thus a very different relation to "outside" influences.

2. Tunapuna is a town running along the East-West corridor of Trinidad, located in the northwest area of the island.

3. Roti is an Indian dish made with curried meat (or vegetables), served with or wrapped in flat bread made from stoneground meal flour. The phrase "rum and roti politics" expresses many farmers' frustration with the ASTT, the oldest of several farmers' organizations in Trinidad. According to some farmers I have interviewed from an opposing organization, the Food Crop Farmers' Association of Trinidad and Tobago, the politics of ASTT, which attempts to co-opt farmers with "rum and roti," overshadows the needs of ordinary farmers. The difference between these organizations is fascinating, and I am hoping to write of these politics in another paper.

4. Professor Dennis Pantin was an economist who established the Sustainable Economic Development Unit at the University of the West Indies. I am grateful I had the opportunity to discuss some of these issues with him before his death after a long illness in July 2010.

5. Vasant Barath, current (2012) Minister of Agriculture in Trinidad and Tobago, recently adopted this strategy. It has been argued however that there is still not enough local production for the project to work in an egalitarian manner. As Emeritus professor of plant pathology, John Spence, said:

> KFC has cassava fries. Now there are no cassava fries in the supermarket. They were expensive, a treat, but now they are not even available! . . . We do not produce enough to have a local market. They need to set up the conditions for a local market before they can start promoting "local". It is not just about people, tastes . . . They are doing this in a hodge-podge fashion . . . We have flat lands with clay soils that work well for sugar cane and citrus. Three-month crops do not grow in these soils

without a drainage system. But they have not yet put this system in place and they want to go local!

Chapter 8: Peasant Resistance to Hybrid Seed in Haiti

1. "Improved seed" refers to seed that has been specifically modified, either through selective breeding (hybrid seed) or genetic alternation (genetically modified seed), to offer an advantage in its cultivation.
2. The term peasant is not a pejorative expression in Haiti. The peasantry refers to a class of the rural population whose livelihood is based on a market-oriented agricultural system and relies on a variety of tenure arrangements to provide access to land (Mintz 1989).
3. The Earth Institute at Columbia University and USAID were selected to distribute the donated seed to Haitian farmers. Both organizations had a relationship with Monsanto to promote agricultural research and technology before the proposed Haiti seed project. Of the total seed that was to be distributed by USAID, 20 percent was provided by Monsanto and the majority was either sourced locally or imported.
4. The decision by Monsanto not to offer GM seed was made because, "Haiti does not have the legal framework in place to approve or use biotech seeds (Monsanto 2010)." The selection of specific conventionally bred hybrid seeds was made in consultation with Haitian Ministry of Agriculture and intended to be the most acceptable to farmers and growing conditions.
5. Second generation (F2) seed is the product of crossing two first generation (F1) hybrid seeds. Since all of the traits selected for in hybrid seeds are Mendelian, the genotypes of the F2 generation will include hybrid traits (Aa) identical to the F1 parent generation and pure dominant (AA) and recessive (aa) traits that may be undesirable to growers. In contrast, GM (genetically modified) seeds, which are not currently used in Haiti, can be replanted generation after generation without the risks posed by hybrids.
6. Most of Haiti has two growing seasons.
7. Agroecological zones are classified by variables such rainfall, altitude, and geography. For example, zone types include coastal dry, humid mountain, irrigated plain, and dry plateau (Baro 2002).
8. This is based on Mazzeo's fieldwork during June 2010 in Gonaives, the major city in the Department of the Artibonite.
9. For a description of the project, see Murray 1984.

Bibliography

Abarca, M. E. (2006), *Voices in the Kitchen: Views of Food and the World from Working-Class Mexican and Mexican-American Women*. College Station: Texas A&M University Press.

Abbott, E. (1988), *Haiti: The Duvaliers and their Legacy*. New York: Simon & Schuster.

Adair, G. (1986), *Myths and Memories*. London: Fontana Paperbacks.

Agamben, G. (1998), *Homo Sacer: Sovereign Power and Bare Life*. Stanford, CA: Stanford University Press.

Albala, K. (2007), *Beans: A History*. New York: Berg.

Alexander, M. J. (2005), *Pedagogies of Crossing: Meditations on Feminism, Sexual Politics, Memory, and the Sacred*. Durham, NC: Duke University Press.

Allen, J. (2007), "Means of Desire's Production: Male Sex Labor in Cuba." *Identities* 14(1/2): 183–202.

Anderson, B. (1991), *Imagined Communities: Reflections on the Origin and Spread of Nationalism*. London: Verso.

Andújar, C. (2006), *La presencia negra en Santo Domingo: un enfoque etnográfico*. Santo Domingo: Breve Letra Gráfica.

Appadurai, A. (1988), "How to Make a National Cuisine: Cookbooks in Contemporary India." *Comparative Studies in Society and History* 30(1): 3–24.

Appadurai, A. (1996), *Modernity at Large*. Minneapolis: University of Minnesota Press.

Apter, A. (2004), "Herskovits's Heritage: Rethinking Syncretism in the African Diaspora," in A. M. Leopold and J. S. Jensen (eds.), *Syncretism in Religion: A Reader*, 160–84. New York: Routledge.

Ardener, E. ([1989]2006), *The Voice of Prophecy and Other Essays*. Oxford: Berghahn Books.

Ayala, C. J. (1999), *American Sugar Kingdom: The Plantation Economy of the Spanish Caribbean 1898–1934*. Chapel Hill: The University of North Carolina Press.

Baldwin, R. (1946), *The Rupununi Record*. Barbados: The Barbados Advocate Co.

Barcia, M. (2008), *Seeds of Insurrection: Domination and Resistance on Western Cuban Plantations 1808–1848*. Baton Rouge: Louisiana State University Press.

Bardenstein, C. (1999), "Trees, Forests, and the Shaping of Palestinian and Israeli Collective Memory," in M. Bal, J. Crewe, and L. Spitzer (eds.), *Acts of*

Memory: Cultural Recall in the Present, 148–68. Hanover: University Press of New England.

Barnett, C., Cloke, P., Clarke, N., and Malpass, A. (2011), *Globalizing Responsibility: The Political Rationalities of Ethical Consumption*. Oxford: Wiley-Blackwell.

Baro, M. (2002), "Food Insecurity and Livelihood Systems in Northwest Haiti." *Journal of Political Ecology* 9: 1–34.

Barth, F. (1969), "Introduction," in F. Barth (ed.), *Ethnic Groups and Boundaries: The Social Organization of Culture Difference*, 9–38. London: Allen and Unwin.

Barthes, R. (1997), "Toward a Psychosociology of Contemporary Food Consumption," in C. Counihan and P. Van Esterik (eds.), *Food and Culture: A Reader*, 28–35. New York: Routledge.

Bauman, Z. (2001), "Identity in the Globalizing World." *Social Anthropology* 9: 121–29.

Beckford, G. L. (1972), *Persistent Poverty: Underdevelopment in Plantation Economies of the Third World*. New York: Oxford University Press.

Behar, R. (1989), "Sexual Witchcraft, Colonialism, and Women's Powers: Views from the Mexican Inquisition," in A. Lavrin (ed.), *Sexuality and Marriage in Colonial Latin America*, 178–206. Lincoln: University of Nebraska Press.

Belasco, W. (2008), *Food: The Key Concepts*. London: Berg.

Bell, B. (2010a), "Groups around the U.S. Join Haitian Farmers in Protesting 'Donation' of Monsanto Seed." http://www.otherworldsarepossible.org/another-haiti-possible/groups-around-us-join-haitian-farmers-protesting-donation-monsanto-seeds (accessed February 14, 2011).

Bell, B. (2010b), "Haitian Farmers Commit to Burning Monsanto Hybrid Seed." http://www.huffingtonpost.com/beverly-bell/haitian-farmers-commit-to_b_578807.html (accessed February 14, 2011).

Bell, B. (2010c), "Haiti: The Clock is Set at Zero." http://www.otherworldsarepossible.org/another-haiti-possible/haiti-clock-set-zero (accessed February 16, 2011).

Benitez-Rojo, A. (1992), "From Plantation to Plantation," trans. James E. Maraniss, in *The Repeating Island: The Caribbean and the Postmodern Perspective*, 33–72. Durham, NC: Duke University Press.

Benjamin, M., Collins, J., and Scott, M. (1984), *No Free Lunch: Food and Revolution in Cuba Today*. Princeton, NJ: Princeton University Press.

Bentley, A. (1998), "Bread, Meat, and Rice: Exploring Cultural Elements of Food Protests and Riots," in A. Bentley (ed.), *Eating for Victory: Food Rationing and the Politics of Domesticity*, 1–24. Chicago: University of Illinois Press.

Bentley, A. (2001), "Reading Food Riots: Scarcity, Abundance and National Identity," in P. Scholliers (ed.), *Food, Drink and Identity: Cooking, Eating and Drinking in Europe Since the Middle Ages*, 179–93. Oxford: Berg.

Berdahl, D. (2005), "Expressions of Experience and Experiences of Expression: Museum Re-Presentations of GDR History." *Anthropology and Humanism* 30(2): 156–70.

Best, L., and Polanyi-Levitt, K. (2009), *Essays on the Theory of Plantation Economy: A Historical and Institutional Approach to Caribbean Economic Development*. Kingston: The University of the West Indies Press.

Bestor, T. C. (2004), *Tukiji: The First Market at the Center of the World*. Berkeley: University of California Press.

Bhabha, H. K. (1994), *The Location of Culture*. New York: Routledge.

Biehl, J., Good, B., and Kleinman, A. (eds.) (2007), *Subjectivity: Ethnographic Investigations*. Berkeley: University of California Press.

Boellstorff, T. (2007), *A Coincidence of Desires: Anthropology, Queer Studies and Indonesia*. Durham, NC: Duke University Press.

Blair, R., and Vermont-Salas, R. (1965), *Spoken Yucatec Maya I* (MCMCA 67 Series X). Chicago: University of Chicago Library.

Borgstede, G. (2010), "Social Memory and Sacred Sites in the Western Maya Highlands: Examples from Jacaltenango, Guatemala." *Ancient Mesoamerica* 21: 385–92.

Bourdieu, P. ([1979]1984), *Distinction: A Social Critique of the Judgement of Taste*, trans. R. Nice. London: Routledge and Kegan Paul.

Bourdieu, P. (1993), *The Field of Cultural Production: Essays on Art and Literature*. New York: Columbia University Press.

Bourgois, P., and Schonberg, J. (2009), *Righteous Dopefiend*. Berkeley: University of California Press.

Bower, A. (ed.) (2007), *African American Foodways: Explorations of History and Culture*. Urbana: University of Illinois Press.

Brenton, B. P. (2007a), "GMO: Benefit or Boondoggle? Part I." *Anthropology News* 48(3): 53–54.

Brenton, B. P. (2007b), "GMO: Benefit or Boondoggle? Part II." *Anthropology News* 48(4): 57–58.

Brenton, B. P. (2011), "Contested Strategies for Defining and Confronting Food Insecurity and HIV/AIDS in Zambia: Rejection of GM Food Aid during the 2002–2003 Food Crisis," in B. P. Brenton, J. Mazzeo, and A. Rödlach (eds.), *HIV/AIDS and Food Insecurity in Sub-Saharan Africa: Challenges and Solutions*, 187–203. Philadelphia: Wiley-Blackwell.

Brenton, B. P., and Mazzeo, J. (2009), "Challenges to Sustaining Local Dietary Biodiversity: Corporate Export of Unhealthy Diets and the Global Paradox of Hunger and Obesity." Paper presented at the 2009 Joint Annual Meeting of the Agriculture, Food and Human Values Society and the Association for the Study of Food and Society, Penn State University, State College, PA.

Brereton, B. ([1981]2009), *A History of Modern Trinidad, 1783–1962*. Champs Fleurs: Terra Verde Resource Centre.

Brotherton, P. S. (2005), "Macroeconomic Change and the Biopolitics of Health in Cuba's Special Period." *Journal of Latin American Studies* 10(2): 339–69.

Brotherton, P. S. (2008), "'We Have to Think Like Capitalists but Continue Being Socialists': Medicalized Subjectivities, Emergent Capital, and Socialist Entrepreneurs in Post-Soviet Cuba." *American Ethnologist* 35(2): 259–74.

Brown, L. K., and Mussell, K. (1984), "Introduction," in L. K. Brown and K. Mussell (eds.), *Ethnic and Regional Foodways in the United States: The Performance of Group Identity*, 3–18. Knoxville: University of Tennessee Press.

Bruner, E. (2004), *Culture on Tour: Ethnographies of Travel.* Chicago: University of Chicago Press.

Buss, T. F. (2008), *Haiti in the Balance: Why Foreign Aid Has Failed and What We Can Do about It*, with A. Gardner. Washington, D.C.: Brookings Institution Press.

Butt Colson, A., and Morton J. (1982), "Early Missionary Work among the Taruma and Waiwai of Southern Guiana: The Visits of Fr. Cuthbert Cary-Elwes, S.J. in 1919, 1922 & 1923." *Folk* 24: 203–61.

Cabezas, A. L. (2009), *Economies of Desire: Sex and Tourism in Cuba and the Dominican Republic.* Philadelphia: Temple University Press.

Caldwell, M. (2004), *Not by Bread Alone: Social Support in New Russia.* Berkeley: University of California Press.

Caldwell, M. (2006), "Tasting the Worlds of Yesterday and Today: Culinary Tourism and Nostalgia Foods in Post-Soviet Russia," in R. Wilk (ed.), *Fast Food/Slow Food: The Cultural Economy of the Global Food System*, 87–93. Lanham, MD: Altamira Press.

Callahan, R. (2005), *Doubt, Shame, and the Maya Self.* Ph.D. dissertation, Department of Anthropology, University of Pennsylvania.

Carnegie School of Home Economics. (2004), *What's Cooking in Guyana*, 2nd ed. Oxford: Macmillan Publishers.

Carney, J. (2001), *Black Rice: The African Origins of Rice Cultivation in the Americas.* Cambridge, MA: Harvard University Press.

Carney, J., and Rosomoff, R. N. (2009), *In the Shadow of Slavery: Africa's Botanical Legacy in the Atlantic World.* Berkeley: University of California Press.

Carrier, J., and Macleod, D. (2005), "Bursting the Buddle: The Socio-cultural Context of Ecotourism." *Royal Anthropological Institute* 11: 315–34.

Castellanos, M. B. (2003), *Gustos and Genders: Yucatec Maya migration to the Mexican Riviera.* Ph.D. dissertation, Department of Anthropology, University of Michigan.

Chevalier, J. M., and Sánchez Bain, A. (2003), *The Hot and the Cold: Ills of Humans and Maize in Native Mexico.* Toronto: University of Toronto Press.

Colchester, M., Rose, J. L., and James, K. (2002), *Mining and Amerindians in Guyana: Final Report on the APA/NSI Project on "Exploring Indigenous Perspective on Consultation and Engagement within the Mining Sector in Latin America and the Caribbean."* Ottawa: The North-South Institute.

Collins, P. H. (1991), *Black Feminist Thought: Knowledge, Consciousness, and the Politics of Empowerment.* New York: Routledge.

Conselho Indigena de Roraima. (1993), *Raposa Serra do Sol: os Indios no futuro de Roraima. Boa Vista, Roraima.* Brazil: Conselho Indigena de Roraima.

da Costa, E. V. (1994), *Crowns of Glory, Tears of Blood: The Demerara Slave Rebellion of 1823.* New York: Oxford University Press.

Counihan, C.M. (1999), *The Anthropology of Food and Body: Gender, Meaning, and Power.* New York: Routledge.

Counihan, C.M. (2004), *Around the Tuscan Table: Food, Family, and Gender in Twentieth-Century Florence.* New York: Routledge.

Counihan, C., and van Esterik, P. (1997), "Introduction," in C. Counihan and P. van Esterik (eds.), *Food and Culture: A Reader*, 1–16. New York: Routledge.

Crenshaw, K.W. (1991), "Mapping the Margins: Intersectionality, Identity Politics, and Violence Against Women of Color." *Stanford Law Review* 43(6): 1241–90.

Currin, F. (2005), "Transformation of Paradise: Geographical Perspectives on Tourism Development on a Small Caribbean Island (Utilla, Honduras)." Thesis, Louisiana State University.

Daly, V.T. (1974), *The Making of Guyana.* New York: Macmillan.

Dávila, A. (2001), *Latinos, Inc: The Marketing and Making of a People.* Berkeley: University of California Press.

DeFillips, R.A., Maina, S.L., and Crepin, J. (2004), *Medicinal Plants of the Guianas (Guyana, Surinam, and French Guyana).* Washington, DC: Smithsonian Institution.

Deive, C.E. (2007), "The African Inheritance in Dominican Culture," in B. Vega (ed.), *Dominican Cultures: The Making of a Caribbean Society*, trans. C. Ayorinde, 87–130. Princeton, NJ: Markus Wiener Publisher.

de Oliveira, A.E. (1994), "The Evidence for the Nature of the Process of Indigenous Deculturation and Destabilization in the Brazilian Amazon in the Last Three Hundred Years: Preliminary Data," in A. Roosevelt (ed.), *Amazonian Indians from Prehistory to Present*, 95–119. Tucson: The University of Arizona Press.

Derby, L. (1998), "Gringo Chickens with Worms: Food and Nationalism in the Dominican Republic," in G. Joseph, C. LeGrand, and R. Salvatore (eds.), *Close Encounters of Empire: Writing the Cultural History of U.S.-Latin American Relations*, 451–96. Durham, NC: Duke University Press.

DeVault, M. (1997), "Conflict and Deference," in C. Counihan and P. van Esterik (eds.), *Food and Culture: A Reader*, 180–201. New York: Routledge.

Diederich, B. (1985), "Swine Fever Ironies: The Slaughter of the Haitian Black Pig." *Caribbean* 14(1): 16–17, 41.

Dodds, D. (1998), "Lobster in the Rain Forest: The Political Ecology of Miskito Wage Labor and Agricultural Deforestation." *Journal of Political Ecology* 5: 83–108.

Dominguez, J.I. (2003), "Constructing Democratic Governance in Latin America: Taking Stock of the 1990s," in J.I. Dominguez and M. Shifter (eds.), *Constructing*

Democratic Governance in Latin America, 351–83. Baltimore: Johns Hopkins University Press.

Douglas, M. (1971), "Deciphering a Meal," in C. Geertz (ed.), *Myth, Symbol, and Culture*, 61–81. New York: Norton.

Douglas, M., and Isherwood, B.C. (1979), *The World of Goods*. New York: Basic Books.

Elias, M., Rival, L., and McKey, D. (2000), "Perception and Management of Cassava (*Manihot esculenta*, Crantz) Diversity among Makushi Amerindians of Guyana (South America)." *Journal of Ethnobiology* 20(2): 239–65.

Ellis, R. (1983), "The Way to a Man's Heart: Food in the Violent Home," in A. Murcott (ed.), *The Sociology of Food and Eating: Essays on the Sociological Significance of Food*, 164–71. Aldershot: Gower Publishing.

Epele, M.E. (2002), "Gender, Violence and HIV: Women's Survival in the Streets." *Culture, Medicine and Psychiatry* 26(1): 33–54.

Erasmus, J.C. (1952), "Agricultural Changes in Haiti: Patterns of Resistance and Acceptance." *Human Organization* 11(4): 20–26.

Escobar, A. (1995), *Encountering Development: The Making and Unmaking of the Third World*. Princeton, NJ: Princeton University Press.

Escobar, A., and Alvarez, A. (eds.) (1992), *The Making of Social Movements in Latin America: Identity, Strategy, and Democracy*. Boulder, CO: Westview Press.

Evans, C., and Meggers, B.J. (1960), *Archaeological Investigations in British Guiana*. Washington, DC: Government Publishing Office.

FAO (Food and Agriculture Organization (1996), "Rome Declaration on World Food Security and World Food Summit Plan of Action." Rome: World Food Summit, November 13–17.

Ferguson, J. (2006), "Globalizing Africa? Observations from an Inconvenient Continent," in J. Ferguson (ed.), *Global Shadows: Africa in the Neoliberal World Order*, 25–49. Durham, NC: Duke University Press.

Fischler, C. (1988), "Food, Self and Identity." *Social Science Information* 27(2): 275–92.

Forte, J. (1996a), *Thinking about Amerindians*. Georgetown: Janette Forte.

Forte, J. (1996b), *About Guyanese Amerindians*. Georgetown: Janette Forte.

Forte, J. (1996c), *Makusipe Komanto Iseru: Sustaining Makushi Way of Life*. Georgetown: North Rupununi District Development Board.

Foster, G.M. (1994), *Hippocrates' Latin American Legacy: Humoral Medicine in the New World*. Langhorne, PA: Gordon and Breach.

Frank, M. (2010), "Cuban Efforts to Reduce Bulk Food Imports on Track." Thomson Reuters, January 3. http://www.reuters.com/article/2010/01/03/cuba-food- (accessed January 2011).

Frazier, E.F. (1957), *Race and Culture Contacts in the Modern World*. New York: Knopf.

Friedman, J. (1994), *Cultural Identity and Global Process.* London: Sage.

Garcia Cuevas, E. (1999), *Mirada en Tránsito (dominicanos, haitianos y puertorriqueños, y otras situaciones en primera persona).* San Juan-Santo Domingo: Isla Negra Editores.

Garth, H. (2009), "'Things Became Scarce': Food Availability and Accessibility in Santiago de Cuba Then and Now." *NAPA Bulletin* 34: 178–82.

Garth, H. (2010), "Toward Being a Complete Woman: Reflections on Mothering in Santiago de Cuba." *Center for Study of Women Newsletter* (December).

Garth, H. (forthcoming), "Disconnecting the Mind and Essentialized Fare: Identity, Consumption, and Mental Distress in Santiago de Cuba," in N. Burke and R. Fernandez (eds.), *In Sickness and Health: Encountering Wellness in Cuba and the U.S.* Berkeley: University of California Press.

Gaskins, S. (2003), "From Corn to Cash: Change and Continuity Within Maya Families." *Ethos* 31(2): 248–73.

Geertz, C. (1983), *Local Knowledge: Further Essays in Interpretive Anthropology.* New York: Basic Books.

Gibson, K. (2003), *The Cycle of Racial Oppression in Guyana.* Lanham, NY: University Press of America.

Gillian, J. (1963), "Tribes of the Guianas and the Left Amazon Tributaries," in J.H. Steward (ed.), *Handbook of South American Indians, Vol. 3 The Tropical Forest Tribes*, 799–860. New York: Cooper Square Publishers.

Gilroy, P. (1993), *The Black Atlantic: Modernity and Double Consciousness.* New Haven, CT: Harvard University Press.

Gomes, P.I. (1981), "The Social and Cultural Factors Involved in the Production by Small Farmers of Trinidad and Tobago of Tomatoes and Cabbage and Their Marketing." *United Nations Educational, Scientific, and Cultural Organisation* 82(2): 3–17.

Goody, J. (1997), "Industrial Food: Towards the Development of a World Cuisine," in C. Counihan and P. van Esterik (eds.), *Food and Culture: A Reader*, 338–56. New York: Routledge.

Gray, N. (2003), "Unpacking the Baggage of Ecotourism: Nature, Science, and Local Participation." *The Great Lakes Geographer* 9(2): 113–23.

Greene, A. (2002), *Huipiles to Spandex: Styling Modernity and Refashioning Gender in the Global Economy of Yucatan.* Ph.D. dissertation, Department of Anthropology, University of North Carolina, Chapel Hill.

Greene, S., and Emanuel, S. ([2000]2001), *Guyana Our Country Our Home* (Levels 5 and 6). San Fernando, Trinidad: Caribbean Educational Publishers.

Gupta, A. (1998), *Postcolonial Developments: Agriculture in the Making of Modern India.* Durham, NC: Duke University Press.

Guyana Bureau of Statistics (2002), "Chapter 2." http://www.statisticsguyana.gov.gy/census.html#popcenfinal (accessed October 31, 2010).

Haenn, N. (1999), "The Power of Environmental Knowledge: Ethnoecology and Environmental Conflicts in Mexican Conservation." *Human Ecology* 27(3): 477–91.

Hall, M. (2003), "Politics and Place: An Analysis of Power in Tourism Communities," in S. Singh, D.J. Tinothy, and R.K. Dowling (eds.), *Tourism in Destination Communities.* Wallingford: CABI Publishing.

Hall, M., and Mitchell, R. (2002a), "The Changing Nature of the Relationship between Cuisine and Tourism in Australia and New Zealand: From Fusion Cuisine to Food Networks," in A.M. Hjalager and G. Richards (eds.), *Tourism and Gastronomy*, 187–206. London: Routledge.

Hall, M., and Mitchell, R. (2002b), "Tourism as a Force for Gastronomic Globalization and Localization," in A.M. Hjalager and G. Richards (eds.), *Tourism and Gastronomy*, 71–90. London: Routledge.

Hall, R.L. (2007), "Food Crops, Medicinal Plants, and the Atlantic Slave Trade," in A. Murcott (ed.), *The Sociology of Food and Eating: Essays on the Sociological Significance of Food*, 17–44. Aldershot: Gower Publishing.

Hall, S. (1994), "Cultural Identity and Diaspora," in P. Williams and L. Chrisman (eds.), *Colonial Discourse and Post-Colonial Theory: A Reader*, 392–401. New York: Columbia University Press.

Hall, S. (1996), "Introduction: Who Needs 'Identity'?" in S. Hall and P. du Gay (eds.), *Questions of Cultural Identity*, 1–9. London: Sage Publications.

Hall, S., and du Gay, P. (eds.) (1996), *Questions of Cultural Identity.* London: Sage Publications.

Hanks, W.F. (1990), *Referential Practice: Language and Lived Space among the Maya.* Chicago: University of Chicago Press.

Hannerz, U. (1990), "Cosmopolitans and Locals in World Culture." *Theory, Culture and Society* 7: 237–51.

Harvey, D. (1989), *The Condition of Postmodernity.* Oxford: Blackwell.

Harvey, D. (2005), *A Brief History of Neoliberalism.* New York.

Hemming, J. (1994), "Indians, Cattle and Settlers: The Growth of Roraima," in J. Hemming (ed.), *Settlement and Change in Brazilian Roraima*, 39–67. New York: Routledge.

Henderson, L. (2007), "'Ebony Jr!' and 'Soul Food': The Construction of Middle-Class African American Identity through the Use of the Traditional Southern Foodways." *Food in Multi-Ethnic Literatures* (MELUS) 32(4): 81–97.

Henfry, T.B. (2002), *Ethnoecology, Resource Use, Conservation and Development in a Wapishana Community in the South Rupununi, Guyana.* Ph.D. thesis, University of Kent at Canterbury.

Hernandez-Reguant, A. (2005), "Cuba's Alternative Geographies." *Journal of Latin American Anthropology* 10(2): 275–313.

Hernandez-Reguant, A. (2006), "Radio Taino and the Cuban Quest for Identi . . . qué?" in D. Sommer (ed.), *Cultural Agency in the Americas*, 178–202. Durham, NC: Duke University Press.

Hernandez-Reguant, A. (2009a), "Writing the Special Period," in A. Hernandez-Reguant (ed.), *Cuba and the Special Period: Culture and Ideology in the 1990s*, 1–20. New York: Palgrave MacMillan.

Hernandez-Reguant, A. (2009b), "Multicubanidad," in A. Hernandez-Reguant (ed.), *Cuba and the Special Period: Culture and Ideology in the 1990s*, 69–88. New York: Palgrave MacMillan.

Herskovits, M. J. (1941), *The Myth of the Negro Past*. Boston: Beacon Press.

Igoe, J., and Brockington, D. (2007), "Neoliberal Conservation: A Brief Introduction." *Conservation and Society* 5(4): 432–49.

Inglis, D., and Gimlin, D. (eds.) (2009), *The Globalization of Food*. Oxford: Berg.

Jackson, J. V., and Cothran M. E. (2003), "Black versus Black: The Relationships among African, African American, and African Caribbean Persons." *Journal of Black Studies* 33(5): 576–604.

Jacobs, M. D. (2009), *White Mother to a Dark Race*. Lincoln: University of Nebraska Press.

Jaffee, J. M. (1990), "Labor, Land, Livestock, and Markets: Persistence and Accumulation in the Peasant Economy of Haiti." M.A. thesis, Cornell University.

Jimenez Solar, G. (2008), "Sobre las costumbres culinarias cubanas." *Catauro: Revista Cubana De Antropologia* 9: 17.

Johns, T., and Eyzaguirre P. (2007), "Biofortification, Biodiversity and Diet: A Search for Complementary Applications Against Poverty and Malnutrition." *Food Policy* 32: 1–24.

Jones, C. R. (1952), *Report of a Medical Survey of Amerindians in British Guiana, 1949–1951*. Colonial Development and Welfare-Scheme D 36.

Joseph, G. M. (1986), *Rediscovering the Past at Mexico's Periphery: Essays on the History of Modern Yucatan*. Tuscaloosa: University of Alabama Press.

Kahn, M. (1986), *Always Hungry, Never Greedy: Food and the Expression of Gender in a Melanesian Society*. London: Cambridge University Press.

Kalcik, S. (1984), "Ethnic Foodways in America: Symbol and the Performance of Identity," in L. K. Brown and K. Mussell (eds.), *Ethnic and Regional Foodways in the United States: The Performance of Group Identity*. Knoxville: University of Tennessee Press.

Kelley, R.D.G., and Lemelle, S. (eds.) (1984), *Imagining Home: Class, Culture, and Nationalism in the African Diaspora*. London: Verso.

Kintz, E. R. (1990), *Life under the Tropical Canopy: Tradition and Change among the Yucatec Maya*. Fort Worth: Holt, Rinehart, and Winston.

Knight, F. W. (1990), *The Caribbean: The Genesis of a Fragmented Nationalism*, 2nd ed. New York: Oxford University Press.

Kracauer, S. (1995), *The Mass Ornament: Weimar Essay*. Cambridge, MA: Harvard University Press.

Kray, C. A. (1997), *Worship in Body and Spirit: Practice, Self, and Religious Sensibility in Yucatan*. Ph.D. dissertation, Department of Anthropology, University of Pennsylvania.

Kray, C.A. (2005), "The Sense of Tranquility: Bodily Practice and Ethnic Classes in Yucatán." *Ethnology* 44(4): 337–55.

Landa, D. de ([1566]1941), *Landa's relación de las cosas de Yucatan*, trans. A.M. Tozzer. Cambridge, MA: Peabody Museum of American Archeology and Ethnology, Harvard University.

Lansing, S.J. (1991), *Priests and Programmers: Technologies of Power in the Engineered Landscape of Bali*. Princeton, NJ: Princeton University Press.

Larner, W. (2000), "Neo-liberalism: Policy, Ideology, Governmentality." *Studies in Political Economy* 63: 5–25.

Larsen, N. (1990), *Modernism and Hegemony: A Materialist Critique of Aesthetic Agencies*. Minneapolis: University of Minnesota Press.

Lea, D.A.M. (1968), "A Socio-demographic Analysis of St. Ignatius-Kumu, Rupununi District." McGill University Savannah Research Project, Savannah Research Series No. 10.

Lentz, C. (1999), *Changing Food Habits: Case Studies from Africa, South America, and Europe*. New York: Routledge.

Lévi-Strauss, C. (1968), "L'Origine des manières de table," in *Mythologiques IV*. Paris: Seuil.

Leyburn, J.G. (1941), *The Haitian People*. New Haven, CT: Yale University Press.

Lichtenstein, A. (1988), "That Disposition to Theft, with Which They Have Been Branded: Moral Economy, Slave Management, and the Law." *Journal of Social History* 21(3): 413–40.

LiPuma, E., and Koelble, T. (2005), "Cultures of Circulation and the Urban Imaginary: Miami as Example and Exemplar." *Public Culture* 17(1): 1153–79.

Littlefield, D.C. (1991), *Rice and Slaves*. Baton Rouge: Louisiana State University Press.

Locher, U., Smucker, G.R., and Woodson, D.G. (1983), *Comparative Evaluation of Three Haitian Rural Development Projects*. Washington, D.C.: Creative Associates.

Logan, J.R., and Molotch, H.L. (1987), *Urban Fortunes: The Political Economy of Place*. Berkeley: University of California Press.

Lowe-McConnel, R.H. (2000), *Land of Waters: Explorations in the Natural History of Guyana, South America*. Sussex: The Book Guild.

Lowenthal, D. (1972), *West Indian Societies*. London: Oxford University Press.

Lundahl, M. (1983), *Man, Land and Markets*. Guildford: Biddles.

Lundahl, M. (1984), "The Roots of Haitian Underdevelopment," in C.R. Foster and A. Valdman (eds.), *Haiti: Today and Tomorrow: An Interdisciplinary Study*, 181–203. Lanham, MD: University Press of America.

MacCannell, D. (1989), *A New Theory of the Leisure Class*. London: Macmillan Press.

Macdonald, J.S. (1986), *Trinidad and Tobago*. New York: Praeger.

Magdoff, F., and Tokar, B. (2009), "An Overview of the Food and Agriculture Crisis." *Monthly Review* 61(3): 1–16.

Maguire, R. (1979), *Bottom-Up Development in Haiti.* Washington, DC: Inter-American Foundation.

Maguire, R. (1984), "Strategies for Rural Development in Haiti: Formation, Organization, Implementation," in C. R. Foster and A. Valdman (eds.), *Haiti: Today and Tomorrow: An Interdisciplinary Study*, 161–72. Lanham, MD: University Press of America.

Marte, L. (2008), *Migrant Seasonings: Food Practices, Cultutural Memory and Narratives of "Home" among Dominican Immigrants in New York City.* Ph.D. dissertation, University of Texas at Austin.

Mazzeo, J. (2009), "Lavichè: Haiti's Vulnerability to the Global Food Crisis." *Annals of Anthropological Practice* 32: 115–29.

McCall, L. (2009), "The Complexity of Intersectionality," in E. Grabham, D. Cooper, J. Krishnadas, and D. Herman (eds.), *Intersectionality and Beyond: Law, Power, and the Politics of Location.* New York: Routledge.

McDonald, M. (2006), "Learning Island Foodways: Tasting Ethnographic Methods." *Florida Gulf Coast University Anthropological Notebooks* 12(1): 35–48.

McGowan, W. F., Rose, J. G., and David, G. (eds.) (2009), *Themes in African-Guyanese History*, 2nd ed. Hertfordshire, UK: Hansib Publications.

McIntyre, B. D., Herren, H. R., Wakhungu, J., and Watson, R. T. (2009), "Agriculture at a Crossroads." United Nations Synthesis Report prepared by the International Assessment of Agricultural Knowledge, Science and Technology for Development (IAASTD). http://www.agassessment.org/reports/IAASTD/EN/Agriculture%20at%20a%20Crossroads_Synthesis%20Report%20(English).pdf (accessed February 17, 2012).

McMichael, P., and Myhre, D. (1991), "Global Regulation vs. the Nation-State: Agro-Food Systems and the New Politics of Capital." *Capital and Class* 15: 83–105.

Mennell, S. (1996), *All Manners of Food: Eating and Taste in England and France from the Middle Ages to the Present.* Chicago: University of Illinois Press.

Messer, E. (1984), "Anthropological Perspectives on Diet." *Annual Review of Anthropology* 13: 205–49.

Miller, D. (1993), "Christmas and Materialism in Trinidad," in D. Miller (ed.), *Unwrapping Christmas*, 134–66. Oxford: Oxford University Press.

Miller, D. (1994), *Modernity, An Ethnographic Approach: Dualism and Mass Consumption in Trinidad.* Oxford: Berg.

Miller, D. (1995), "Consumption and Commodities." *Annual Review of Anthropology* 24: 141–61.

Miller, D. (2005), "Materiality: An Introduction," in D. Miller (ed.), *Materiality*, 1–50. Durham, NC: Duke University Press.

Miller, D., and Slater, D. (2000), *The Internet: An Ethnographic Approach.* Oxford: Berg.

Milne, S. W., and Ateljevic, I. (2001), "Tourism, Economic Development, and the Global-Local Nexus: Theory Embracing Complexity." *Tourism Geographies* 3(4): 369–93.

Mintz, S.W. (1961a), "The Question of Caribbean Peasantries: A Comment." *Caribbean Studies* 1: 31–34.

Mintz, S.W. (1961b), "Pratik: Haitian personal economic relationships." *Proceedings of the Annual Spring Meetings, American Ethnological Society*: 54–63.

Mintz, S.W. (1971), "The Caribbean as a Sociocultural Area," in M.M. Horowitz (ed.), *Peoples and Cultures of the Caribbean: An Anthropological Reader*, 17–46. Garden City: American Museum of Natural History Press.

Mintz, S.W. (1985a), *Sweetness and Power: The Place of Sugar in Modern History.* New York: Penguin Group.

Mintz, S.W. (1985b), "From Plantations to Peasantries in the Caribbean," in S.W. Mintz and S. Price (eds.), *Caribbean Contours*, 127–53. Baltimore: Johns Hopkins University.

Mintz, S.W. ([1974]1989), *Caribbean Transformations.* New York: Columbia University Press.

Mintz, S.W. (1993), "Goodbye Columbus: Second Thoughts on the Caribbean Region at Mid-Millennium." Walter Rodney Memorial Lecture, Centre for Caribbean Studies, University of Warwick, May.

Mintz, S.W. (1996), *Tasting Food, Tasting Freedom.* Boston: Beacon Press.

Mintz, S.W. (2003), "Remembrance of Repasts: An Anthropology of Food and Memory," David E. Sutton (Review). *American Ethnologist* 30(3): 474–75.

Mintz, S.W., and Du Bois, C.M. (2002), "The Anthropology of Food and Eating." *Annual Reviews of Anthropology* 31: 99–119.

Mintz, S.W., and Price, R. ([1976]1992), *The Birth of African-American Culture: An Anthropological Approach.* Boston: Beacon Press.

Mintz, S.W., and Price, S. (eds.) (1985), *Caribbean Contours.* Baltimore: Johns Hopkins University Press.

Mohanty, C.T. (2003), "Genealogies of Community, Home, and Nation," in *Feminism without Borders: Decolonizing Theory, Practicing Solidarity*, 124–36. Durham, NC: Duke University Press.

Momsen, J.H. (ed.) (1993), *Women and Change in the Caribbean: A Pan-Caribbean Perspective.* Bloomington: Indiana University Press.

Moore, B.L. (2009), "The Social and Economic Subordination of the Guyanese Creoles after Emancipation," in W.F. McGowan, J.G. Rose, and D.A. Granger (eds.), *Themes in African-Guyanese History.* London: Hansib Publications.

Moore, R.D. (1997), *Nationalizing Blackness: Afrocubanismo and Artistic Revolution in Havana, 1920–1940.* Pittsburgh, PA: University of Pittsburgh Press.

Moreno, P. (2005), "Ecotourism Along the Meso-American Caribbean Reef: The Impacts of Foreign Investment." *Human Ecology* 33(2): 217–44.

MPP (Mouvman Peyizan Papay) (2010), MPP History. http://www.mpphaiti.org (accessed February 15, 2011).

Mullings, L. (2002), "The Sojourner Syndrome: Race, Class, and Gender in Health and Illness." *Voices* 6(1): 32–26.

Murcott, A. (1983), *The Sociology of Food and Eating: Essays on the Sociological Significance of Food.* Aldershot: Gower.

Murray, G. F. (1977), "The Evolution of Haitian Peasant Land Tenure: Agrarian Adaptation to Population Growth." Ph.D. dissertation, Columbia University.

Murray, G. F. (1984), "The Wood Tree as a Peasant Cash-Crop: An Anthropological Strategy for the Domestication of Energy," in C. R. Foster and A. Valdman (eds.), *Haiti—Today and Tomorrow: An Interdisciplinary Study*, 141–60. Lanham: University Press of America.

Myers, I. (1993), "The Makushi of the Guiana-Brazilian Frontier in 1944: A Study of Culture Contact." *Antropologica* 80: 3–99.

Naipaul, V. S. (2001), *A Way in the World.* London: Vintage.

Nestle, M. (2002), *Food Politics: How the Food Industry Influences Nutrition and Health.* Berkeley: University of California Press.

New York City Department of City Planning (2000), http://www.nyc.gov/html/dcp/html/census/nny_exec_sum.shtml#sco (accessed September 24, 2011).

Nina, J. B. (2004), *El organ de la cocina dominicana.* Santo Domingo: Mediabyte.

Nina, J. B. (2007), *Folklore Gastronomito Del Sur: Historia y Recetas Típicas de la Región Sur de La Republica Dominicana.* Santo Domingo: Mediabyte.

Olwig, K. F. (1985), *Cultural Adaptation and Resistance on St. John: Three Centuries of Afro-Caribbean Life.* Gainesville: University of Florida Press.

Omi, M., and Winant, H. (1986), *Racial Formation in the United States from the 1960s to the 1980s.* New York: Routledge.

ORE (Organization for the Rehabilitation of the Environment) (2011), "Program History." http://www.oreworld.org (accessed February 11, 2011).

Orozco Melgar, M. E. (1994), "La desruralización de Santiago de Cuba: Génesis de una ciudad moderna (1788–1868)." Doctoral thesis, Departamento de Historia del Arte, Universidad de Oriente.

Ortiz, F. ([1940]1963), "Los factores humanos de la cubanidad." *Revista Bimestre Cubana* 21: 161–86.

Ortiz, F. ([1947]1995), *Cuban Counterpoint of Tobacco and Sugar*, trans. H. De Onís. Durham, NC: Duke University Press.

Ortiz-Cuadra, M. (2006), *Puerto Rico en la Olla, ¿somos aún lo que comimos?* España: Doce Calles.

Ortner, S. B. (1974), "Is Female to Male as Nature is to Culture?" in M. Z. Rosaldo and L. Lamphore (eds.), *Woman, Culture and Society*, 66–88. Stanford, CA: Stanford University Press.

Palacio, J. O. (1995), "Aboriginal Peoples—Their Struggle with Cultural Identity in the Caricom Region." *Bulletin of Eastern Caribbean Affairs* 20(4): 25–40.

Pattullo, P. (1996), *Last Resorts: The Cost of Tourism in the Caribbean.* New York: Monthly Review Press.

Peet, R., and Hartwick, E. (1999), *Theories of Development.* New York: The Guilford Press.

Perez, G. (2004), *The Near Northwest Side Story: Migration, Displacement, and Puerto Rican Families.* Berkeley: University of California Press.

Pérez, L.A., Jr. (2003), *Cuba: Between Reform and Revolution.* Oxford: Oxford University Press.

Pérez Firmat, G. (1987), "From Ajiaco to Tropical Soup: Fernando Ortiz and the Definition of Cuban Culture," in R. Tardanico (ed.), *Dialogues 93.* Miami: University of Florida Press.

Pérez Firmat, G. (1997), "A Willingness of the Heart: Cubanidad, Cubaneo, Cubanía." Cuban Studies Association Occasional Paper Series 2.7. Miami, Florida, October.

Pertierra, A.C. (2008), "En Casa: Women and Households in Post-Soviet Cuba." *Journal of Latin American Studies* 40: 743–67.

Pichardo, J. (2007), "Immigration in the Late 19th Century and Early 20th Century and its Contributions to Dominican Culture," in B. Vega (ed.), *Dominican Cultures: The Making of a Caribbean Society*, trans. C. Ayorinde, 161–208. Princeton, NJ: Markus Wiener Publisher.

Pilcher, J.M. (1998), *¡Que vivan los tamales! Food and the Making of Mexican Identity.* Albuquerque: University of New Mexico Press.

Pilcher, J.M. (2006), "Taco Bell, Maseca, and Slow Food: A Postmodern Apocalypse for Mexico's Peasant Cuisine?" in R. Wilk (ed.), *Fast Food/Slow Food: The Cultural Economy of the Global Food System*, 69–82. Lansing: Altamira Press.

Pollan, M. (2006), *The Omnivore's Dilemma: A Natural History of Four Meals.* New York: Penguin Press.

Pollan, M. (2008), *In Defense of Food: An Eater's Manifesto.* New York: Penguin Press.

Prosterman, L. (1984), "Food and Celebration: A Kosher Caterer as Mediator of Communal Traditions," in L.K. Brown and K. Mussell (eds.), *Ethnic and Regional Foodways in the United States: The Performance of Group Identity*, 127–42. Knoxville: University Tennessee Press.

Rabe, S.G. (2005), *U.S. Intervention in British Guiana: A Cold War Story.* Chapel Hill: The University of North Carolina Press.

Raulin, A. (1990), "Consummation et adaptation urbaine. Des minorites en region parisienne." *Sociétés contemporaines* 4: 19–36.

Ray, K. (2004), *The Migrant Table: Meals and Memories in Bengali-American Households.* Philadelphia: Temple University Press.

Re Cruz, A. (1996), *The Two Milpas of Chan Kom: Scenarios of a Maya Village Life.* Albany: State University of New York Press.

Red Dominicana (2007), "Precios de plátanos." http://www.reddominicana.com/comun/foros/topic.asp?TOPIC_ID=33898 (accessed January 1, 2011).

Redfield, R., and Villa Rojas, A. (1934), *Chan Kom: A Maya Village.* CIW Pub. 448. Washington: Carnegie Institution of Washington.

Renvoize, B.S. (1972), "The Area of Origin of *Manihot esculenta* as a Crop Plant—A Review of the Evidence." *Economic Botany* 26: 352–60.

Ricardo, C.A. (1996), *Povo indegenas no Brazil: 1991–1995.* Sao Paulo: Instituto Socioambiental.

Richards, G. (2002), "Gastronomy: An Essential Ingredient in Tourism Production and Consumption?" in A. Hjalager and G. Richards (eds.), *Tourism and Gastronomy*, 3–20. New York: Routledge.

Richards, P. (1985), *Indigenous Agricultural Revolution: Ecology and Food Production in West Africa.* Boulder, CO: Westview.

Richards-Greaves, G. (2012), "'Cook-up Rice': Constructing Guyanese Identities with Rice and Beans," in R. Wilk and L. Barbosa (eds.), *Rice and Beans: A Unique Dish in a Hundred Places*, 192–225. London: Berg.

Richardson, B. (1992), *The Caribbean in the Wider World, 1492–1992: A Regional Geography.* Cambridge: Cambridge University Press.

Riviere, P. (1963), "An Ethnographic Survey of the Indians on the Divide of the Guianese and Amazon River Systems." Ph.D. thesis, Oxford, University of Oxford.

Riviere, P. (1984), *Individual and Society in Guiana: A Comparative Study of Amerindian Social Organisation.* Cambridge: Cambrige University Press.

Robotham, D. (1998), "Transnationalism in the Caribbean: Formal and Informal." *American Ethnologist* 25(2): 307–21.

Rosario, N. (2007), "Feasting on Sancocho Before Night Falls: A Meditation." *Callaloo* 30(1): 259–81.

Roseberry, W. (1996), "The Rise of Yuppies Coffees and the Reimagination of Class in the United States." *American Anthropologist* 98(4): 762–75.

Roth, W.E. (1915), "An Inquiry into the Animism and Folklore of the Guiana Indians." 30th Annual Report of the Bureau of American Ethnology, Washington, DC.

Rottmann, S.B., and Marx Ferree, M. (2008), "Citizenship and Intersectionality: German Feminist Debates about Headscarf and Antidiscrimination Laws." *Social Politics* 15(4): 481–513.

Rowland, E.D. (1892), "The Census of British Guiana." *Timehri* 6: 40–68.

Rowlands, M. (1995), "The Material Culture of Success," in J. Friedman (ed.), *Consumption and Identity*, 147–66. London: Harwood Academic.

Royce, A.P. (1982), *Ethnic Identity: Strategies of Identity.* Bloomington: Indiana University Press.

Ryer, P. (2006), "Between La Yuma and África: Locating the Color of Contemporary Cuba." Ph.D. thesis, University of Chicago, Department of Anthropology.

SACAD (Systèms Agraires Caribéens et Alternatives de Développement) and FAMV (Faculté d'Agronomie et de Médecine Vétérinaire) (1994), *Paysans, Systèms et Crise: Travaux sur l'agriare Haïtien.* Pointe-á-Pitre, Guadeloupe: Université des Antilles et de la Guyane; Port-au-Prince, Haiti: Université d'Etat d'Haïti.

Sahlins, M. (1990), "Food as Symbolic Code," in J.C. Alexander and S. Seidman (eds.), *Culture and Society: Contemporary Debates*, 94–101. Cambridge: Cambridge University Press.

Said, E. (1978), *Orientalism*. New York: Vintage.

Sayer, A. (2001), "For a Critical Cultural Political Economy." *Antipode* 33(4): 687–708.

Schlosser, E. (2002), *Fast Food Nation: The Dark Side of the All-American Meal*. New York: Houghton Mifflin Company.

Scholliers, P. (ed.) (2001), *Food, Drink, and Identity: Cooking, Eating, and Drinking in Europe Since the Middle Ages*. Oxford: Berg.

Schomburgk, R.H. (1840), *A Description of British Guiana, Geographical and Statistical: Exhibiting its Resources and Capabilities, Together with the Present and Future Condition and Prospects of the Colony*. London: Simpkin, Marshall and Co.

Scott, J.C. (1985), *Weapons of the Weak: Everyday Forms of Peasant Resistance*. New Haven, CT: Yale University Press.

Scott, J.C. (1990), *Domination and the Arts of Resistance*. New Haven, CT: Yale University Press.

Scott, D. (2004), "Modernity That Predated the Modern: Sidney Mintz's Caribbean." *History Workshop Journal* 58(1): 191.

Simmel, G. ([1907]2004), *The Philosophy of Money*, trans. T. Bottomore and D. Frisby. London: Routledge.

Singer, M. (2011), "Toward a Critical Bio-Social Model of Ecohealth in Southern Africa: The HIV/AIDS and Nutrition Insecurity Syndemic." *Annals of Anthropological Practice* 35(1): 8–27.

Smith, J.M. (2001), *When the Hands are Many: Community Organization and Social Change in Rural Haiti*. Ithaca, NY: Cornell University Press.

Smith, L.M., and Padula, A. (1996), *Sex and Revolution: Women in Socialist Cuba*. Oxford: Vilma Press.

Smith, M.G. (1962), *West Indian Family Structure*. Seattle: University of Washington Press.

Smith, R.T. (1956), *The Negro Family in British Guiana*. London: Routledge.

Smucker, G.R. (1982), "Peasants and Development Politics: A Study in Haitian Class and Culture." Ph.D. dissertation: New School for Social Research, New York.

Smucker, G.R., and Noriac, D. (1996), *Peasant Organizations in Haiti: Trends and Implications*. Rosslyn, VA: Inter American Foundation.

Smucker, G.R., and Thomson, J. (1999), "Social Capital and Development in Haiti." Technical Report. Port-au-Prince, Haiti: USAID.

Soler Puig, J. (1975), *El Pan Dormido*. La Habana: UNEAC.

Stewart, S. (1993), *On Longing: Narratives of the Miniature, the Gigantic, the Souvenir, the Collection*. Durham, NC: Duke University Press.

Stone, G.D. (2010), "The Anthropology of Genetically Modified Crops." *Annual Review of Anthropology* 29: 381–400.

Stoner, K. L. (1991), *From the House to the Street: The Women's Movement for Legal Reform 1898–1940.* Durhman, NC: Duke University Press.

Stonich, S. (1998), "Political Ecology of Tourism." *Annals of Tourism Research* 25(1): 25–54.

Stonich, S. (2000), *The Other Side of Paradise: Tourism, Conservation, and Development in the Bay Islands: Cognizant Communication Corporation.* Elmsford, NY: Cognizant Communications.

Stricker, P. (2007), *Toward a Culture of Nature.* Lanham: Lexington Books.

Sutton, D. E. (2001), *Remembrance of Repasts: An Anthropology of Food and Memory.* Oxford: Berg.

Sutton, D. E. (2009), "Tradition and Modernity Revisited." *Leituvos Etnologoja* 9: 55–76.

Tomczyk, T. (2004), "65,000 and Growing." *Bay Islands Voice,* September 1.

Tonkin, E., McDonald, M., and Chapman, M. (eds.) (1989), *History and Ethnicity.* New York: Routledge.

Torres-Saillant, S. (2000), *Diasporic Disquisitions: Dominicanists, Transnationalism, and the Community.* Dominican Studies Working Paper Series 1. CUNY Dominincan Studies Institute.

Torres-Saillant, S. (2006), *An Intellectual History of the Caribbean.* New York: Palgrave Macmillan.

Trouillot, M. R. (1990), *Haiti, State Against Nation: Origins and Legacy of Duvalierism.* New York: Monthly Review Press.

Trouillot, M. R. (1992), "The Caribbean Region: An Open Frontier in Anthropological Theory." *Annual Review of Anthropology* 21: 19–42.

Trouillot, M. R. (1995), *Silencing the Past: Power and the Production of History.* Boston: Beacon Press.

Trouillot, M. R. (1998), "Culture on the Edges: Creolization in the Plantation Context." *Plantation Society in the Americas* 5(1): 8–28.

Trouillot, M. R. (2001), "The Anthropology of the State: Close Encounters of a Deceptive Kind." *Current Anthropology* 42(1): 125–38.

Trouillot, M. R. (2003), "Anthropology and the Savage Slot: The Poetics and Politics of Otherness," in *Global Transformations: Anthropology and the Modern World,* 7–28. New York: Palgrave McMillan.

USAID (U.S. Agency for International Development) (2010a), "Haitian Farmers Increase Agriculture Productivity through Support of U.S. Government." Press Release. October 19, 2010. http://www.usaid.gov/press/releases/2010/pr101019.html (accessed February 7, 2011).

USAID (U.S. Agency for International Development) (2010b), "Seed System Security Assessment: Haiti." Technical Report. Port-au-Prince, Haiti: USAID.

USDA (U.S. Department of Agriculture) (2008), "Cuba's Food and Agriculture Situation Report." Office of Global Analysis, FAS. March. http://www.fas.usda.gov/itp/cuba/cubasituation0308.pdf (accessed February 17, 2012).

Veloz Maggiolo, M., and Tolentino Dipp, H. (2007), "Gastronomia Dominicana: Historia del Sabor Criollo." http://www.claro.com.do/libros_pdf/Gastronomia/gastronomia_1.pdf (accessed February 17, 2012).

Vereecke, J. (1994), "National Report on Indigenous Peoples and Development." Georgetown: UNPD.

Via Campesina (2011), *The International Peasant's Voice*. February 9. http://viacampesina.org/en/index.php?option=com_content&view=article&id=1029:the-international-peasants-voice&catid=27:what-is-la-via-campesina&Itemid=44 (accessed April 29, 2011).

Villa Rojas, A. (1981), "Terapéutica tradicional y medicina moderna entre los mayas de Yucatán." *Anales de Antropología* 18(2): 13–28.

Villa Rojas, A. (1983), "Enfermedad, pecado y confesión entre los grupos mayenses." *Anales de Antropología* 20(2): 89–110.

Wade, R. (2006), "Choking the South." *New Left Review* (March/April): 38.

Walker Bynum, C. (1997), "Fast, Feast and Flesh: The Religious Significance of Food to Medieval Women," in C. Counihan and P. van Esterik (eds.), *Food and Culture: A Reader*, 138–58. New York: Routledge.

Walters, E., and Brick, D. (2010), *A Rapid Seed Assessment in the Southern Department of Haiti: An Examination of the Impact of the January 12 Earthquake*. Port-au-Prince, Haiti: Catholic Relief Services.

Walton, J.K., and Seddon, D. (1994), *Free Markets and Food Riots: The Politics of Global Adjustment*. Oxford: Wiley-Blackwell.

Warde, A. (1997), *Consumption, Food and Taste*. London: Sage.

Waterton, C. (1825), *Wanderings in South America*. London: J. Mawman.

Waterton, C. (1925), *Wanderings in South America*. London: J.M. Dent and Sons.

Watson, J.L. (ed.) (1997), *Golden Arches East: McDonald's in East Asia*. Stanford, CA: Stanford University Press.

Weaver, D.B. (1998), *Ecotourism in the Less Developed World*. New York: Cab International Publications.

Weaver, D.B. (2004), "Manifestations of Ecotourism in the Caribbean," in D.T. Duval (ed.), *Tourism in the Caribbean: Trends, Development, Prospects*, 172–86. New York: Routledge.

Weismantel, M.J. (1988), *Food, Gender, and Poverty in the Ecuadorian Andes*. Philadelphia: University of Pennsylvania Press.

Whit, W.C. (2007), "Soul Food as Cultural Creation," in A. Bower (ed.), *African American Foodways: Explorations of History and Culture*, 45–58. Urbana: University of Illinois Press.

Whitehead, N.L. (1994), "The Ancient Amerindian Politics of the Amazon, the Orinoco, and the Atlantic Coast: A Preliminary Analysis of Their Passage from Antiquity to Extinction," in A. Roosevelt (ed.), *Amazonian Indians from Prehistory to Present*, 33–54. Tucson: The University of Arizona Press.

Wilk, R. (1999), "Real Belizean Food: Building Local Identity in the Transnational Caribbean." *American Anthropologist* 101(2): 244–55.

Wilk, R. (2006a), *Home Cooking in the Global Village: Caribbean Food from Buc-caneers to Ecotourists.* Oxford: Berg.

Wilk, R. (ed.) (2006b), *Fast Food/Slow Food: The Cultural Economy of the Global Food System.* Lanham: Altamira Press.

Williams, B. F. (1991), *Stains on My Name, War in My Veins: Guyana and the Poli-tics of Cultural Struggle.* Durham, NC: Duke University Press.

Williams-Forson, P. (2006), *Building Houses out of Chicken Legs: Black Women, Food and Power.* Chapel Hill: University of North Carolina Press.

Wilson, D. J. (1999), *Indigenous South Americans of the Past and Present: An Eco-logical Perspective.* Oxford: Westview Press.

Wilson, P. (1973), *Crab Antics.* New Haven, CT: Yale University Press.

Witt, D. (1999), *Black Hunger: Food and the Politics of U.S. Identity.* New York: Oxford.

Wolf, E. (1982), *Europe and the People without History.* Berkeley: University of California Press.

Wood, R. (2004), "Global Currents: Cruise Ships in the Caribbean Sea," in D. Duval (ed.), *Tourism in the Caribbean: Trends, Development, Prospects,* 152–71. New York: Routledge.

Woodson, D. G. (1987), "Problems and Prospects of Small-Scale Rural Credit Pro-grams in Haiti: A Preliminary Anthropological Study of the Experiences and Performances of Selected Private Voluntary Organizations." Technical Report. Port-au-Prince, Haiti: USAID.

Woodson, D. G. (1990), "Tout Moun se Moun, Men Tout Moun pa Menm: Micro-level Sociocultural Aspects of Land Tenure in a Northern Haitian Locality." Ph.D. dissertation, University of Chicago.

Woodson, D. G. (1997), "*Lamanjay,* Food Security, *Sécurité Alimentaire:* A Lesson in Communication from BARA's Mixed-Methods Approach to Baseline Research in Haiti, 1994–1996." *Culture and Agriculture* 19(3): 108–22.

World Food Programme (WFP) (2011), "Haiti Overview." http://www.wfp.org/countries/Haiti/Overview (accessed July 18, 2011).

World Tourism Organization (n.d.), http://www.unwto.org/destination/bordeaux/en/web_e.pdf (accessed November 2008).

World Wildlife Fund (n.d.), http://www.worldwildlife.org/home-full.html (accessed April 2011).

Yelvington, K. A. (2001), "The Anthropology of Afro-Latin America and the Carib-bean: Diasporic Dimensions." *Annual Review of Anthropology* 30: 227–60.

Zimmerer, K., and Carter, E. (2002), "Conservation and Sustainability in Latin America and the Caribbean," in K. S. Zimmerer and E. D. Carter (eds.), *Latin America in the 21st Century: Challenges and Solutions,* 207–50. Austin: Univer-sity of Texas Press.

Index

in Trinidad, 111, 114, 118
in Yucatán, 42
igusi soup, 83
imagined community, Dominican Republic as, 73
IMF *see* International Monetary Fund
imports, 109
to Caribbean, 109, 110
to Cuba, 98, 101, 104–5
to Haiti, 13, 127
to Trinidad, 107–8, 111, 118
improved seed, 122
distribution of, 134
production costs with, 132
production system influence by, 130–2
resistance to, 126–7
risks with, 132
see also hybrid seed
indentured servitude, 18
Indians *see* Amerindian society and culture; East Indians
indigenous people
of Caribbean, 4
extermination of, 109
see also Amerindian society and culture
individualism, 2
international aid organizations, 121, 126
International Monetary Fund (IMF), 7
intersectionality, 6
Islam, 18

Jagdeo, Bharrat, 77
Jean-Baptiste, Chavannes, 126
Juubche, 31–2, 44

Kanuku Mountains, 16, 23
Keens-Douglas, Paul, 115
Kentucky Fried Chicken (KFC), 13
slogan for, 117
in Trinidad, 107–8, 116–19
kinship, ix, 8
kipi, 64
ki'waaj, 33–4
kool (cornfield), 32
kweh-kweh, 76, 88

la libreta, 97
liming, 117

loans, in Haiti, 130
lobster, 48
localization, 115–16

MacCannell, Dean, 47
Makunaima, 22
Makushi tribe, 10–11, 15–16
in Brazil, 20
creation beliefs of, 22–3
farming practices of, 23–5
gender specialization and, 26–8
population of, 19
slave-raids of, 17, 28
struggle of, 2
la mancha del plátano (the stain of the plantain), 60, 69, 73
mangú, 12, 57
domestic, 62
in Dominican Republic, 12, 57–8
as gendered cultural performance, 71–2
identity and, 71
ingredients in, 63, 65
in New York City, 2, 58, 62–70
origins of, 59
preparation of, 69
re-valorization of, 74
as staple food, 58
as symbol of resistance, 66
versions of, 61–70
marine species, degradation of, 46
Marte, Lidia, 12
matapi, 27
Maya, 31
mayu, 26
Mazzeo, John, 13
memory
food, 45
seafood, 45–6, 53–4
social, 55
men
eating expectations of, 90
food preparation by, 65–6
Guyanese, 89–90
Mesoamerica, 31
mestizaje, Cuba as, 95, 105
metemgee, 82–4
Mexico, 1, 11
see also Yucatán

Yucatec Maya, 31
  age and, 38, 42, 44
  gender roles in, 32–3
  identity of, 42
  women of, 31, 33–4
Yucatecan cuisine, 33–4
  consensus and criticism in, 34–5

  novel innovations in, 39–41
  recent additions to, 36–8,
    41
  texture in, 37–8
  uniformity in, 34, 38

Zambia, 123